DEMOCRACY AND DICTATORSHIP IN GHANA AND TANZANIA

Also by Robert Pinkney

DEMOCRACY IN THE THIRD WORLD

GHANA UNDER MILITARY RULE

RIGHT-WING MILITARY GOVERNMENT

Democracy and Dictatorship in Ghana and Tanzania

Robert Pinkney
Senior Lecturer in Government
University of Northumbria at Newcastle
Newcastle

First published in Great Britain 1997 by
MACMILLAN PRESS LTD
Houndmills, Basingstoke, Hampshire RG21 6XS and London
Companies and representatives throughout the world

A catalogue record for this book is available from the British Library.

ISBN 0–333–63175–7

First published in the United States of America 1997 by
ST. MARTIN'S PRESS, INC.,
Scholarly and Reference Division,
175 Fifth Avenue, New York, N.Y. 10010

ISBN 0–312–17518–3

Library of Congress Cataloging-in-Publication Data
Pinkney, Robert.
Democracy and dictatorship in Ghana and Tanzania / Robert Pinkney.
p. cm.
Includes bibliographical references and index.
ISBN 0–312–17518–3 (cloth)
1. Democracy—Ghana.   2. Ghana—Politics and government.
3. Democracy—Tanzania.   4. Tanzania—Politics and government.
I. Title.
JQ3036.P56 1997
320.9667—dc21   97–9157
                                                         CIP

© Robert Pinkney 1997

All rights reserved. No reproduction, copy or transmission of this publication may be made without written permission.

No paragraph of this publication may be reproduced, copied or transmitted save with written permission or in accordance with the provisions of the Copyright, Designs and Patents Act 1988, or under the terms of any licence permitting limited copying issued by the Copyright Licensing Agency, 90 Tottenham Court Road, London W1P 9HE.

Any person who does any unauthorised act in relation to this publication may be liable to criminal prosecution and civil claims for damages.

The author has asserted his right to be identified as the author of this work in accordance with the Copyright, Designs and Patents Act 1988.

This book is printed on paper suitable for recycling and made from fully managed and sustained forest sources.

10 9 8 7 6 5 4 3 2 1
06 05 04 03 02 01 00 99 98 97

Printed in Great Britain by
The Ipswich Book Company Ltd
Ipswich, Suffolk

Contents

List of Tables and Figures viii

Acknowledgements ix

1 Introduction 1
Why democracy? 1
Why Ghana? Why Tanzania? 4
The art and science of comparative politics 5

2 Democracy in a Hot Climate 8
The varied forms of democracy 8
Who wants democracy? 17
Democratic prospects 20
An end to authoritarianism or a beginning of democracy? 31

3 Ghana: Pluralist Democracy, Socialism, Populism and Democracy 33
A socialist experiment? 35
A liberal restoration? 37
The emergence of populism 40
Could any political system be made to work? 47
Economic constraints 48
Cultural constraints 52
Behavioural weaknesses 53
Populists into democrats? 58

4 Ghana: Political Structures, Civil Society and Democracy 62
The state and civil society 62
The Civil Service 68
The army 70
Constitutional checks and balances: the legislature and the judiciary 74
Local government 77
Conclusion 85

5	**Tanzania: the Search for Socialism and Pluralism**	87
	The making of a socialist ideology	88
	A party of the revolution?	96
	Theory into practice?	104
	Socialism and pluralism: allies or enemies?	108
6	**Tanzania: Political Structures, Civil Society and Democracy**	112
	The state and civil society	112
	Civil and military bureaucracies	118
	Constitutional checks and balances: the legislature and the judiciary	123
	Local government	126
	Trade unions and industrial relations	129
	Conclusion	132
7	**The Politics of Democratic Transition and Consolidation: Some Preliminary Thoughts**	137
	The elements in a transition	138
	The seeds of challenge to authoritarianism	139
	The configuration of interests	145
	The resolution of conflicts and the consolidation of democracy	151
8	**Ghana: Democratic Transition and Consolidation**	158
	A long march or trench warfare?	158
	The seeds of challenge to authoritarianism	162
	The configuration of interests	165
	The resolution of conflicts	170
	The consolidation of democracy	175
9	**Tanzania: Democratic Transition and Consolidation**	184
	A long and lonely march	184
	The seeds of challenge to authoritarianism	185
	The configuration of interests	189
	The resolution of conflicts	195
	Democracy as who chooses what, why and how	198
	The prospects for democratic consolidation	205

10 Conclusion	**209**
Bibliography	220
Index	228

List of Tables and Figures

Tables

3.1	Different ideological tendencies in Ghana	34
5.1	The interests, ideologies and policy positions of the Tanzanian President, party leaders, ministers and state bureaucrats	93
9.1	Perceptions of 'very important' influences on Tanzanian voters	199
9.2	'Very important' influences on Tanzanian voters: perceptions of two-way channels	199
9.3	Reasons for voting for the CCM (the ruling party)	200

Figures

4.1	State, society and economic change: some suggested relationships	65
7.1	Sources of initiative for democratisation: government and opposition; elites and masses	147
8.1	Sources of initiative for democratisation in Ghana: government and opposition; elites and masses	166
9.1	Sources of initiative for democratisation in Tanzania: government and opposition; elites and masses	190

Acknowledgements

Many people have made the completion of this book possible. The University of Northumbria at Newcastle granted me sabbatical leave to carry out the research, and colleagues there took over additional teaching and administrative responsibilities in my absence. Dr Austin McCarthy, our Faculty Librarian, was as always invaluable in pointing me in the direction of the relevant literature. The British Academy financed my fieldwork in Africa.

Professor Dennis Austin of the University of Manchester and Professor James Read of the School of Oriental and African Studies briefed me on recent events in Ghana and Tanzania respectively, and Tim Kelsall, also of SOAS, provided useful information on the Tanzanian elections. Professor Kwame Ninsin, Dr Joseph Ayee and Dr Mike Oquaye of the Department of Politics at the University of Ghana were all generous in giving up their time to help me, and Mrs Valerie Sackey at Osu Castle helped to put me in touch with many members of the Ghana government.

In Tanzania, academics were equally helpful in guiding me through their country's politics, especially Professor Sam Maghimbi, Professor Ralph Masenge and Dr Max Mmuya. Professor Marion Doro was a constant source of help both as a political scientist and as a kindly neighbour, and Mr H. Mtanga and his staff at the University of Dar es Salaam Links Office were always willing administrative helpers. Miss Fauzia Mohamed and Mr David Majura helped as interpreters in interviews with voters, and Mr Revocatur Kamilwa translated the questionnaire responses. Mr Melchior Assey, the Clerk to the National Assembly, arranged for me to meet some of the newly-elected MPs in Zanzibar.

In both countries, busy ministers, civil servants, MPs, judges, party officers and officers of pressure groups were generous with their time, and in both countries numerous individuals not holding any public office helped to make me feel welcome. People who had previously been strangers to me took trouble to help in such ways as providing transport and first aid, guiding me through unfamiliar terrain and recovering lost luggage. Much may change in African politics, but African hospitality remains undiminished.

My wife coped with additional work at home in my absence, and corrected many errors in the first draft of the book. To all those who helped, I am very grateful. I take full responsibility for the contents of the book, and for any errors of fact or opinion.

ROBERT PINKNEY

1 Introduction

WHY DEMOCRACY?

On the walls of Siena Town Hall are two fourteenth-century frescos. One depicts *The Allegory of Good Government*, the other *The Allegory of Bad Government*. The former shows a well-ordered, prosperous city, and a well-cultivated countryside beyond the city wall. The latter shows figures representing such sins as greed, pride and arrogance which are serving a devil-like figure labelled 'tyranny'. While 'bad government' is equated with tyranny, there is nothing in the first picture to equate good government with democracy. The presentation of stately buildings, well-tilled land, healthy animals, and industrious people engaged in farming, building and marketing, conjures up a vision of what later generations would have called 'development' rather than democracy.

This should serve to remind us that democracy has not always been a primary objective of human endeavour, whether in fourteenth-century Italy or twentieth-century Africa. The well-being produced by development, buttressed by a stable peaceful environment, have often appeared to be more attractive goals than the nebulous one of democracy. Yet if the artist implies that human misbehaviour leads to tyranny, what political arrangements should be associated with 'good' government? A pragmatic answer might be that, as long as people enjoy peace and prosperity, the form of government is not important, and that a benevolent dictatorship would serve as well as democracy. There were many in Africa who held this view in the early years after independence, but the benevolent version of dictatorship has proved even more elusive than democracy. Politicians with extensive power over their subjects have frequently fallen prey to the sins depicted in *The Allegory of Bad Government*, and their subjects have thus become the victims of poverty, violence and disease. They have also suffered something which might have been less comprehensible to medieval Italians – the loss, or absence, of 'human rights'. In much of the modern world there are expectations that people should be free from arbitrary arrest, torture or execution, and should be free to express their political opinions, and combine with others to pursue political demands.

If tyranny deprives people of perceived rights, and frequently produces material degradation, what alternatives can they seek? There may be a yearning for 'traditional' forms of government which were not always democratic, but in which the king or chief had responsibilities to his subjects that prevented him from behaving like a tyrant, but such a past cannot be re-created once the traditional loyalty to the chief has gone and his kingdom has been absorbed into a larger nation state. There is also the alternative of 'theocracy' within which 'God given' laws regulate the political, and other, behaviour of ruler and ruled alike. Such a system may limit human rights, as generally perceived, but still provide a stable environment within which people can prosper as they did under 'good government' in medieval Italy, but such a system requires widespread commitment to religious discipline, and adequate agreement on the nature of the God-given laws, which is seldom found outside the Middle East. There have also been the more recent secular religions of communism and fascism which offered apparently attractive alternatives to democracy, as commonly understood in the West, but governments based on these, like many earlier forms of tyranny, have fallen as they have failed to provide either material sustenance or individual freedom.

Almost by default, 'democracy' has become a rallying cry as other forms of government have failed. It is seen to be practised in nearly all of the world's most prosperous countries, even if the causal relationship between democracy and prosperity remains unclear, it offers relief to people denied human rights, and it affords people the opportunity to change their governments by peaceful means if their performances are found wanting. At first sight it might seem remarkable not so much that democracy has extended to more countries in recent years, but that it has not swept much further and faster, if it has so many advantages over other forms of government. To explain why it has not, and why the advance of democracy is such a tortuous process in 'difficult' countries such as Ghana and Tanzania, is one of the purposes of this book.

Without attempting to define democracy at this stage, we may note some of the more obvious barriers in the way of its advance. If democracy is desired by the majority of citizens, it may not be desired by incumbent authoritarian rulers who will use their power to resist it. If this resistance can be overcome, will the populace be able to reach a consensus on what democracy is and what form it should take? Should it, for example, allow substantial autonomy to particular groups or areas? Should it give rulers latitude to curb the freedom of troublesome minorities? How far should it facilitate, or require, the redistribution of power and wealth from the privileged to the underprivileged? How far should it allow judges to overrule elected politicians? Even if a consensus can be achieved on these matters, there is the problem of the durability of democracy once it has been established. If the performances of elected politicians fail to match people's expectations, can we be certain that people will limit their dissent to peaceful protest and to voting the government out when the opportunity arises, or will they regard the satisfaction of their immediate demands, especially in times of acute hardship, as more important than the preservation of democracy? There is the possibility that people will bring democracy down directly by taking to the streets, or at least remain passive bystanders as soldiers extinguish democracy through a *coup d'état*.

All this still assumes that, in view of the unattractiveness of the alternatives, most people want democracy most of the time, but how confident of this can we be? There is the immediate problem, especially in largely illiterate rural societies, of a 'parochial' political culture in which there is little grasp of the concept of democracy, at least at a national level, and where people's attitude to the political system is one of extracting the maximum benefits for themselves and their immediate communities without much concern for how rulers are chosen or held accountable. Beyond such parochial attitudes there may be, even amongst educated people, a belief that, whatever the theoretical advantages of democracy as an ultimate ideal, more authoritarian political structures are necessary to deal with immediate material problems. Democracy, in this view, may be divisive by encouraging conflict between ethnic or religious groups, or may be a recipe for indecisive government based on compromise rather than bold decisions. And at a more personal level, there may be individuals who do not necessarily have any strong views on the merits or otherwise of democracy, but who think in terms of their immediate interests. They may undermine the democratic process through such practices as bribery, tax evasion, theft or misuse of public property, or violence.

WHY GHANA? WHY TANZANIA?

An obvious reason for studying attempts at democratisation in Ghana and Tanzania is that they represent difficult, though not impossible, cases. The prospects are not as bleak as in, for example, Iraq or Zaire, where the underlying political cultures, social divisions, the distribution of wealth and civil–military relations all make a democratic settlement unlikely in the foreseeable future. Yet Ghana and Tanzania have lagged well behind the countries most prominent in what Huntington calls the 'third wave' of democratisation which began in the 1970s and gained momentum in the 1980s (Huntington 1991–2). For some countries, such as Greece and Uruguay, democratisation was little more than a return to 'business as usual' after brief periods of authoritarian rule. For Spain and Portugal, the authoritarian interlude was much longer, but social and economic development had reached a level comparable with that found in other countries which were able to sustain democracy. In other countries, including Argentina, Brazil and Chile, the struggle for democratisation was tough, but the pro-democracy groups were built on solid bases of support in societies where the extent of industrialisation and urbanisation, and per capita income, were much greater than in Tropical Africa.

Occupying an intermediate position between the countries which have apparently democratised successfully and those that have little immediate prospect of doing so, Ghana and Tanzania thus provide us with an opportunity to explore the outer frontiers of democracy. Can explanations of democratisation based on the experience of the successful cases be stretched to these more difficult cases, or have those countries which have had difficulty in climbing ashore during the third wave been inadequately equipped for a democratic transformation? Many other countries in Tropical Africa, in Central America and possibly East Asia, could have been chosen as case studies, and the final choice must be put down to the personal preferences of the author. I had become acquainted with Ghana when working there in the early days of the First Republic, had returned to study the first military government and tried to keep in touch with subsequent political developments, and there can be few political scientists who would not be fascinated by these developments. The establishment of four civilian republics and three periods of military government in less than 40 years is indicative of the delicate balance between democratic and authoritarian forces.

Tanzania, in contrast, appears to offer a picture of stability and continuity, with the same party in power throughout the period since independence in 1961. Yet it is a country in which the question of what constitutes democracy, and how such a condition might be achieved and sustained, has seldom been far below the surface. Tanzania began with a competitive party system, but one in which the electorate chose to give a virtual monopoly of the representation to one party. It then became a *de jure* one-party state, with an attempt to institutionalise democracy by allowing voters to choose between competing candidates from the same party. This helped voters to press for resources for their constituencies, by electing only those able to demonstrate their ability to deliver the goods, but it gave voters little control over the direction of national policy. A combination of pressures from dissident groups, from within the ruling party and from external sources, then led to the legalisation of multi-party politics in 1992, but with question marks over whether opposition parties could hope to compete effectively when the ruling party and the state had been so intertwined for over 30 years. While in Ghana a major institutional problem in attempting democratisation is to confine the army to narrower boundaries, in Tanzania it is to transform the ruling party into one that competes with others on something approaching equal terms.

THE ART AND SCIENCE OF COMPARATIVE POLITICS

This study falls broadly within the discipline of comparative politics, but it does not attempt a mechanical point-by-point comparison of the two countries. This is partly because of the unevenness of my own knowledge and research, but also because the political features which are significant in one country are not necessarily so important in the other. On the first point, I have made varied contacts with Ghanaian public servants and academic observers of the political scene over the years, whereas my links with their Tanzanian counterparts have been fewer and more recent. My good fortune in being in Tanzania in 1995 gave me an opportunity to study political parties and the electoral process at a crucial moment, and in greater detail than in Ghana, where I had to rely more on secondary sources. There will thus be detours into different types of highway and byway in each of the two countries. On the second point, the political structures and attitudes which are fundamental to the understanding of one country may have counterparts in the other which are much less significant. The Ghanaian army has played the roles of ruler, kingmaker, and arbiter of what is politically acceptable for over 30 years, whereas the Tanzanian army has sometimes been a power behind the throne, but has never ruled or decided who should rule. In contrast, the ruling party in Tanzania and the ideology (or ideologies) it has propagated has been a major, if not the major, determinant of the working of the political system, while no Ghanaian party since 1966 has been much more than a loose and transitory coalition of interests, with little ability to give direction to government policy. Chiefs in Ghana are an ever-present political force, whereas in Tanzania the title 'chief' carries little status and no authority.

Before looking at the individual countries I sketch out in Chapter 2 some of the general problems of defining democracy, considering the extent to which it has become a valued form of government, and discuss some of the variables which are said to be conducive to the existence of democracy. The next four chapters look at the fortunes of democracy and dictatorship in Ghana and Tanzania since independence. Chapters 3 and 5 focus mainly on political ideas, political culture and economic constraints, while Chapters 4 and 6 concentrate on the extent to which the political structures in each country have taken on a life of their own. Chapter 7 views the subject from a more dynamic point of view, with some preliminary thoughts on the ways in which countries can make a transition from dictatorship to democracy, and considers some frameworks for analysis, and Chapters 8 and 9 then relate this to the specific cases of Ghana and Tanzania.

Ghana ushered in a new multi-party democracy in 1992, Tanzania in 1995. It is thus early days to make any judgement on the success or durability of democracy. As in so much of Africa, the unthinkable and the unexpected have occurred too frequently since the early 1980s for us to make any confident predictions. Ghana had seemed destined for either prolonged military dictatorship, or continued alternations between military, and weak democratic civilian, governments, while in Tanzania there had been little reason to doubt the continuation of one-party rule. The ending of the Cold War, and the subsequent concern of Western governments to encourage democratic development, put new pressures on authoritarian governments, but the nature, extent and pace of democratisation depended very much on indigenous forces, as will the ability of each country to 'consolidate' democracy. Each country provides a fascinating range of groups, political structures, personalities and beliefs, and each has provided a stage for a fascinating political drama. I hope that some of this emerges in the pages which follow, even if we are no nearer to knowing how, if at all, the drama will end.

2 Democracy in a Hot Climate

THE VARIED FORMS OF DEMOCRACY

According to a survey in *The Economist* in 1994, Ghana belonged to the group of countries classified as 'partly free' while Tanzania belonged to the 'not free' group (*The Economist* 1994: 18). Yet Tanzanians could claim that they had held competitive elections every five years since 1960, whereas Ghana has held only three competitive elections, of which only one was acknowledged as free and fair by all the main participants. This should serve as a reminder that there is no unanimity on what constitutes democracy, or even partial democracy. I have suggested elsewhere a rough classification of the different types of democracy (Pinkney 1993: 5–17), and adherents of any one type may reject the others as not being the genuine article. For the purposes of this study we can eliminate 'radical democracy', where the will of the elected majority prevails without checks and balances to protect minorities from the tyranny of the majority (Dodd 1979: 176–8). There were elements of this in Ghana under Nkrumah between 1957 and 1966, with the government justifying virtually any action it took on the grounds that it had received a mandate from the people. The absence of checks and balances can quickly transform democracy into tyranny, as it did in Ghana, and few politicians today will admit to seeking or practising this form of democracy. We can also dismiss 'guided democracy', where rulers claim to be executing the 'general will' without even asking the electorate whether its perception of this will coincides with the government's. The concept might be stretched to embrace Tanzania under one-party rule, with the electorate confined to making a parochial choice of MPs while the presidency went uncontested, but the more frequent defence of the pre-1995 Tanzanian system was that the party provided ample opportunity for democratic participation, and that the absence of challengers for the presidency was more a matter of accident, or satisfaction with the single nomination, than a matter of ideology. One could even stretch the concept of guided democracy to the form of government in Ghana under Flight Lieutenant Rawlings from 1981 to 1992, where the rulers never tired of pointing out the widespread opportunities for popular participation through bodies such as the Committees for the Defence of the Revolution (CDRs), while the government in its wisdom controlled the economy, internal security and foreign policy, but the absence of competitive elections at even the local level for the first seven years suggests something closer to authoritarianism than democracy.

More important from our point of view are the liberal, socialist and consociational models of democracy. Much of the disagreement about what constitutes democracy in Africa hinges on the extent to which each of these types is regarded as legitimate.

> In 1966 the military [in Ghana] ... claimed to be preparing the ground for the restoration of democracy, the latter seen in terms of an electoral competition between two or more parties in periodic election [sic] and the restoration of the economy. By which they meant the restoration of capitalism for the recruitment of political elites in whom the task of running the affairs of state would be entrusted for a period of four years till the next round of electoral contests.
> (Hansen 1991: 15)

Here is the classic objection to liberal democracy as a system which merely enables people to make periodic choices as to who shall rule, and possibly exploit them, but without really enabling the people to participate in the taking of significant political decisions. Yet this was the form of democracy which had been practised by the former colonial powers in their own countries, and the form which African nationalist politicians generally demanded, almost without question, with the coming of independence. Why should there be so much enthusiasm for a form of democracy which apparently gave people so little control over their own destiny? A cynical answer might be that nationalist politicians merely aspired to step into the shoes of the departing colonial elites, but managed to fool their followers into believing that they would be able to exercise democratic control over their leaders. A practical answer might be that demanding a liberal democratic constitution was the simplest way of easing the departure of the colonial powers. They would not willingly have handed over power to a blatant dictatorship, and would probably have had qualms about leaving Africa in the hands of egalitarian, participatory democrats where the security of private property, including the property of foreigners, was uncertain. Liberal democracy might thus be seen as a blank cheque. The donors and recipients might both hint that they expected it to be used for certain specific purposes, but with the recipients ultimately able to adapt it to suit their own needs, including perhaps the plundering of public property, the suspension of civil liberties, the rigging of elections and the destruction of opposition, while the donors disclaimed any responsibility for these actions, having handed over an impeccable constitution at the time of their departure.

Political expediency and naked ambition no doubt played a part in such transactions, but there were good reasons for valuing liberal democracy in itself, and not simply as an expedient for disposing of unwanted colonies, or as a stepping stone to authoritarian rule. Liberal democracy, more than most forms of democracy, acknowledges the diversity of groups in society and the need to protect them from exploitation, whether by one another or by the state. It places much emphasis on constitutional checks and balances to prevent this exploitation, and recognises that there are large 'non-political' spheres in society where people should be free to go about their business with a minimum of interference from the state. The 'democratic' element comes in the freedom for all citizens to vote in competitive elections, buttressed by freedom of expression and association so that all contenders for power are able to convey their messages to the electorate. The 'liberal' element comes in the attempts to safeguard the rights of citizens, whether against the tyranny of the majority or of a minority, so that people are free from arbitrary arrest, imprisonment or the confiscation of their property.

Presented in this way, liberal democracy is not just a fad of wealthy Western Europeans and North Americans. There is no reason why Africans should not be equally anxious to step into the political sphere, when they wish to choose between competing party programmes offered by rival contenders for power, or when they want to influence political decisions which impinge on their interests or beliefs, and to step out of that sphere when they wish to pursue their family, social, cultural, business or religious interests, unencumbered by political interference. The difficulty lies in the difference between liberal democracy as an ideal concept and liberal democracy as something that can be translated into an everyday process in the real world. If Hansen's description of (presumably liberal) democracy as a system in which rival elites compete for power and, by implication, use that power to advance their own interests, is not universally applicable, it is clearly recognisable in many parts of the world. Leaving aside the question of how easily African rulers have been able to jettison liberal democracy altogether, in favour of arbitrary, authoritarian government, there appear to be at least two major difficulties in adapting the liberal democratic model to Africa: the question of whose freedom and property is being protected and the question of who is able to participate effectively in the political process. Critics from Marx onwards have seen constitutional checks and balances as a smokescreen for protecting the 'rights' of the already privileged rather than the common people. 'Freedoms' beyond the control of the political system may include the freedom for employers to hire workers at starvation wages, for landlords to evict tenants and for monopolists to extort large profits. On participation, the common criticism is that it may not extend much beyond making a narrow choice between competing elites once every four or five years. Liberal democracy in the West may well be a long way from resolving either of these problems, but devices have evolved, which one may regard as either extensions of the political system or something running parallel to it, which offer the citizen extra-constitutional protection. Thus capitalist exploitation has been blunted by social welfare provisions, by reasonably well-policed laws that protect workers and tenants, and possibly by social norms and conventions which discourage the exploitation of economic advantages to the full. The 'participatory deficit' may also be narrower in practice than a crude reading of models of liberal democracy would suggest. Participation, beyond the act of voting in periodic elections, may not be written into constitutions, but politicians and bureaucrats in the West are in frequent contact with representatives of a variety of groups which have sufficient expertise, resources and perceived legitimacy to be able to influence political decisions. Even if only a minority of the population belongs to, or is active in, these groups, the many may benefit from the pressures of the few. And the *potential* power of the many to participate, should circumstances warrant this, is an important resource in itself.

If we turn to liberal democracy in Africa, we cannot be so confident that an extended or a parallel structure will go nearly so far in protecting the weak against the strong, or in enabling the many to participate to extract concessions from the few. Even if governments want to curb the activities of the wealthy and powerful, and frequently they do not because it is these groups that sustain them in power and court them with 'gifts', their ability to do so will be limited. How, for example, would a Tanzanian government be able to prevent the owner of a transport business from employing his drivers for long hours at low wages, given the inadequacy of the bureaucracy and the police service to enforce the law, and the inadequacy of trade unions to defend the workers. Where the business is foreign-owned, as is much of the economy in Tropical Africa, the scope for control via representative government is even more limited, as the firm can escape by transferring its activities to another country.

If liberal democracy in practice is seen as entrenching, or at least failing to provide public control over, indigenous or foreign elites, the search for alternative forms of democracy is understandable. Nyerere in Tanzania, and Nkrumah and perhaps even Rawlings in Ghana, saw democracy as ineffective unless it relieved the masses of poverty and gave more political participation to the underprivileged. Their alternative might be described as 'socialist democracy' in that it implied a redistribution of wealth and greater state control over the economy but, if we look at the intended political outcomes, the ultimate result might be to make Africa closer to Western Europe than to either a totalitarian or a utopian model. McHenry makes a useful distinction between liberal democracy's concern with means, such as civil liberties, majority rule, political equality and elections, and what he calls 'popular democracy's' concern with ends, and especially with whether decisions accord with the wishes of the majority (McHenry 1994: 17). Built-in state controls or participatory structures in Africa might help to reduce inequalities of power and wealth which have already been reduced in Western liberal democracies through the social institutions, operating largely autonomously from the state, which we have already described. Socialism in Africa might thus be seen as the functional equivalent of corporate arrangements between government, business and trade unions in the West, in attempting to curb economic exploitation. Participation within the African mass party might be seen as compensating for the absence of the varied informal participatory structures found in the West, and exhortations and directives against corruption in Nkrumah's Dawn Broadcast in 1961 and Nyerere's Arusha Declaration in 1967 might be seen as substitutes for the largely unwritten codes of ethics which are supposed to guide politicians in the West. Some advocates of African socialism might object that they were not merely trying to create functional equivalents of Western political structures but to give expression to egalitarian, participatory aspirations which were rooted in their own culture. They might also observe that the financial discipline and moral rectitude which Nyerere expected of his followers was much more rigorous than the standards which normally prevail in the West. But this does not alter the fact that African states were starting from a baseline at independence at which inequality and exploitation were generally greater than in the West, and that socialist policies would have to close that gap before moving on to any higher state of society.

But what sort of animal is, or was, African socialism, and to what extent did it advance democracy? We have suggested that, on paper, it might have established and protected citizens' rights in ways which would not otherwise have been possible, but the results in practice have been rather less impressive. In its ideal form, socialism might imply extensive state intervention to meet the needs and wishes of the majority of citizens who would otherwise be exploited by the privileged few, but in practice it could mean the manipulation of state structures by politicians and elites to retain their own power bases. State corporations ostensibly designed to promote indigenous productivity might be used to provide employment for friends and relations of politicians, health and educational facilities ostensibly designed to improve the quality of life might be allocated to communities of the right tribe or political persuasion at the expense of others, and party structures ostensibly designed to stimulate political participation might be used as conduits for central patronage and control. It is not our purpose in this chapter to look at the actual workings of proclaimed socialist policies in Ghana or Tanzania, but we need to note that, just as liberal democracy has functioned imperfectly in the absence of extra-constitutional checks and balances, socialist democracy may be equally difficult to apply if there are few checks on those who seek to impose it. Not only that, but the situation may be worsened by the dismantling of some of the admittedly inadequate checks of liberal democracy. In the political sphere, the prohibition of opposition parties on the grounds that they advocate tribalism, sectarianism or capitalism, can leave voters with little or no electoral choice if they are dissatisfied with their current rulers, thus pushing the system closer to 'guided democracy'. In the economic sphere, reductions in the scope of the private sector not only increase the danger of inefficient or corrupt state monopolies which misuse the nation's resources, but leave a larger number of citizens dependent on the goodwill of the state, or more narrowly of the ruling politicians, and therefore less able to challenge authority without risking their livelihood.

It therefore seems unlikely that the ideal of, or the attempts to practice, socialist democracy would have survived, even without the collapse of the Communist Bloc and external pressure for economic liberalisation. One can argue about whether or not socialism, as interpreted by African political leaders, was the best of the imperfect alternatives available to them in the 1960s and 1970s, but by the mid-1980s it did not appear to offer any great prospect of economic advancement or democratic choice and participation. Where were African democrats now to look for inspiration? There were some, notably among the opposition politicians in Ghana, who kept faith with the Western model of liberal democracy, but many others remained unhappy about the inequality, limited participation and divisiveness which appeared to go with this model. Without generally mentioning its name, some African leaders showed a growing interest in 'consociational democracy'. The term was originally coined by Lijphart to describe coalition politics in the Low Countries and Switzerland (Lijphart 1977: 25–103), and applied by Apter to attempts in Nigeria to ensure that all significant groups were incorporated in government without being frozen out by crude majoritarianism (Apter 1961: 20–8). The objection to classical liberal democracy here is not just that it limits public participation to periodic elections and perpetuates powerful elites but that, in the African context, where people frequently vote on ethnic or religious lines, a 'winner takes all' system will leave many groups excluded from power indefinitely, whether they be Europeans in South Africa or ethnic or religious minorities in Tropical Africa. Military rulers, such as Acheampong and Rawlings in Ghana and Museveni in Uganda, took the argument to extremes by advocating the creation of no-party states, on the grounds that parties are intrinsically divisive. Internal pressures from civilian politicians and external pressures from donor countries have ultimately made the permanent no-party state unattainable, but the desire to enhance citizen participation, and to build a broad consensus on the basis of it, remain as ideals which appear to have been elusive under both multi-party politics and single-party, nominally socialist, states. The inclusion of the (mainly Afrikaans) National Party in a broad coalition in South Africa until 1996 might be seen as a significant step towards consociationalism, but multi-party politics and national consensus have seldom gone together in Africa. Indeed the 'winner takes all' principle was taken to extremes in Zanzibar in 1995 when the Civic United Front (CUF) won 49.8 per cent of the vote but was not invited to join a government of national unity on the grounds that this would compromise its oppositional role. As CUF won every seat on Pemba, the second largest of Zanzibar's islands, the politics of exclusion are illustrated here in dramatic form. Is there, then, an authentically 'African' form of democracy which can provide better solutions than the imported models?

> Sandbrook defined liberal democracy as 'a political system characterised by regular and free elections in which politicians organised into parties competing to form a government, by the right of virtually all adult citizens to vote, and by guarantees of a range of familiar political and civil

rights'. Others would prefer a broader definition of democracy so as to involve key ideals such as political choice, social equality, and empowerment. Other sources of democratic ideals, and institutions, within Africa include the democratic aspirations of some key nationalist figures, such as Leopold Senghor who evoked the African idea of democracy as involving the *palaver*, dialogue or discussion, followed by unanimity of decisions. More contemporary academic analyses have pointed to the positive effects of ethnic heterogeneity, and the surprising resilience of a democratic political culture or a democratic ethic underneath the authoritarian model

(Riley 1992: 540, quoting Sandbrook R. (1988) 'Liberal Democracy in Africa', *Canadian Journal of African Studies*, 22(2))

African politicians face a dilemma. Pressed by Western donors to follow the letter of liberal democracy by engaging in multi-party politics, they may then be condemned for not following the spirit, by proclaiming 'winner takes all', without the losers being protected by the checks and balances commonly found in the West, but the dilemma is easier to highlight than the solution. No one has yet found a way of transplanting the village palaver tree in the capital city to provide a meeting point for all those seeking consensus in national politics. Pragmatists might argue, like Aristotle, that we should not waste our time pursuing any one political system in its extreme form, but should seek a synthesis of the best features of each: in our case a synthesis of liberal, socialist and consociational democracy. Sklar suggests the possible emergence of 'developmental democracy', which accommodates the goals of social reconstruction implicit in socialist democracy, the resistance to authoritarianism implicit in liberal democracy, as in the struggle for trade union autonomy in Zambia, and the recognition of cultural diversity implicit in consociationalism, as in federal experiments in Nigeria (Sklar 1983: 19–21), and Imam argues that

The 'capitalist path', which puts public resources in the hands of a few entrepreneurs who were supposed to generate economic development, has not worked. The 'socialist path', whereby public resources were controlled to mobilise and canalise mass energies for development, has also not achieved substantial results. These failures should signal the end of the theoretical war between 'central planners' and 'free marketeers'. The time has come to develop new theoretical and practical perspectives which go beyond the old boundaries. In this regard popular needs should be defined by emancipated individuals and economies planned by free people acting together to produce what they decide they need. (Imam 1992: 103)

Such sentiments no doubt appeal to a broad spectrum of intellectual opinion, but we may demanding more and more of democracy at a time when economic conditions and the external environment place growing burdens on governments and their subjects. Before looking at the conditions most likely to sustain or undermine democracy, we need to consider the extent to which, and the ways in which, Africans see democracy as an immediate priority.

WHO WANTS DEMOCRACY?

Democracy by consensus undoubtedly takes a charitable view of society and is based on optimistic assumptions concerning human nature ... . Consensual democracy seeks inexorably to achieve its goal of unanimity. It assumes either that people are perfect, very much aware of their rights and obligations ... or, on the contrary that they are bereft of willpower and without freedom. In other words, consensual democracy can only exist in a society of gods or among slaves. (Nzouankeu 1991: 374)

Nzouankeu reports that the demand in Africa, in countries ranging from Zaire to Tunisia, is specifically for pluralist democracy, by which is meant multi-party, competitive democracy, with winners and losers and, therefore accountability. One of the central reasons for this widespread wave of demands is a perception of the failure of forms of democracy which were emancipalist and collectivist rather than individualist and competitive. Africans have had enough, according to this account, of African Rousseauism, of 'the legend of the palaver tree', of the myth of monolithic consensus evolved by debate and requiring no party competition; they reject the claim of purely 'African' ideas of democracy and rights in favour of the universal ('western') forms. In short, what they want is what the West has already got, not what it aspires to (Allison 1994: 15–16).

Discovering 'what Africans want' is not an easy process, but such opportunities as public opinion has had to express itself in both Ghana and Tanzania might suggest a rejection not only of the palaver tree but of competitive party politics, or at least its relegation below other priorities. In the Ghanaian election of 1992, voters had the opportunity to remove a leader who had previously overthrown a democratically-elected government and who had then presided over an authoritarian regime for the next eleven years, yet they re-elected him with 58.3 per cent of the vote. The fairness of the election remains a matter of dispute, but one could question whether a coalition of military leaders, technocrats and party thugs would have been sufficient to produce such a result without a widespread public feeling that Rawlings had produced material benefits where others had failed. Jeffries and Thomas suggest that voters regarded 'social rights' as more important than 'human rights', and that relative economic success, together with a hope that constitutional rule would moderate Rawlings's illiberal policies, were the major factors in his re-election (Jeffries and Thomas 1993: 361–2).

In Tanzania in 1991 the Nyalali Commission toured the country to discover whether people wanted a continuation of the one-party state. After holding 1061 meetings and receiving 36 199 responses, it found that 77.2 per cent of the respondents favoured such a continuation, although not necessarily in its current form (United Republic of Tanzania 1992: 7–8). Even when the government acceded to the commission's recommendation that multi-party politics should be permitted, on the grounds that the 21.5 per cent who favoured this should not be disenfranchised, the 1995 general election gave opposition parties barely 20 per cent of the seats in Parliament, and less than 40 per cent of the presidential vote. As in Ghana, the opposition parties questioned the fairness of the election, and one might also question the extent to which the respondents to the Nyalali Commission's questions said what they thought the government wanted them to say, but it is still difficult to believe that fear, indoctrination and election rigging would have been sufficient in either country to secure the re-election of politicians whose past records cast doubt on their respect for the democratic process. In Tanzania, as in Ghana, the results may be explained partly by at least implicit acknowledgements by ruling politicians of previous authoritarian excesses, allegedly made necessary by the circumstances of the time, and of promises that they would now respect democratic standards. It might also be argued that we should remark on how many, rather than how few, people voted for opposition parties in both countries as evidence of a commitment to pluralist democracy, in spite of prolonged periods of government propaganda and intimidation, and the superior resources of the incumbents. To this we could add the tone of opposition leaders' pronouncements, which dwelt at least as much on the alleged iniquities of authoritarian rule as on bread and butter questions, though it is not clear how far the votes they received were the result of such anti-authoritarian appeals.

The question of whether there has been an upsurge of demands for democratic government in Ghana and Tanzania remains a difficult one. It is tempting to return to Dunn and Robertson's assessment of Ghanaian political attitudes:

In 1969 – and very possibly still today – the legitimacy of the Ghanaian state in the eyes of its ordinary rural citizens appeared to depend on its long-term conformity to the model of representative democracy. But it was also clear that the prudential and moral requirement of obedience to whatever was currently the government was a much more definite and salient political precept than any vague conception of how the polity ought legitimately to be ordered.
(Dunn and Robertson 1973: 314)

No one would dispute the heroic deeds performed by some opposition politicians, lawyers, journalists, academics, trade union leaders and others in the quest for democratisation. Nor can one doubt the anger of a wider public at the frequent incompetence, corruption and bullying of authoritarian governments, but this is not the same as saying that there is a clear majority of the population of Ghana or Tanzania with a clear perception of, and a willingness to defend, democratic values. The incumbent authoritarian government in Ghana offered itself as the party of economic recovery, that in Tanzania as the party of internal peace and stability. Against these attractions, concerns about the desirability of a democratic order could easily become obscured.

DEMOCRATIC PROSPECTS

The possible absence of a widespread public commitment to democracy is not in itself an insuperable barrier to democratic development. Much of the literature on the subject suggests that democracy may evolve not so much because the majority of people consciously want it, but because it appears to be the best means of resolving immediate political conflicts. Without going through all the explanations of the emergence of democracy (some of which I have examined elsewhere; see Pinkney 1993: 18–38), we shall look at influences which seem especially relevant to Ghana and Tanzania, especially the impact of colonial rule, the underlying political cultures, the relationship between the state and civil society, and the economic background.

The colonial background

> The colonial state is the indispensable framework for any prospect of democratic government that may emerge. There is no alternative in either African tradition or pan-Africanist sentiment. (Austin 1993: 204)

> [Under colonial rule] Everything began and ended with the government, as demonstrated by the ludicrous practice of officials commissioning pit-latrines in villages. In effect local creativities and initiatives were blunted, and any sense of personal responsibility was detrimentally skewed. Many commonly refer to public property as '*aban*' – 'it belongs to the aban' – with the implication that it can be stolen, abused or destroyed with no direct consequences. The government

is still considered to be a foreign entity, and too many people feel no compunction or obligation to protect its property or services. Those officials who enriched themselves by corruption were not stigmatised in the eyes of society. *The entrenched and pervasive system of government, after all, had no effective means of making public servants accountable for their misdeeds.* Their lack of accountability, therefore, promoted social vices like embezzlement and corruption. Post-colonial leaders have generally not sought to redress the social contradictions bequeathed by colonialism.

(Agyeman-Duah 1987: 614–15. Emphasis added)

These statements are not necessarily incompatible, but they emphasise different aspects of the colonial inheritance. In terms of political structures, the colonial powers established distinctive nation states, however ill-conceived their boundaries might have been, and bequeathed constitutions and administrative structures which at least provided a framework for political interaction until something better could be found. On the other hand, colonial rule might be seen as emphasising order at the expense of democratic participation, and the notion that the state was something alien, 'above' the people, rather than an expression of their own aspirations. There was certainly an element of 'Do as I say, don't do as I do' as colonial rulers locked up nationalist agitators, and left no room for any notion of public servants being 'politically neutral' as between government and opposition, yet urged the adoption of liberal democratic constitutions. If colonial rule offered any 'preparation' for post-independence democracy, it was not mainly through offering trial runs, since the interval between the first nationwide elections on a broad franchise and the granting of independence in Africa (unlike India) was generally short, and few conventions had evolved on matters such as the rights of minorities, judicial and legislative checks and balances, or the handling of dissent. More important were the administrative and constitutional structures already mentioned which were necessary, though not sufficient, for any democratic system to function, and possibly the growing contacts between the metropolitan country and at least the wealthier and more talented members of the indigenous population. When some of them went to Europe or America as students or aspiring politicians, these people often became victims of racial discrimination and humiliation, but they also gained insights into the workings of pluralist political systems, which they were not allowed to operate at home, and this often provided an inspiration for incipient nationalist movements. These movements advanced the cause of democracy in the early years at least to the extent of presenting alternatives to rule by colonial powers or traditional elites, and by pressing for competitive elections. The return from Britain of Kwame Nkrumah and Julius Nyerere to Ghana and Tanganyika, where they both quickly established themselves as leaders of nationalist movements, can still be seen as an important landmark in the history of each country.

Political culture, the state and civil society

The different perspectives of Austin and Agyeman-Duah lead us on logically to two other inter-related variables frequently cited as having a bearing on democratic development: firstly the nature of indigenous political culture and secondly the relationship between the state and civil society. Agyeman-Duah's reference to the blunting of local creativities and initiatives might imply the existence of a participant culture which would have flowered but for the heavy hand of colonialism, whereas Austin's assertion that there is no democratic alternative in 'African tradition' suggests that any such culture is a blind alley when it comes to modern national politics. The enthusiasm of Ghanaians for local political participation can hardly be in doubt. There is a long tradition of faction fighting over the destoolment and succession of chiefs, with those who have helped the winning contender expecting their due rewards, and more recently writers have remarked on the contrast between the high turnout in the non-party local elections of 1988–9 and the lack of interest in the previous parliamentary and presidential elections of 1979 (Oquaye 1992: 283). National constitutions, parties and juntas have come and gone, but local politics endure, where people have a clearer perception of what is due to them and how they can obtain it.

No party politician or military ruler has dared to proclaim the republic of the common man at village level, or to abolish the office of chief; and ordinary illiterate Ghanaians have ... been moved to violent action in defence of 'rights'.

(Austin 1976: 157)

As Crook has observed 'The strength and mobilisation of Ghanaian civil society could, if better harnessed and integrated, provide a stronger basis for a participative and civic order' (Crook 1990: 34), but harnessing these forces has proved as problematic as harnessing the power of the Volta River to generate an industrial revolution. In both cases there is room for argument about whether the 'failure' to realise the potential is the result of mismanagement or of unrealistic expectations. If, as Agyeman-Duah argues, colonial rule has led Ghanaians to see national authority as something alien, which may be feared or exploited but seldom loved, the difficulties in sustaining democracy may be attributed to more than the misfortune of having the wrong politicians taking the wrong decisions.

Tanzanian political culture is in many ways the mirror image of the Ghanaian. With a large number of small tribes, Tanzania never had powerful chiefs comparable with the Asantahene or the Okyenhene of Akim Abuakwa, and the chieftaincy was abolished with little difficulty after independence. While occasional insults of 'tribalism' were exchanged between presidential candidates in 1995 when they could think of no other ammunition to fire, there are no real foci of ethnic or local loyalty comparable with those found in Ghana. In the absence of chiefs, or of ethnic groups large enough to demand autonomy, there is a relative absence of social hierarchy but also a relative inability to resist penetration by national institutions. A more egalitarian society appears to make it easier to achieve consensus, and Van Donge and Liviga have illustrated the way in which a consensual political culture provides for continuity in policy making (Van Donge and Liviga 1986: 619–39). More recent writers have highlighted a more authoritarian fist within the apparently consensual glove (especially Baregu in Widner 1994: 158–81), but there do not seem to have been any obvious lines of political conflict comparable with those between Akans and

Ewes, or between the rival heirs to the Nkrumah and Danquah-Busia traditions in Ghana. The problem for democracy in Tanzania may lie in lack of conflict, whereas in Ghana it has been the intensity of conflict that has been the problem. The absence of chiefs, or of powerful ethnic groups which might dominate other groups, may make for egalitarianism but it may also make it easier for the ruling party or government to dominate society in the absence of adequate intermediate institutions.

This leads us on to the whole question of the balance between the state and civil society. An over-bearing state which attempts to control every aspect of political life, as in the totalitarian model, and a weak state which is unable to convert popular demands into policy outputs, can both be equally harmful to democracy. The former stunts independent political participation, and the latter renders such participation futile. As for the concept of civil society, this has been used in a variety of ways but Harbeson's suggestion that civil society, as distinct from society in general, 'is confined to associations to the extent that they take part in rule setting activities' (Harbeson in Harbeson, Rothchild and Chazan 1994: 4) seems a useful starting point, especially if we substitute the word 'convention' for rule. This approach emphasises that in most, if not all countries, the values of different groups in society and the sanctions which they can bring to bear to enforce them, play a part in determining political outcomes alongside the outcomes determined by formal structures such as votes in parliament or executive decisions carrying the force of law. Thus explanations of public policy towards the treatment of religious minorities needs to take into account not only laws relating to freedom of worship or public money voted for religious schools, but the extent and intensity to which different beliefs are held, attitudes towards the beliefs of others and the resources and sanctions which different denominations may be able to bring to bear, from withholding votes to excommunication or violence against heretics.

State–civil society relations have fluctuated in both Ghana and Tanzania. During the height of one-party rule in Tanzania it seemed that the state was either throttling civil society or filling the vacuums existing on account of the weakness of civil society, bearing in mind what we have said about the absence of a chieftaincy or effective autonomous groups. More recently Rothchild and Lawson have suggested that there has been 'societal disengagement' from the state as retrenchment has reduced the role of the state in areas such as policing, education and agriculture (Rothchild and Lawson in Harbeson, Rothchild and Chazan 1994: 270–1), but the disengagement was from an initially high level of state activity by African standards, and it is by no means certain that some political equivalent of the economic 'invisible hand' will stimulate democratic participation where there was previously a largely passive consumption of state services. One opposition politician claimed in an interview that vigilante groups which had been set up, when policing became inadequate, had subsequently been taken over by the ruling party which used them to run protection rackets. While I could not verify this, the story is indicative of a Tanzanian expectation that ruling politicians and bureaucrats will, or even should, be the focus of political activity rather than an autonomous civil society. The concern of opposition politicians about obtaining adequate subsidies from the state for the 1995 election, rather than going out and raising their own funds, appears to reflect a similar attitude.

In Ghana our description of a flourishing chieftaincy, and the existence of strong business and professional groups, suggests a more autonomous civil society. There was also a strong state, built on the foundations of colonial rule by Nkrumah's Convention People's Party (CPP) between 1951 and 1966, with favourable economic conditions facilitating an expansion of state activities in economic management and social welfare. But the growing political instability which accompanied economic decline, and alternations between civilian and military governments which varied from the incompetent to the kleptomaniac, meant that the retreat of the state in the 1980s was much more dramatic than in Tanzania, with a collapse of social provision and an abandonment of many attempts to manage the economy. In a country with a stronger tradition of autonomous groups, this collapse might have been seen as a signal for a revival of civil society and of participatory activities which could provide a basis for democratic revival, but again the state's loss was not necessarily civil society's gain. This is partly because many of the activities carried out by groups of individuals in the absence of state aid, such as mutual self-help or marketing schemes, had little connection with political activity but were more strategies for survival, and impoverished people struggling for survival have little time for political activity (see especially Herbst 1993: 172). In time greater self-reliance might lay the foundations for a growing entrepreneurial class which could seek a new role in the political system, but there is little evidence that this has happened so far.

> A number of academics have sought to romanticise various forms of popular political expression, together with the local-level arrangements to which some communities have turned for the (often very inadequate) performance of functions no longer performed effectively by the state ... There is a danger here of mistaking an intellectual fad for real progress in popular participation and influence.
> (Jeffries 1993: 32–3)

Not only is there a danger of over-estimating the extent to which civil society is encouraging democratic development, but there is also a danger of assuming that, because the state in many parts of Africa has been repressive, corrupt and inefficient, its weakening or contraction should be welcomed by democrats. Jeffries argues that a stronger, more administratively efficient state may be necessary to provide an environment in which government policies, even those directed towards economic liberalisation, can be put into effect (ibid: 20–25). For the present and the immediate future, democratic development appears to be inhibited by both weak states and civil societies with limited resources.

Economic influences

While history, political culture, the state and civil society have all made an impact on the nature and extent of democratic development, the influence of economic performance is always lurking in the background. Writers from Lipset onwards have been interested in the relationship between material prosperity and democracy (Lipset 1959: 69–105), and many have pointed to the juxtaposition of wealth and democracy. There have not been many military governments or personal dictatorships in Scandinavia, and stable liberal democracy has not been the norm in Central America, though we can point to exceptions such as the flourishing of democracy in a poor country such as India or the survival of authoritarianism in wealthy Arab states. Material wealth can make a direct contribution to democracy by making politics less of a life and death struggle for limited resources, and leaving people less dependent on political outcomes for their prospects in life. In a poor country it is often governmental decisions that determine whether a school is located within travelling distance for a particular child, and thus whether the child can grow up literate and enjoy better career prospects; whether a business man will be awarded a contract that may make a difference between affluence and bankruptcy; or whether a motorable road will be built that will enable villagers to market their crops. In wealthier countries, in contrast, the differences are frequently of quantity rather than quality. The closure of a village school may be an inconvenience, but there will be another one down the road; the inability to win a government contract will reduce profits but there will be other customers in the market; roads to the nearest market town may be in a poor state of repair but farmers will not normally be reduced to carrying their produce on foot. Supporting the winning side in politics, whether through votes or bribes, is therefore less crucial to one's life chances. Economic prosperity also frequently enhances democracy because it is not just a matter of per capita incomes increasing, but of accompanying processes such as industrialisation, urbanisation, improved communications, expanded education and the growth of a variety of groups in society representing producer interests, local communities or commonly-held beliefs, which enhance pluralist political participation.

On the basis of these indicators of development, the prospects for democracy in Ghana and Tanzania do not look promising. Tanzania has a literacy rate of over 60 per cent, which is high by African standards though declining (*Observer*, Dar es Salaam, 15 October 1995: 7) while that in Ghana is less than 40 per cent. On most indicators of development these countries are among the world's poorest, with low levels of per capita income, industrialisation, urbanisation and life expectancy. In 1992 the World Bank reported that Tanzania was the second poorest country in the world, second only to Mozambique (Lofchie in Callaghy and Ravenhill 1993: 400), though the wealth produced by the 'black economy', which cannot easily be estimated, was probably significant in a country where it had made economic sense to escape from the heavily-regulated formal sector. Twenty years ago, the economic handicaps we have described would have been regarded as insuperable barriers to democracy, yet the 1980s and 1990s have seen the undermining of authoritarian regimes and the holding of competitive elections in range of unlikely settings, including much of Eastern Europe, Latin America, South Africa and, of course, Tropical Africa. There is a wealth of literature offering explanations of this phenomenon, but most writers are on firmer ground when they offer explanations for the collapse of authoritarian regimes, or even the holding of free, competitive elections, than when they seek to explain why, and to what extent, the absence of authoritarianism and the holding of free elections will make for a new era of sustained democratic politics.

If economic backwardness is not conducive to democracy, it is equally true that economic decline is bad for authoritarianism, and especially the sort of authoritarianism which has been common in Tropical Africa in recent years. The severity of the decline could not but have political consequences. In Ghana the terms of trade, based on an index of 100 in 1961–2, had deteriorated to 60 by 1983–4. The price per ton of cocoa, the major export, by 1983–4 was only 28 per cent of the 1960–1 value (Kraus in Rothchild 1991: 127), while the import trade was hit by rising oil prices from 1973 onwards. By 1982 per capita income in Ghana was 15 per cent lower than it had been at the time of independence in 1957 (Herbst 1993: 17–18). Tanzania experienced a later and less dramatic economic decline, but had begun from a position of greater poverty. Per capita income grew at a rate of 6.4 per cent per year between 1961 and 1967, and at 4.8 per cent to 1973, but the economy was then hit by the oil crisis and by a decline in agricultural production, with droughts and the ill-fated attempts to re-settle isolated farmers in villages (Berg-Schlosser and Siegler 1990: 89). With deteriorating terms of trade and a costly war with Uganda in 1979, gross domestic product failed to keep pace with population growth and per capita income fell by 2.4 per cent a year between 1981 and 1985 (Cleary 1989: 6–25; Barkan 1994: 22).

Some types of authoritarian government may be able to withstand economic decline. Colonial governments can, within wide limits, deploy more coercive forces from the metropolitan country to quell popular discontent. 'Traditional' rulers do not base their claim to rule on indicators of economic growth, and are not normally held responsible for a poor economic performance, but governments based on military juntas or single parties are much more vulnerable. A military government's claim to legitimacy may be based on its ability to establish or restore order and stability where others have failed, in which case it will lose that legitimacy if it fails to fulfil its promise within a limited time span, or it may be based on its superior ability to promote economic growth when freed from the petty squabbling and short-term vote seeking of politicians. This again means that 'doing' rather than 'being' is the key to legitimacy, and the doing may be limited by world economic forces and the inadequate administrative capacity of the state. There are also the internal dynamics of the army to consider, as the small minority of soldiers who have usurped power, and enjoy the fruits of office, may provoke some of the majority in the army outside the government into carrying out a coup to enjoy similar benefits. For all these reasons military government has a limited shelf life, and the rulers may feel that an early return to barracks is preferable to the risk of a loss life, liberty or personal property in a violent overthrow. Even in exceptional cases where the military rulers are relatively successful in managing the economy, as in Ghana between 1983 and 1992, they will not go unchallenged. People will begin to ask why authoritarian government is necessary if there is no longer an economic crisis.

Single-party rule is designed as a longer term political solution than military government. It had already endured for over 40 years in the Soviet Union and nearly 20 years in Eastern Europe when Nkrumah and Nyerere began to preach its virtues in Ghana and Tanzania. There seemed to be no reason why a government should not base its legitimacy on the will of a single party with a mass base, especially if any potential opposition could be portrayed as tribalist and divisive, as in Ghana, or electorally insignificant, as in Tanzania. But the superficial similarities with Eastern Europe were misleading. Nkrumah's CPP lacked the discipline of a coherent ideology or a selective membership, and quickly degenerated into a gravy train for people seeking to share the spoils of office. As the spoils became scarcer with economic decline, there were few people left with the will to defend the party by 1966, and the coup of that year met with virtually no resistance. Nyerere's Tanganyika African National Union (TANU) was a more coherent force, and the holding of regular intra-party parliamentary elections gave it a sense of purpose in facilitating electoral choice and political recruitment. It even attempted, though probably too late, to impose ideological qualifications on people seeking membership. But ideological purity based on a state-controlled economy failed to produce material benefits, and when Ali Mwinyi succeeded Nyerere as President in 1985 he had little alternative but to liberalise the economy. Having had to abandon most of its ideological baggage by the 1990s, with the implicit admission that many of its policies had been mistaken, if not disastrous, the ruling party was hardly in a position to claim that it had a monopoly of political insight. Ruling parties elsewhere have, of course, survived after abandoning previously sacrosanct policies and principles, but the break-up of the Soviet Bloc and the insistence by Western donors on political pluralism as a condition for aid, left Tanzania with little alternative but to permit multi-party elections.

It is tempting to see Western pressure, especially after the ending of the Cold War, as the crucial factor in ending authoritarian rule in Africa, but the fact that the pressure was successful must, in turn, be related to the economic performances of African governments which led them to seek aid on terms largely dictated by outsiders. One does not hear so much about Western pressure for democratisation in Saudi Arabia, Singapore or Taiwan. It does not, of course, follow that the economic hazards of the 1970s and 1980s would have been negotiated any better by democratically elected governments in multi-party systems, but our concern here is with why authoritarianism collapsed rather than whether in some circumstances it might be the lesser evil.

AN END TO AUTHORITARIANISM OR A BEGINNING OF DEMOCRACY?

What of the prospects for the consolidation of democracy rather than the repelling of authoritarianism, bearing in mind the pessimism in earlier literature about the limited scope for democracy in the midst of poverty? The apparent 'thinness' of civil society, the paucity of groups with sufficient resources to stand up to the state and the absence of a widespread or deep commitment to democratic values, are phenomena which will not change overnight. What may be changing is, on the one hand, the extent to which governments are still able to dominate the political process and, on the other, the extent to which their opponents or critics are learning to exploit the freer political conditions.

With economic liberalisation, the ability of governments to retain support through political patronage is more limited. With political liberalisation – at least partially underwritten by foreign donors – press comment, public protest and organised campaigns become easier, as witness the successful pressure to abandon value added tax in Ghana in 1995. Governments and their supporters may still try to rig elections, but such rigging is likely to be only one of several factors which will influence the outcome. What seems to vary is the skill with which those outside the government operate. Opposition parties have displaced incumbent governments in recent years in Benin, Burundi, the Congo, Lesotho, Madagascar, Malawi, Mali, Niger, Sao Tome, Principe and Zambia, but not in Cameroon, Cote d'Ivoire, Gabon, Ghana, Kenya, Mauritius and Tanzania (see especially Wiseman 1993: 439–49). It is obviously not a requirement of democracy that citizens should vote their governments out regardless, but there does seem to be a difference, at least in English-speaking countries, between those where there was a determination on the part of opposition groups to overcome all their handicaps in order to bring about a change (notably in Malawi and Zambia) and those where the opposition was too fragmented or too narrowly-based to mount an effective challenge (Ghana, Kenya and Tanzania). The proverbial playing field may be far from level, but the ability of governments to win political battles, whether through the ballot box or in the course of day-to-day politics, can no longer be taken for granted. It used to be part of British political folklore that 'Oppositions don't win elections, governments lose them'. In much of Africa it is tempting to argue that 'Governments don't win elections, oppositions lose them', but it may be more complicated than that. Incumbent governments still retain a formidable array of resources. A test of the effectiveness of democracy will be the ability of opposition parties to defeat not only ageing tyrants and ineffective rulers who have lost control of the political process, but also to defeat effectively organised incumbents.

3 Ghana: Pluralist Democracy, Socialism, Populism and Dictatorship

They bury the past more thoroughly in the former Communist Bloc. Few towns or streets still bear the name of Stalin, and statues of Lenin have been removed one by one. Berliners no longer live in streets named after leaders of the German Democratic Republic, and not even the prophets of the revolution have been spared. Trains no longer stop at Marx–Engels Strasse, but at Heckescher Market.

The visitor to Ghana, in contrast, can land at Kotokta Airport (named after the general who ousted President Nkrumah), and travel via Danquah Circle (named after Nkrumah's leading opponent who died in gaol) and along Kwame Nkrumah Avenue (named after the President of the First Republic), before stopping to shop at 31 December Makola Market (which commemorates Flight Lieutenant Rawlings's second coup). Only the leaders of the unstable Third Republic and the unloved second military government, the National Redemption Council (NRC), remain uncommemorated. National Redemption Circle has been renamed Thomas Sankara Circle, after Rawlings's opposite number in Burkina Faso.

Ghanaian politicians do obviously fall from grace, and Nkrumah's solitary statue enjoyed a much shorter life than the many in Lenin's likeness, but ideological divides between one regime and the next are generally less sharp than those in Eastern Europe. Yet Ghanaian politics are clearly more than a series of personal or 'tribal' conflicts, and ideology does provide us with some guide through the multiplicity of party and military acronyms of the past 40 years. At the risk of crude over-simplification, we can attempt to unravel three

Table 3.1 Different ideological tendencies in Ghana

State socialist	Populist	Liberal
CPP (Nkrumah) 1949–66		UGCC, NLM, UP (Danquah, Busia) 1947–66
NAL (Gbedemah, Agama) 1969–72		NLC (Gen. Ankrah, Gen Africa) 1966–9; PP (Busia) 1969–72
	NRC/SMC (Gen. Acheampong, Gen. Akuffo) 1972–79.	
PNP (Limann) 1979–81	AFRC (Flt. Lt. Rawlings) 1979.	PFP (Owusu) 1979–81.
	PNDC (Flt. Lt. Rawlings) 1981–92.	
NCP (Agyekum) 1992 –(Plus other extra-parliamentary parties)	NDC (Rawlings) 1992 –	NPP (Boahen) 1992–

ideological strands, and call them state socialism, liberalism and populism. We omit conservatism since virtually all political tendencies claim to believe in 'development', with all its implications for social change and state intervention. While there are institutions which many, if not most, Ghanaians want to conserve, such as the chieftaincy and varied tribal traditions, there is no clearly recognisable attempt to defend a 'traditional' social order where such an order conflicts with material progress.

Table 3.1 attempts to plot the evolution of the state socialist, liberal and populist strands. The intention of this chapter is not produce a detailed political history of Ghana, which is covered well by such writers as Austin (1964) on the First

Republic, Austin and Luckham (1975) on the first military government and the Second Republic, Oquaye (1980) on the second military government, and Ninsin and Drah (1993) and Rothchild (1991) on events after 1979, but to illustrate the evolving lines of conflict which have a bearing on the ability, or otherwise, of Ghanaian politics to develop a system of institutionalised democratic competition. The liberal element can be traced back to the elite groups which sought self-government for the then Gold Coast in the early post-war years, and who formed the United Gold Coast Convention (UGCC). As with many early nationalist movements, the overriding objective of self-government was more important than detailed consideration of the actual form of government, but it was generally assumed that an independent Ghana would enjoy a liberal democratic political order, with political parties competing freely, and with checks and balances to limit the power of politicians.

A SOCIALIST EXPERIMENT?

Kwame Nkrumah, who had already established a reputation as an African nationalist in Britain and the United States, was invited to return to Ghana to lead the UGCC in 1947. He soon became dissatisfied with the pace at which the Convention wanted to move, and in 1949 broke away to form the Convention People's Party (CPP). Although the immediate attraction of the CPP was its demand for 'self-government now', it also proclaimed itself to be socialist and pan-Africanist, and cultivated the support of lower social groups which the UGCC had largely ignored.

> The future leaders if the CPP still held relatively humble positions – relative that is, to the lawyers, newspaper owners and merchants among the intelligentsia. They were primary school teachers, clerks in government and commercial offices, petty traders, storekeepers, local contractors, not very successful businessmen with a one-man, one-lorry transport enterprise or a small import-export trade. And their immediate following was still more humble. The junior school leaver, and those who failed to complete the full

senior course – who lacked the all important Standard VII certificate – were hardly employable at all.

(Austin 1964: 16)

The CPP's promise of national independence, secured in 1957, and of the national development which would (it mistakenly believed) follow it, enabled it to win decisive victories in three pre-independence elections. Helped by a buoyant economy with rising export prices, the CPP government quickly expanded the public service in both the economic and the social spheres, and set itself the objective of rapid development through industrialisation.

The rump of the UGCC toiled in the shadows, first as the National Liberation Movement (NLM) and then as the United Party (UP). Leaders, such as Joseph Danquah and Kofi Busia, remained impeccable advocates of liberal democracy, limited government and civil liberties, but political conflict soon revealed Ghanaian roots that were at least as important as imported ideologies. Regions such as Ashanti, and to a lesser extent the North and the Volta Region, feared a concentration of power in Accra, so the lines of political conflict polarised around centre versus periphery as well as state socialism versus liberalism. It was but a short step from regional claims to the claims of the dominant ethnic group within a region, so that politics could be portrayed in 'tribal' terms. Thus the NLM might be seen as articulating the demands of the Asante as a tribe, and not merely Ashanti as an administrative region. But tribalism was never more than part of the story. Political conflict never revolved around monolithic groups, which at other times and places has been a recipe for civil war or national disintegration. Within each group there were dissenting minorities, some based on long-standing chieftaincy disputes, some on social class and some on ideology. This may have made for a more quarrelsome society, with the newly-established political parties exploiting, and being exploited by, a range of local conflicts, but it also provided the 'cross-cutting cleavages' which many textbooks regard as necessary in a pluralist polity.

The CPP overcame demands for regional autonomy and separatism. Opposition politicians were 'bought off' through patronage or silenced through preventive detention. A *de jure* one-party state was declared in 1964, and the party won all the seats in Parliament in the 1965 'election' in which all its candidates were returned unopposed. The rhetoric of the Leninist single party was frequently employed, but the reality was different. According to one senior party member:

> On ... all important questions of policy ... discussion begins at branch level. The arguments, pro and con, move on to the District Executive Committee of the Party, and then on to the Regional Executive Committee, and from there to the National Executive Committee. Next the Cabinet gives assent, probably with some modifications and interpretations to ensure the fullest possible consensus of party opinion. (Armah 1965: 96)

The reality was that the party structure decayed once there were no elections to contest. The combined effects of worsening terms of trade after 1960, and the dissipation of public resources in largely unproductive, and often corruptly incurred, public expenditure, led to growing economic hardship and public discontent. One can argue about whether there had ever been a genuine attempt to establish socialist state, and indeed about what the term means, but the years before 1966 were distinctive in the extent to which state control over the economy was imposed, and to which a single party claimed a monopoly of the truth and a right (imperfectly exercised in practice) to penetrate all sections of society. The experiment worked only patchily in relatively prosperous years, and had little chance of survival once the economic tide turned.

A LIBERAL RESTORATION?

In the absence of competitive elections or of conditions conducive to a popular uprising, the only obvious way of removing the government was through a *coup d'état*. This occurred in February 1966. The army had its own grievances, including the loss of resources to the President's Own Guard Regiment and the recent dismissal of two of its most senior officers, but the leaders of the coup were very much in the mould of the liberal democratic opposition (see especially the memoirs of one of the coup leaders, Afrifa [1966]). The rule of the new National Liberation Council (NLC) might almost be seen as a period of liberalism without democracy. The retreat from state economic intervention was mild by present-day standards, but political detainees were released, a variety of pressure groups were encouraged to contribute to the policy-making process, the expertise of civil servants was treated with greater respect and a National Advisory Committee was created, consisting largely of former opposition politicians, to act like a parliament without legislative power (see especially Pinkney 1972: 66–88). Liberal tolerance did not, however, extend to the now-proscribed CPP. Its leaders were put in 'protective custody' immediately after the coup and, although the majority did not remain there for very long, the government ensured that the party did not re-surface when an election was called in 1969. Hundreds of CPP members were disqualified from standing for office on the grounds of corruption during the First Republic. To that extent, the military 'fixed' the election in favour of the liberal democratic element, which re-emerged as the Progress Party (PP) under Dr Busia, but again the battle lines were not entirely clear cut. Two of the eight members of the military government belonged to the Ewe tribe, and favoured Komla Gbedemah, a fellow tribesman who led the rump of the CPP under the confusing title of the National Alliance of Liberals (NAL), while some other members of the government remained agnostic. While the general tone of the most prominent military leaders was that Ghana must not go back to the days of one-party dictatorship, it would be fanciful to imagine that a small group of soldiers and police officers with no popular base could have swayed millions of voters. The PP had to earn its votes by persuading opinion leaders, ultimately the ordinary voters, that its claim to moral probity was a stronger asset than its opponents' claims to experience in government (see especially Twumasi in Austin and Luckham 1975: 140–63).

Did the experience of PP rule between 1969 and 1972 provide Ghana with experience of pluralist democracy which might throw light on the country's ability to sustain democracy? There was certainly an 'openness' which had been lacking under the CPP, with no preventive detention, a free press, an opposition in Parliament, and freely-contested by-elections won by the opposition. On the economic front, the government claimed to be laying the foundations of development where it mattered, in the rural areas, in contrast to the CPP's policies of 'prestige spending' on a multi-million pound conference centre, the Accra–Tema motorway and numerous uneconomic factories. But, as in subsequent periods of pluralist democracy, the spectre of previous authoritarian rulers led democrats to behave in ways not conducive to democracy. Gbedemah was deprived of his parliamentary seat on the grounds that previously corrupt behaviour disqualified him. While this was nominally a judicial decision, greater magnanimity on the part of the government might have done more for political consensus. Not only did Nkrumah remain in exile, but displaying his likeness became a criminal offence, so that the legitimacy of a major political tendency in Ghana was effectively denied. A belief that the country had suffered under the previous rule of uneducated 'bully boys' was extended into a belief in the innate wisdom of the lawyers, academics and members of chiefly families who now dominated the government. Critics were treated with a certain condescension, and policy positions became inflexible, whether on the expulsion of 'alien' business men (some of whose families had been in Ghana for several generations), the dismissal of 568 allegedly inadequate public servants, or the opening of a dialogue with (white) South Africa. Even a judicial ruling on the impropriety of dismissing the public servants was brushed aside on the grounds that it was for the government to decide which people it should employ.

In these ways the PP lost the support of much of what should have been its 'natural' constituency. Local businesses found that the expulsion of entrepreneurs from other African states and the Middle East meant the loss of essential supplies, lawyers disliked the disregarding of judicial rulings, and students and other intellectuals were critical of any appeasement of apartheid. The government was thus already in a weak political position at a time when world economic conditions were turning against Ghana. A balance-of-trade surplus of 28 million cedis in 1968 had turned into a deficit of 65.1 million cedis by 1972 (Austin 1976: 7), and the terms of trade deteriorated sharply after 1971 (Kraus in Rothchild 1991: 127). The government was forced to devalue the cedi, thus creating hardship among the working population, and to curtail some of the amenities previously enjoyed by army officers. The latter decision was sufficient to provoke another military coup, led by (the then) Colonel Ignatius Acheampong.

The circumstances of the 1972 coup were different from those of 1966. In 1966 the army could rightly claim that there was no other way of removing an authoritarian government, and it kept its promise to allow the people to choose a new government. The 1972 coup, in contrast, was against a government which might have been insensitive or unimaginative, but which was not denying people basic human rights, including the right to vote it out. That such a coup could succeed with minimal resistance, if not on any great wave of support, and on a pretext which scarcely concealed the self-interest of the military as the main driving force, did not say much for the prospects of sustaining democracy. At best democracy seemed to be something which might arouse the passions of a small politically active minority and a few intellectual observers, but to the bulk of the population its demise was something of little interest, or seen as beyond their control.

THE EMERGENCE OF POPULISM

The new National Redemption Council (subsequently renamed the Supreme Military Council [SMC]) not only had few qualms about extinguishing democracy, but had very different views from the first military government on the type of political system appropriate to Ghana. It is here that what we term a 'populist' attitude to politics emerges in competition with the state socialist and liberal strands. The term may be difficult to define, but it implies a suspicion of party politicians as a whole, and not just one-party regimes, as vehicles for articulating the popular will. Party politicians, in this view, are not representatives of the people but entrepreneurs who exploit the masses so as to win power and wealth for themselves, often creating discord between different groups in society in order to win votes. Ways must therefore be found of hearing the authentic voice of the people without it being distorted by political parties. The committee established by the government to work out the detailed proposals for a no-party state argued that 'Historical data and journalistic accounts abound as to the acrimony, the near disintegration of Ghana and the fanning of discordant ethnic feeling as a result of party politics.'(Ghana 1977: 33). General Acheampong, it reported, envisaged a type of government other than 'the party type of government that brings in its trail division, hatred, sectional and tribal interest' (Ghana 1977: 33). There were also elements of populism in the economic sphere which earned the government immediate support. Busia's devaluation of the cedi was reversed, some foreign debts were repudiated, Nkrumah's reputation was rehabilitated, and an ambitious 'Operation Feed Yourself' scheme was launched with a view to making Ghana self-sufficient in food.

As a short-term expedient there is nothing remarkable about an African military government banning political parties and seeking to communicate with the population via chiefs, bureaucrats and organised groups. What was distinctive about the Acheampong government was its attempt to establish a permanent no-party state in which corporate groups, including the army, would be represented in government alongside non-party representatives chosen by voters.

Was 'populism', which resurfaced in a different form under Rawlings, an ideology which deserves serious attention, alongside socialism and liberalism, or merely a smokescreen created by the military to justify the curtailment of pluralist politics? It is certainly an ideology which can be, and has been, perverted by rulers. The rulers, in turn, have had no lack of sycophants, able to admire the latest style in the emperor's new clothes. Yet beyond crude self interest there is a serious point. Political parties in Ghana, as in much of the Third World, have been both too strong and too weak for the effective functioning of democracy. They have been too strong in the sense that, in the absence of strong countervailing institutions, parties can win votes relatively easily through bribery, intimidation and the exploitation of local and personal conflicts, if they have the necessary financial backing and key individuals in the right places. This is in contrast to party politics in most Western countries, where the power of a potentially dominant party is checked by other parties, whose supporters may have an ingrained loyalty and may not be 'bought off' easily, and partly by other institutions such as the state bureaucracy, labour, business, religious and voluntary groups, which all play a major role in determining the distribution of resources, largely irrespective of which party is in power. At the same time parties in Ghana (and in much of the Third World) are weak in the sense that they lack a large core of committed supporters to sustain them in times of economic difficulties, and are therefore more likely to resort to bribery, patronage and coercion to retain power. Party support is, for the most part, 'instrumental' in the sense of being based on the expectation of tangible benefits, rather than 'solidaristic' in the sense of being built on the loyalty of groups such as social classes or religious denominations.

In such a situation, one does not have to be a megalomaniac military ruler to have reservations about the efficacy of party politics. It was easy to argue that, far from giving voice to the people's aspirations, parties were a means by which the few exploited the many. Keep them out of politics, and the true wishes of the people would be articulated, whether through Acheampong's corporate groups or Rawlings's District Assemblies and Committees for the Defence of the Revolution. As an ideal, one could argue that populism was no more alien to Africa than liberal democracy but, in terms of practical application, no one has yet found a means of achieving the elusive consensus that party politics is supposed to have destroyed. In Acheampong's case, the fact that the government was already unpopular by the mid-1970s on account of its corruption and economic mismanagement, meant arguments about the relative merits of a no-party state became tangled up debate on the merits of the government itself, and a referendum in 1978 on 'union government', as the proposed arrangements were called, was easily turned into a referendum on the popularity of the government.

Fierce public resistance soon surfaced, centred largely on supporters of the erstwhile Busia regime. People who had gone to prison for opposing a one-party state under Nkrumah now paid a return visit for opposing a no-party state. Despite the virtual prohibition of any open 'No' campaign, and the dubious ways in which the votes were actually counted, the government's opponents won 45 per cent of the vote, which amounted to a moral victory.

By this time the economic benefits of the early years of military government, when cocoa prices had been rising and agricultural output growing, had been offset by negative economic growth, huge balance of payments and budget deficits, shortages of essential goods and a rate of inflation of nearly 100 per cent. Real wages were estimated to have fallen to a quarter of their 1972 value. In an economic world of shortages and a political world of unaccountable government, black markets and corruption flourished (see especially Jeffries in Cruise O'Brien et al. 1989: 77–81). With the government unpopular for its denial of democratic rights, the ever-growing economic hardship and corruption amongst the military leadership, the military responded by replacing General Acheampong with General Akuffo (for a detailed account of the government's record see Oquaye 1980: 17–55). The new administration promised the holding of multi-party elections, but public dissatisfaction had reached the point where there were demands not just for civilian government but for the punishment of Acheampong and his colleagues for their corruption and mismanagement. This was the pretext for the coup led by Flight Lieutenant Jerry Rawlings on 4 June 1979.

While the 1966 coup was motivated largely by concern with democratic rights, and that of 1972 with the corporate interests of the officer corps, the 1979 coup was much more an uprising of the junior officers and other ranks against the corruption and mismanagement of their superiors. The aim was not to impose another spell of military government, but to purge the corrupt army elements so that justice was done before the multi-party elections were held. If the Acheampong government was populist in the sense of bypassing politicians in seeking public support, Rawlings was a populist in the more radical sense of appealing to the increasingly impoverished masses against a selfish and incompetent ruling elite. In pursuit of such an appeal, ends mattered more than means. If the masses wanted corrupt officers punished, and the judicial process was too cumbersome to establish their guilt, then bypass the judiciary. If existing laws did not make corruption a capital offence, then ignore the law, try people in private and execute them in public. If market women were deemed to be responsible for hoarding, shortages and high prices (and a more refined economic analysis might see them as a symptom rather than a cause), then send soldiers to beat up the market women and burn down their stalls.

We should, however, beware of crediting the Rawlings Government with too coherent a strategy or ideology. The weeks that followed the coup were a period in which the army's internal hierarchy and discipline broke down, so that much depended on who happened to have a gun at a particular time or place. Rawlings is sometimes portrayed as a 'moderating' influence. While Acheampong, Akuffo, Afrifa and four other officers were executed, and many others were imprisoned or deprived of their assets, it has been suggested that these punishments were necessary to appease discontent in the lower ranks, and perhaps among the civilian population, before a semblance of normality could be restored and elections held (Jeffries in Cruise O'Brien et al. 1989: 85).

The 1979 parliamentary and presidential elections were the only post-independence elections to have been accepted as fair by all the losers as well as the winners. Victory went to Dr Hilla Limann's People's National Party (PNP), which was generally seen as an ideological reincarnation of the CPP, even though most of the personnel were different, and the leader's main power base was now in the north, his own area, rather than the south or west. The new Third Republic enjoyed an impeccable human rights record throughout its existence; a lively opposition operated in Parliament and on one occasion even defeated the government's budget proposals. Why, then, did 1979, like 1969, prove to be a false democratic dawn?

Limann, like Busia before him, spent much of his time fighting the spectre of a former head of state. But whereas Busia's adversary, Nkrumah, was in exile in Guinea, Limann's adversary, Rawlings, was closer at hand, despite attempts to give him a diplomatic posting. The de-stabilising influence of Rawlings was aggravated by the government's inability to tackle the country's continued economic weaknesses. An impeccable human rights record proved to be of little value in preserving a democratic regime if it could not provide its citizens with basic necessities, especially when Rawlings had acquired a reputation as the man who was on the side of the poor. And it was Rawlings who appeared to be a more plausible alternative leader than any civilian politician.

A coup on new year's eve 1981 brought Rawlings back to power, and the populist element in Ghanaian politics returned to the ascendancy. The diagnosis of Ghana's ills was no longer one of a ruling party or senior army officers behaving corruptly, but of a failure of a whole political/bureaucratic class. Rawlings shared Acheampong's distaste for competitive party politics, which were seen as an elitist activity that exploited the masses rather than offering them democratic choice, but his alternative was not merely to bypass politicians, but to establish populist structures that would articulate the 'real' voice of the common people. People's Defence Committees (PDCs), based on geographical areas, and Workers' Defence Committees (WDCs), based on workplaces, were thus established, although the word 'committee' suggests a more formal organisation than generally existed. Anyone was free to join these organisations, apart from such 'enemies of the revolution' as chiefs, capitalists, former politicians and members of the professions. Rawlings's new regime, the Provisional National Defence Council (PNDC), thus started with a very different power base from any previous Ghanaian regime. The PDCs and WDCs were designed to shore up mass support, while at the centre Rawlings relied on trusted military colleagues, drawn largely from junior officers and other ranks, and radical intellectuals.

The extent to which the 1981 coup was a 'popular revolution' remains a matter of dispute. The drastic reduction in living standards since the mid-1970s had undoubtedly produced greater anger with the incompetence and dishonesty of ruling politicians, and perhaps with the elite as a whole, but the change of government manifested itself as an old-fashioned coup, involving a relatively small number of soldiers and few civilians, rather than a 'revolution'. According to one (subsequently disaffected) member of the PNDC, only twelve loyal soldiers entered Burma Camp (the headquarters of the Ministry of Defence) with Rawlings on the day of the coup (Yeebo 1991: 47–8). The subsequent political changes were revolutionary in the sense that most of the building blocks on which previous Ghanaian governments had been based – party leaders, civilian bureaucrats, senior army officers, the chieftaincy and the professions – were largely dispensed with. But was there a viable alternative 'revolutionary' structure? And were there viable revolutionary policies around which people could unite? By 1983 the answers to both questions seemed to be in the negative. The romantic notion of turning back the tide of world capitalism and establishing a self-reliant economy soon lost its appeal as economic conditions worsened still further, and the government fell back on the non-revolutionary strategy of seeking assistance from the International Monetary Fund (IMF). The ideological compromises implicit in this shift of policy alienated many of the radical intellectuals in the government, and the hardships caused by the austerity measures, which IMF aid required, alienated much of the working-class constituency in the PDCs and WDCs. These organisations, which had initially been useful to the government in pillorying capitalists, senior army officers, party politicians and other opponents, were now becoming an embarrassment as they disrupted the minimal order which the government was trying to restore. With the radical intellectual and working-class constituencies largely lost, the government was now trying to repair relations with erstwhile 'enemies of the revolution' such as technocrats, employers, the professions and chiefs. Even in the army, much of the traditional command structure was restored, following the purges of senior officers.

At this point one might have been tempted to conclude that the PNDC was just another military government which had come to terms with political and economic reality, and would soon revert to the traditional cycle by handing over power to elected civilians, once the weight of the burden of office and the limited scope for political choice became apparent. But the actual outcome was very different. Instead of a continuation of the cycle of weak elected civilian governments, inhibited by the fear of military intervention, and military governments unable to resolve the problems for which they claimed greater competence than civilians, the course of Ghanaian politics was altered more profoundly by the Rawlings regime than by any other since Nkrumah. The reasons for this appear to be two-fold. Firstly, when the government did resort to 'orthodox' economic policies after 1983, it was a relatively successful orthodoxy. The gross domestic product had been declining at an annual rate of over 4 per cent in the first two years of PNDC rule. From 1984 to 1989 the annual rate of growth averaged over 6 per cent (Kraus in Rothchild 1991: 128). This relative economic success gave Rawlings a degree of legitimacy which General Acheampong had not enjoyed when presiding over a collapsing economy, and enabled Rawlings to claim that any hasty transfer of power to civilians might put the economic recovery in jeopardy, especially in the light of the performance of previous civilian governments. Secondly, there were strong ideological and practical reasons for not returning to competitive party politics. At a practical level, a regime which had retained power not only through relative economic success, but through arbitrary arrest, detention, torture and execution, must have given some thought to the possible consequences of an anti-Rawlings government being elected and taking its revenge on the men responsible for repression. At an ideological level, there was still a genuine belief that liberal democracy had not served Ghana well, and that a more participatory form of democracy should be sought. The PDCs and WDCs, subsequently transformed into Committees for the Defence of the Revolution (CDRs), were one manifestation of this, and district assemblies, elected on a non-party basis, were another. Fora such as these, it was argued, were open to members of all social groups, with rival candidates for the district assemblies sharing common platforms and thus incurring few election expenses. This was in contrast to party competition, where it was said that electoral success depended on the ability to spend money, and thus excluded the poor. The hostility to party politics, in terms of both its allegedly elitist nature and its damaging effects when practised in Ghana, continued almost up to the drafting of the Fourth Republic constitution. Yet the alternative of a populist no-party state, for all its achievements in stimulating interest in local government, seemed increasingly implausible as a basis for national government.

COULD ANY POLITICAL SYSTEM BE MADE TO WORK?

Before going on to look at the incongruous attempts by self-declared opponents of bourgeois democracy to establish a liberal democratic order, we need to take stock of the circumstances which had brought Ghana to such a pass. Every type of political arrangement attempted since independence appeared to have failed, not only in the sense of failing to maintain material prosperity and civil liberties, but in the sense of failing to sustain any framework within which political conflict could be resolved, resources allocated or governments held accountable for their actions. Socialism, liberal democracy and populism had all initially offered new paths out of the maze, but each time Ghana had ended up apparently more disoriented than before. Was this because of the failings of individual political actors? Were world economic conditions too hostile for any government to keep its constituents satisfied for long? Was the underlying political culture unconducive to any rapport between government and governed? Or did political structures, especially the army, political parties and the state bureaucracy, take on a life of their own to the extent that the political system lost any equilibrium that it might have had? We shall look at political structures in more detail in the next chapter. Here we shall look at the extent to which economic conditions, political culture and political behaviour made life difficult for authoritarians and democrats alike.

ECONOMIC CONSTRAINTS

Civilian governments certainly seem to have been unlucky in presiding over periods in which the terms of trade were moving against Ghana. Based on a 1961–2 base of 100, the terms of trade deteriorated under the CPP from 107 in 1960–1 to 68 in 1965–6, only to revive under the next three years of military government. After reaching 109 during the Progress Party's first full year in power, they had fallen to 72 by the time Dr Busia was deposed. There was a continuous improvement to 186 under the next seven years of military government, followed by a sharp deterioration during Dr Limann's brief two year reign (Kraus in Rothchild 1991: 127). World prices are something over which the government of a small country has virtually no control, and for which it could not be blamed directly. Yet worsening terms of trade are likely to lead to unpopular austerity measures which may be the final straw for a government which already enjoys only limited legitimacy in the eyes of the population. Austin suggests that economic failure was more important than loss of 'loyalty' in explaining the demise of civilian governments and that 'when the goods run out the traders are discredited' (Austin 1976: 158). If there is agreement on nothing else about Ghanaian political attitudes, it is generally accepted that 'loyalty' to elected governments is a very scarce commodity. There may, as Dunn and Robertson suggest, be a belief in democracy as an ideal (Dunn and Robertson 1973: 314) but few Ghanaians are willing to lie down in front of the tanks when the military decide to depose a civilian government that is no longer able to distribute extensive material benefits.

If world commodity prices were beyond the control of Ghanaian politicians and soldiers, could they still be blamed for political choices which made the economy still worse, and thus undermined their own positions? After all, neighbouring Cote d'Ivoire faced a similar world economy, yet its political system remained remarkably stable, if undemocratic. Much depends on the extent to which one believes that political actors have 'free will'. It is easy to pick on the 'economic irrationality', or even the socially irresponsibility, of politicians but, like everyone else, they live in world in which some actions are rewarded and others punished, no matter how unjust these outcomes may seem. The most rewarding decisions will not necessarily be those which produce the greatest good for the greatest number. Jonathan Frimpong-Ansah, a former Governor of the Bank of Ghana, offers a damning critique of Ghanaian government policies from Nkrumah to Rawlings in his radical phase. Nkrumah's emphasis on rapid industrialisation and centralised state control, coupled with crippling taxes on cocoa which weakened the agricultural sector, are seen as sowing the seeds of economic decline (Frimpong-Ansah 1991: 97–8, 144–6), and Dr Busia, despite his different ideological position, could do little to reverse the decline. He sat at the centre of 'an essentially Nkrumaist state that he did not identify with and could not control' (ibid.: 100). General Acheampong, faced with falling cocoa prices after 1975, contributed to Ghana's most spectacular fall in per capita income through a long delay in the devaluation of the cedi (ibid.: 95). These are strong criticisms, but could the rulers have behaved otherwise in the circumstances? Having built up a mass party rapidly in the 1950s which depended on satisfying the demands of certain key groups, Nkrumah could not suddenly have switched to a more 'rational' economic policy if this left the main beneficiaries of government patronage impoverished. Busia, as Frimpong-Ansah hints, was also inhibited by the need to retain his urban power base, and Acheampong was a prisoner of his past in the sense that he had captured power following an unpopular devaluation by Busia, and feared that a similar action would hasten his own demise. No doubt more honest and competent administration would have reduced the damage done but, if the first priority of rulers is to survive in power, the price of that survival may have been a range of policies which did not necessarily reflect their own preferences and which did not reflect the national interest, however loosely defined.

The period in which economic policy appeared to be most successful, at least in terms of raising the gross national product, was the decade after 1983, and it is no coincidence that this was the period in which the government was least constrained by the need to satisfy influential groups. The PNDC's first year in power appeared to be devoted largely to a moral crusade against those who had exploited the country's economic weaknesses, rather than any concerted attempt to tackle the weaknesses themselves, but from 1983 onwards the government accepted the retrenchment and economic liberalisation which assistance from the IMF and World Bank required. In the 1983 budget the producer price of cocoa was raised by 65 per cent, petrol prices doubled and the cedi devalued by 990 per cent, while the budget deficit was cut substantially (Jeffries in Cruise O'Brien et al. 1989: 94). The wisdom of the policies may be disputed, but what was remarkable is that policies which caused so much hardship, at least in the short term, and which reduced the capacity of the government to 'buy' support through patronage, could be executed with so little effective resistance, especially in view of what we have said about the previous constraints on Nkrumah, Busia and Acheampong. Any civilian government needing votes and the support of opinion leaders would certainly have been more inhibited than the PNDC, but even previous military governments had felt the need to satisfy their militiary constituency and key civilian groups. Why did the PNDC regime appear to be a 'dictatorship' in the narrower sense? The army itself appeared to be more pliable than in the 1960s and

1970s, after a period of near anarchy in which arms had been distributed freely and the authority of officers undermined. The purge of officers both during Rawlings's brief interregnum in 1979, and after 1981, left him with an army more in his own image, and the lessons learnt from earlier indiscipline and lack of arms control may have strengthened the resolve to maintain a tightly controlled army after 1982. There was also the somewhat less disciplined violence which the revolutionary committees could mete out to 'enemies of the revolution'. While these bodies were often an embarrassment to the government because they retained their radical beliefs while the government lost many of its, they were still a useful line of defence (or attack) against any group which challenged the government.

The virtual monopoly of force under the control of the PNDC was clearly important in helping it to impose its will, but these coercive instruments would hardly have been sufficient on their own. At least as significant was the way in which economic decline had shattered the patron–client relationship between the government and its key supporters. The previous payouts to contractors, urban elites and rural opinion leaders, and the sinecures given to party supporters, were no longer available now that the cupboard was bare. The response of society to this loss of resources is subject to different, if not entirely contradictory, interpretations. According to Azarya and Chazan, the population became more self-reliant, and economic decisions taken in Accra (one infers) became less important as local groups organised their own production and distribution, including widespread smuggling, independently of state-imposed price controls, marketing boards or customs posts (Azarya and Chazan 1987: 121–31). Herbst, on the other hand while acknowledging the growth of the black market and the informal sector, perceives a decline of 'associational life', as the longer working hours necessary for survival, and the shortages of fuel, spare parts for vehicles and even writing paper, reduced the means of communication necessary for group activity so that 'every organisation in Ghana fell apart' (Herbst 1993: 172). Whether one accepts the interpretation that there was less resistance to the government because people felt less affected by its activities, or because they had lost such resources as they had had to resist it, the outcome was a period, probably unique in Ghana's history, in which the government could pursue its economic policies (or, more cynically, the IMF's policies) with little need to take public opinion into account. Unfortunately, from the PNDC's point of view, this golden age of authoritarianism could not survive once the fruits of economic recovery began to show.

CULTURAL CONSTRAINTS

Different perspectives on group autonomy are paralleled by different perspectives on the nature of Ghanaian political culture. Chazan sees 'a deeply ingrained culture of consultation, autonomy, participation and supervision of authority', with particular groups such as lawyers, students, unions and traders having 'evolved a liberal culture of resistance to interference in their affairs' (Chazan in Diamond, Linz and Lipset 1988: 14. Quoted by Riley 1992: 541). Ansah-Koi, in contrast, sees a non-confrontational, submissive and compliant attitude towards authority, a preference for unanimity and consensus, with no tradition of prolonged and sustained debate (Ansah-Koi in Ninsin and Drah 1993: 65–6), while Austin suggests an instrumental attitude towards political authority once one gets beyond the local community, with people at lower levels giving support 'to those who can look after them' (Austin 1976: 157). There seems to be a problem in reconciling the private thoughts of Ghanaians with their often pragmatic assessment of how to respond to authority in particular circumstances. Leaving aside the 'professional' dissidents in opposition movements, and in parts of the army, who are constantly waiting for a moment to strike, the bulk of the population is capable of putting on a show of compliance, or even sycophancy, for remarkably long periods, such as the early 1960s and early 1980s, when the government has all the trump cards. But there have been other periods such as the mid-1950s under Nkrumah, the early 1970s under Busia and the late 1970s under Acheampong, when either a relatively liberal regime or an extremely incompetent one has brought the 'liberal culture of resistance' to the surface. Professional, labour and 'traditional' groups may then activate networks of contacts which can embarrass, or even undermine, the government. It is here that we come back to the fragile basis on which government by consent, or the promise of future government by consent, rests. People may suffer in apparent silence for long periods, but a storm of protest or resistance can build up remarkably quickly. Democratic and authoritarian governments seem equally vulnerable. Neither the claim of a popular mandate, nor that of a mission to liberate the country from civilian politicians, has been enough to save governments from public wrath. If we exclude the brief Rawlings government of 1979, which was less concerned with taking over the machinery of state than with demolishing it, only one Ghanaian government (that of 1966–9) has departed at a time of its own choosing, and none has departed on account of electoral defeat. It may be objected that this has more to do with the propensity of the military to intervene than with political culture, but the coups of 1966, 1971, 1979 and 1981 all occurred after periods of hardship and government unpopularity, and were not merely the result of a soldierly spirit of adventure. Indeed if the coups had not occurred, the country might have endured even longer periods in which the withdrawal of public consent and co-operation would have exposed the fragility of government still further.

BEHAVIOURAL WEAKNESSES

Finally there is the argument that virtually every attempted political arrangement has failed not so much on account of the faulty political structures but because individual political actors failed to act out the appropriate roles adequately. Ghanaian leaders have certainly had their share of human weaknesses, including Nkrumah's detachment from reality, the patronising attitude of Busia and his colleagues, and the greed of Acheampong and his fellow officers. Austin has suggested that a combination of a feeling of insecurity, a desire to enjoy the fruits of office, and a feeling that no one had the right to challenge the legitimacy of a nationalist movement, made for intolerance of dissent and opposition under Nkrumah (Austin 1976: 98–9; Austin 1985: 10–11), with the result that government could only be removed by undemocratic means. Busia was intolerant of the practice of opposition, if not its existence, largely because it came from the people who had extinguished democracy in the First Republic, and Acheampong was intolerant of opposition because he saw it as intrinsically divisive. Limann's regime in the Third Republic has been praised for its greater willingness to respect the constitution (see especially Boafo-Arthur in Ninsin and Drah 1993: 234–40), but an impeccable record of obedience to the rule of law and the authority of Parliament was of little use in the face of an economic decline which the government could not control, of party financiers who demanded similar rewards to those which they had enjoyed in more prosperous times, and of soldiers who felt it wise to 'get their retaliation in first' as their relations with the government became increasingly strained.

Insofar as individual political choices did have a bearing on the general failure to establish stable, effective government, the scope for choice probably narrowed over time. The CPP could conceivably have permitted a more pluralist political system in the 1950s, and possibly a more decentralised one to give more autonomy to Ashanti and the peripheral regions. Ghana might then have enjoyed more of the political competition and freedom of expression in Nigeria in the early years, but without the ethnic tensions suffered in a larger, more heterogeneous country. Busia after 1969 might have made his peace with the rump of the CPP, after isolating those responsible for the greatest amount of repression and corruption. But after his overthrow, relations between the two main political tendencies, and between the military and politicians in general, appeared to have passed a point of no return. The military regimes of the 1970s and 1980s were reluctant to let go of power at all in view of their experience of elected governments, yet neither of them was able to establish a secure power base. Acheampong's failure was spectacular, as the economy collapsed and his attempt to legitimise his authority through a no-party state ended in a moral victory for his opponents. To speak of Rawlings 'failing' seems more perverse, since he weathered several coup attempts and then legitimised his rule by winning a presidential election in 1992. In personal terms he succeeded, but only at the cost of abandoning his attempt to establish a populist political system, and reverting to the bourgeois democracy which he had previously attacked so vehemently. In interviews Rawlings asserted that:

The kind of elections held under former regimes gives no real opportunity for participation. The ballot box was used to usurp people's power, allowing them only a meaningless choice, making spectators of us, after which people could only look on helplessly as the politicians lined their own pockets and thereby systematically destroyed the social and economic fabric of the nation. (Novicki 1984: 6)

Our move toward a new democratic order has already involved the following processes: one, re-awakening of the consciousness and confidence of our own people through calls on them to wake up and play their rightful roles. We have attempted this through processes of mass sociopolitical and economic mobilisation involving the majority of ordinary people of our country who, in the past, were driven into limited and marginalised roles which their circumstances compelled them to accept. Two, the creation of appropriate frameworks and platforms for all sections of the population to express their views on the way forward in our search for functional sustainable democracy.
(Novicki 1991: 35)

Yet there is little in the constitution which came into force in 1993 which is fundamentally different from that which Rawlings usurped in 1981. Indeed the most significant innovation was probably the establishment of a Commission on Human Rights, which owed more to liberal ideology than populism (Ghana Government 1992: 143–8).

Why did the vision of a populist, participatory democracy fade? We have already dwelt on the severe economic constraints, which meant that major decisions were more likely to be made in Washington than under the palaver tree or through revolutionary committees. Secondly, there was a vagueness in what Rawlings wanted to achieve, and in his perception of what other political actors might want. Folson suggests that he was critically concerned more with failings in individual behaviour than with correcting the political and economic weaknesses that might contribute to such behaviour (Folson in Gyimah-Boadi 1993: 76–94). Thus allegedly corrupt soldiers were shot, market women hoarding scarce goods were beaten and business men had their property confiscated, but no attempt was made, when the opportunity was available in 1979, to amend the Third Republic constitution to prevent the abuse of power, and little was done to tackle the economic causes of shortages, corruption and falling production, at least until 1983 when the remedies were then those of the free market rather than populism. As for other political actors, the main props of the regime in the early years were the Marxist intellectuals co-opted into government and the revolutionary committees which were supposed to mobilise the masses. From Rawlings's point of view, the former group put too rigid an interpretation on the prevailing ideology, and the latter too flexible an interpretation. At one extreme a disillusioned member of the government claimed that Rawlings could have chosen the alternative of building 'an independent economy, and attain self-sufficiency in food production and other material needs' (Yeebo 1991: 146) – a view based on faith in the 'dependency school' of political analysis which few practising politicians shared by the mid-1980s. By 1983 most of the radicals in the government had either deserted Rawlings, been dismissed or come to accept a more pragmatic view of economic policy, and the revolutionary committees were no longer so dependable.

> The PDCs are ... mass organs of the oppressed sections of society; organs through which the oppressed must organise and educate themselves and mobilise people to destroy oppressive power relations and institutions.
> (Rawlings, quoted by Ninsin in Gyimah-Boadi 1993: 101)

The creation of PDCs and WDCs as an immediate power base made ideological and political sense. The Marxist intellectuals had few resources other than their ideas, political parties were banned, chiefs and businesses were seen as part of the old order, and trade union leaders had proved fickle friends of governments in the past. As for the army, it had undergone purges after the 1979 and 1981 coups, and could offer little as a corporate body, even though the individual soldiers might be important. Reaching out to the unorganised masses therefore seemed an attractive alternative and, up to a point, it worked. When trade unions protested against devaluation and price increases, and the government feared an imminent coup in 1983, it was the WDCs that supported the government (Herbst 1993: 65). Revolutionary committees controlled prices and rents, interim management committees controlled businesses in both the public and private sectors, and citizens' vetting committees and public tribunals meted out 'justice' to corrupt officials and tax evaders (Rothchild and Gyimah-Boadi 1989: 223). In the early days there seemed to be little conflict between the activities of these revolutionary bodies and the aims of the government but, with no clearly defined functions and no regularised procedures governing the election or accountability of their officers, the government had little control over the directions in which the committees went. Some of the more articulate leaders fell out of favour because they were close to the radical bodies such as the June 4 Movement, which now saw Rawlings as a traitor to the revolution. Some took the government at its word and demanded participation in areas of policy, such as economics and national security, where the government did not want them to trespass. According to one radical former member of the government:

> Popular organisations of students and workers are subject to routine harassment and repression. Centralisation and distrust of local initiatives are symptomatic of an underlying predilection against participatory politics. And this is reflected in the policy making process at all levels.
> (Hansen 1991: 153)

Other revolutionary bodies upset their constituents by attacking chiefs, harassing any individuals who happened to be out of favour, or using their positions to channel food and other government aid to their friends and relations (see especially Jeffries in Rothchild 1991: 165–6; Oquaye 1992: 422). The government had created loosely structured mass organs but it had not destroyed the older elite power bases, even though some individual members of these elites had been removed. As the revolutionary bodies lost popularity with government and governed alike, searching for new power bases again became a process of elimination. Chiefs were needed to maintain order in rural areas, private business was needed to implement the free market policies, technocrats were needed in government, in place of ideologues, and a restored military hierarchy, led once again by senior officers, was necessary to enforce unpopular policies and fend off counter coups (Kraus 1987: 205–7; Drah in Ninsin and Drah 1993: 101).

Some of the revolutionary bodies survived even into the Fourth Republic but, in Bagehot's terminology, they now belonged more to the decorative than the efficient part of the political system, able to recite revolutionary myths on state occasions, but with real political power in the hands of those at the centre of government, and with economic privileges, though on a diminished scale, securely in the hands of the groups that had enjoyed them for most of the period since independence.

The most obvious absentees from the feast in the late 1980s were the party politicians. According to Kraus the preponderance of technocrats in the government was largely due to the difficulty in recruiting 'moderate' politicians (Kraus 1987: 206–7). Rawlings's contempt for politicians was largely reciprocated. Whereas the first military government had been anti-Nkrumah and the second had been anti-Busia, and each had been able to attract some politicians from the other side of the divide, Rawlings had alienated Nkrumaists by displacing their party in the 1982 coup, and alienated Busia's heirs by attacking the chiefs and the professions. Rawlings subsequently sought their support to shore up the government, but this was little more than a temporary marriage of convenience.

POPULISTS INTO DEMOCRATS?

One of the consequences of the PNDC's hostility to party politics was thus to shift the main lines of cleavage in Ghanaian politics from those of the liberal Danquah/Busia element versus the socialist Nkrumah/Limann element, to a conflict between the PNDC on the one hand, and virtually all party politicians right across the political spectrum, on the other. It was as if two teams of bitter rivals had suddenly united in pursuit of someone who had stolen their ball and stopped the game.

By 1992 it was clear that a no-party state was not feasible. The PNDC might dislike parties, but a military government based on coercion could not continue indefinitely, and foreign donors had made it clear that aid to Africa depended on 'free and fair' elections. Populist participatory democracy anyway seemed less attractive to the government as it came to realise that this could mean popular resistance to government policies. Yet it would have been foolhardy for Rawlings to retire to cultivate his garden and allow voters to choose whom they would to replace him, bearing mind the hostility to Rawlings of virtually aspiring party leaders, and their possible desire to punish him for his misdeeds. Not only that, but there was clearly substantial civilian support for Rawlings from people who, for the most part, had not previously been involved in politics, and who wanted him to lead an elected civilian government. This group included those who had been co-opted into political positions by Rawlings, and whose association with him might therefore make them too 'tainted' to retain office under any alternative leader. Beyond them were almost 'apolitical' people who felt that the ends achieved by Rawlings, in reviving the economy and rooting out corruption, justified the sometimes unsavoury means. These people were less likely to be lawyers, academics or big businessmen, many of whom continued to favour the resuscitation of the old political parties, and more likely to be technocrats, school teachers, retired servicemen or the self-employed. Such people ultimately provided the bulk of pro-Rawlings parliamentary candidates when an election was held. Beyond these emerging activists were would-be voters who might also feel that a government that can bring bread back into the markets is closer to their aspirations than one that respects the rule of law but cannot manage the economy. There was in short the possibility that, just as Rawlings the anti-capitalist had shown that he could pursue capitalist policies more effectively than his predecessors, so Rawlings the anti-politician could lead a party to victory in a free election. This he succeeded in doing in 1992, though we shall have to reserve judgement for the moment on the 'fairness' of the election.

Ghana had apparently restored democratic politics for the third time in 23 years, but the nature of this democracy requires careful scrutiny. The problem was not just the opposition allegation that the 1992 presidential had been rigged by the PNDC, now transformed from a junta into a political party – the National Democratic Congress (NDC). This allegation, whatever its basis, led to most opposition parties boycotting the subsequent parliamentary election, thus giving the NDC and its allies a monopoly of the seats. The foundations of a democracy may be shaky if a president with a substantial constitutional powers is sustained by a one-party parliament, but such a situation may be seen as a symptom of a bigger problem – that of a polarisation between the Rawlings camp and most other political groups. In terms of actual policy the differences were not substantial, with Rawlings having already stolen many of his opponents' free market clothes in response to external pressure, and having given way to demands for a liberal democratic constitution rather than a no-party state. But in terms of questions of who had a legitimate right to rule, and in relation to which power bases, the gulf between Rawlings and his opponents was immense. On the NDC side, it was a question of a caring egalitarian, if authoritarian, government proving its economic competence and legitimising its position by gaining a mandate from the electorate. On the opposition side, this was merely a continuing military government masquerading as a democratic civilian one. As for the extra-parliamentary party, this was portrayed as a continuation of the groups of thugs who belonged to the CDRs and other 'revolutionary' groups such as the June 4 Movement and the 31st December Women's Movement. Since these people had used violence and intimidation to sustain the previous military government, it was not implausible to believe that they used similar methods to ensure victory in the presidential election. Whether such a characterisation was correct is not our immediate concern. What is important is the implications for pluralist democracy if the government's opponents see it not as a legitimately elected government but as a continuing authoritarian regime which has retained power by rigging one election, and which will have no scruples about rigging subsequent elections.

Thus if we look at the nature of the interaction between government and opposition, there are few obvious reasons to be optimistic about the prospects for pluralist democracy. While the conflict between the broadly socialist and broadly liberal elements in the first three republics had a certain logic about it, and might even have provided the foundations for a more durable pluralist democracy under more favourable economic conditions, or in the absence of power-hungry soldiers, the conflict between the NDC and 'the rest' in the Fourth Republic is much more problematic.

But this still leaves us with the question of whether we are looking in the right places for sources of durable democracy. Is the nature of party conflict necessarily the most important factor in sustaining or destroying democracy, or should parties be seen as more transitory actors on a broader stage? Do other political institutions, such as the state bureaucracy, the army and the judiciary, and the wider society beyond, have at least as important a bearing on the prospects for democracy? And are these forces strong enough to transform the party system into one that is more conducive to democracy? It is to these questions that we shall turn in the next chapter.

4 Ghana: Political Structures, Civil Society and Democracy

Political and social structures have the capacity to strengthen or weaken moves towards stable democracy. They may eventually become strong enough to regulate the various pressures on the political system, and to limit the powers of governments and their leaders. But each structure may also have a perception of its own role and interests that will lead to destabilisation. What happens if the state bureaucracy lacks the will or ability to implement the policies for which people have voted? Or if soldiers decide that it is their prerogative, and not that of the electorate, to remove governments? Or if non-democratic forces in the wider society carry more weight than democratically-chosen political parties? Or if parties which came to power with democratic intentions find that the checks and balances provided by the legislature and judiciary are weak, and that parties are not punished if they stray from the democratic path?

In the case of Ghana, I have already suggested that the lines of party conflict since 1992 have not, on the whole, been conducive to pluralist democracy. The need for other political and social structures to establish and consolidate the democratic process is therefore especially important. In this chapter we shall explore the evolution of state–society relations, and then look at the working of specific state structures.

THE STATE AND CIVIL SOCIETY

Even before the recent wave of literature on 'civil society', it was widely accepted that democracy functioned more effectively if there were adequate autonomous institutions in society which could bridge the gap between government and governed. The absence or inadequacy of such institutions might be the result of deliberate policy, as in totalitarian countries where groups autonomous from the state were not permitted, or a reflection of a situation in which there is incongruence between the values and beliefs of government and governed. This was generally the case under colonial rule, where the colonial power sought to exploit the territory's resources, and possibly impose new beliefs such as Christianity or loyalty to the imperial throne, in the face of resistance or indifference from the indigenous population. In contrast, there are countries in which government and governed, or at least government and elites outside the government, share common values, so that much 'political' participation can be left to institutions in the wider society, whether they be trade unions co-operating in wage restraint, charities supplementing welfare provision or doctors contributing to the administration of a health service. Recent literature highlights the distinction between society in general and the area designated 'civil' society which, according to Harbeson 'is confined to associations to the extent that they take part in rule-setting activities' (Harbeson in Harbeson, Rothchild and Chazan 1994: 4), though traditional writers might prefer the word 'convention' to 'rule', to emphasise that much political activity is based on accepted norms rather than legally-enforceable directives. If it is generally agreed that democracy fares better if there is a flourishing civil society, there are still three questions which produce less clear-cut answers:

1. Does democracy require a strong state as well as a strong civil society?
2. Are the strengthening of the state and the strengthening of civil society complementary to, or competitive with, one another?
3. How have the state and society fared in relation to one another in Ghana, and with what implications for democracy?

On the first question, one has to cut through many of the myths current in Western democracies about the desire of governments to 'roll back the state', or their achievements in doing so. There are few votes to be won by openly advocating a stronger state. But the reality is often different from the rhetoric. States in the West not only have the strength to defend their frontiers and police their communities more effectively than most of their counterparts in Africa, but they are generally better able to facilitate the implementation of government policies on such matters as the provision of education, health and social services, the control of pollution, the planning of cities and the collection of taxes. This relative efficiency of the state does not, of course, guarantee democracy, but democracy would not mean very much if governments lacked the capacity to translate at least some of the promises on which they were elected into policy outputs. Jeffries contrasts the 'hopelessly weak' states in Africa with the development of a strong state in South Korea, a country which had the same per capita income as Ghana in 1957 but which has now risen above Third World status (Jeffries 1993: 25, 32). He sees a clear link between the weakness of the state and the frequent absence of democracy: 'Government is frequently authoritarian because it is so markedly non-authoritative' (ibid.: 32). The ability to execute or imprison opponents, or to grant patronage to favoured groups and withhold it from troublesome ones, is not the same as the ability to carry out a range of innovations which broadly reflect the popular will. The fact that aspirations, such as self-sufficiency in basic foodstuffs, the provision of safe water for the majority of the population or the achievement of universal literacy, have remained just aspirations is some indication of the limited capacity of the state in Africa. If elected politicians are unable to 'deliver' these policies, people may begin to question the value of democratic elections.

Are strong states and strong civil societies complementary or competitive? Crook suggests that many of Ghana's problems have arisen not because of an imbalance between the relative strengths of state and society, but because of the strength of both, and of the failure to find an adequate institutionalised means of resolving conflicts between them (Crook 1990: 24–34). Chazan, on the other hand, sees more of a zero-sum game, with society flourishing in the early 1980s as the capacity of the state declined under the influence of political upheavals and economic decline. Economic, religious and communal networks served as vehicles for the expression of alienation from the existing political order (Chazan in Rothchild 1991:

26–7). This conflicts with Herbst's view, noted in the previous chapter, that 'every organisation in Ghana was falling apart' during this period (Herbst 1993: 172) as people concentrated on individual survival in the face of shortages of basic necessities – a weak society under a weak state.

This does not exhaust the range of possibilities. A range of possible state–society relationships, varying with political and economic circumstances, is suggested in Figure 4.1. It is conceivable that state–society relations in periods of economic recovery are different from relations in periods of decline. A drying up of resources in both the public and private sectors may well weaken both state and society, but improved conditions may then enable the state to control much of the trickle down of new resources, and thus impose the conditions on which society functions. Gyimah-Boadi suggests that this is

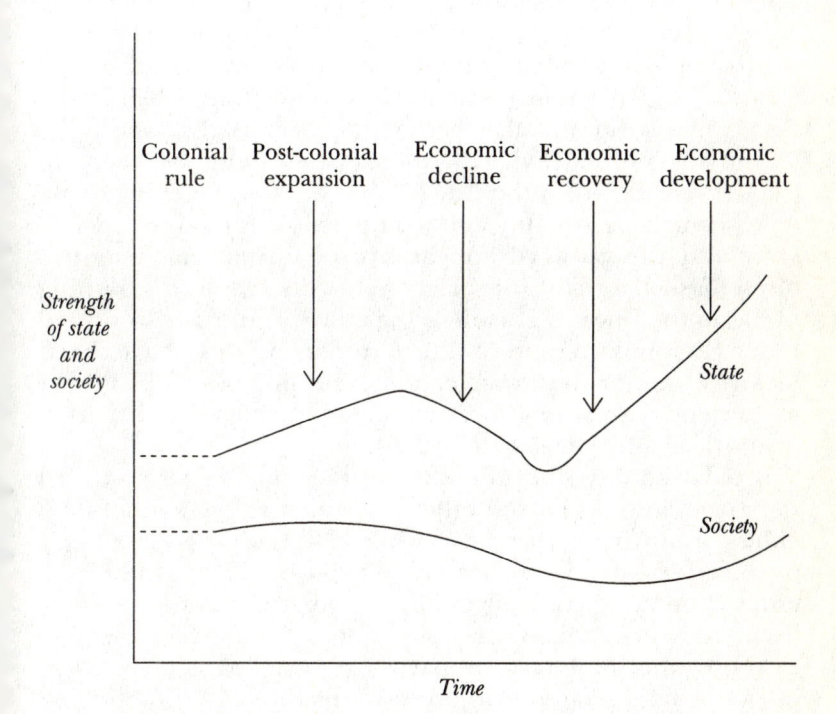

Figure 4.1 State, society and economic change: some suggested relationships

what happened in Ghana with the economic recovery of the mid-1980s, with the state weakening associational life by wielding more carrots and sticks (Gyimah-Boadi in Harbeson, Rothchild and Chazan 1994: 143–4). If the trickle of new resources becomes a flood, society may regain much of the lost ground as it is able to become more autonomous from the state, but Ghana has never achieved that happy situation.

We now need to bring these pieces of the jigsaw together to explore the broad relationship between state, society and democracy in Ghana since independence. One hypothesis is that Ghana emerged from colonial rule with a strong civil society, that the CPP overpowered that society by imposing state control over previously autonomous institutions, and that society has never really recovered, hence the failure of attempts to establish a democratic order. Drah speaks of 'a nascent civil society' at independence, covering occupational, self-help, social, recreational and political activities, which was largely destroyed as the CPP centralised power and took control of groups such as the trade unions, co-operatives and farmers' organisations (Drah in Ninsin and Drah, 1993: 76–7). Even when it did not take over existing groups, the party often set up in competition with them. The Young Pioneers attracted recruits from the Boy Scouts, and party ideology, with its Nkrumah personality cult, competed with established religion. But the outward appearance of formal party control often masked a reality of society setting its own terms. Writing of life in the town of Larteh in the 1960s, Brokensha reported that 'Nationalism and political independence have been factors of minor importance, and even the powerful CPP has to contend with strong localism, emerging almost as a Larteh institution' (Brokensha 1966: 266).

Brokensha describes the way in which a party rally showed the ascendancy of Larteh values over the CPP, with chiefs and elders occupying a raised dais while CPP leaders erected their own platform at a lower level (ibid.: 125–6). The sight of comrades from an apparently omnipotent party showing humility in the presence of their social superiors may have been pleasing to those who deplored the party's growing arrogance, but it does not immediately conjure up a picture of a functioning democracy. It does, however, remind us of the pluralist nature of Ghanaian society, and gives grounds for hope to democrats who see democracy as evolving through compromises between powerful groups, which may subsequently be pressed into accommodating less powerful groups. (In the European context, see Rustow in Lewis and Potter 1973: 117–32.)

We have already charted much of the ebb and flow of the strengths of the state and society since the demise of the CPP. No government has dared to tamper with the institution of the chieftaincy, even though overtly anti-government chiefs have often been de-stooled (Austin 1976: 157), and even a populist like Rawlings had to make his peace with the chiefs when other power bases began to crumble. In the 'modern' sector, the churches and the professions, especially lawyers and teachers, help to reinforce widely held values, and occasional government attempts to downgrade these groups by deporting bishops, setting up people's tribunals outside the judicial framework or sending party thugs to wreck university campuses, are exceptions that prove the rule. The state has seldom been the outright winner in such confrontations, and has generally had to retreat at the end of them. This might lend support to Crook's thesis that Ghana's problems have not arisen so much from an imbalance between the relative strengths of state and society, as from the strength of both (Crook 1990: 24–34). The state has proved its ability to use its powers of patronage and coercion; particular individuals, or even communities, are easily rewarded or punished, but society as a whole still goes its own way, frequently pursuing goals which are incongruent with those of the government, whether elected or military. Crook concludes that 'the strength and mobilisation of Ghanaian civil society could, if better harnessed, provide a stronger bases for a participative and civic order' (Crook 1990: 34). The lack of harnessing and integration might be traced back partly to the common African problem of an 'artificial' nation state whose boundaries were drawn by outsiders, and whose inhabitants frequently have a greater loyalty to sub-national institutions than to the state, but is Ghana any more 'artificial' than Belgium, Switzerland or South Korea? A sense of loyalty to the state, and thus to the nation which it claims to embody, depends largely on the ability of the state to produce concrete benefits for its citizenry, and not merely selective rewards and punishments. The Belgian, Swiss and South Korean states have been relatively successful in producing concrete benefits, whereas Ghana is poorer today than it was on the morrow of independence. Ghanaian citizens may thus retain loyalties to a variety of entities other than the 'national interest', as defined by those who control the state. There are ample signs of democratic values and practices within ethnic, religious, professional and cultural organisations, yet Ghana's first elected government was able to develop into an autocracy with little public resistance, the second and third elected governments were overthrown by the army with even less resistance, and the democratic credentials of the fourth are challenged by a substantial section of the population. Pluralism has flourished, but the political miracle of transforming pluralism into pluralist democracy has still to be performed effectively.

If the performance of most Ghanaian governments has not matched public expectations, what does this tell us about specific state structures? We can concede that world economic conditions have been unfavourable to much of the Third World over the past three decades, with worsening terms of trade, rising oil prices, and the burden of debts which seem more imprudent in retrospect that they did when they were incurred. But within this generally hostile context, specific state structures can perform competently or incompetently, honestly or corruptly, altruistically or selfishly, and their performance in turn may depend on the extent to which they are constrained, coerced or even abandoned by other state structures. Below we take a brief look at some of the major state structures in an attempt to assess their contribution, if any, to the evolution of democracy.

THE CIVIL SERVICE

> Authority is ... a basic problem in the sense that many officials do not always do what they are told. They do not comply with the routines of their official duties, and do not accept the goals or the hierarchy of the organisation as, at the least the parameters within which they might pursue their interests. (Crook 1983: 188)

Heavy sums have been voted annually by previous governments for road maintenance. No one knows how such maintenance votes have been used in the past and it may be asking too much of the Ghana Highways Authority to justify the expenditure made and also their very existence. (*Legon Observer*, 21 November 1980: 290, quoting President Limann)

The Ghanaian Civil Service has never lacked detractors. As the quotations above indicate, it is a long way from the 'legal rational' model of bureaucracy. Under the CPP it was criticised, at least by implication, by writers such as Adu who wished to preserve the Whitehall model of a 'non-political' civil service (Adu 1965: 180–90), and by ruling politicians for being too close to the colonial tradition. Under the first military government it enjoyed some renaissance, as the military placed greater value on technocratic skills than high flown ideology, but Busia's dismissal of 568 civil servants in the Second Republic further undermined morale. Rawlings's contempt in his early years for bureaucrats, as part of the larger exploitative bourgeoisie, was reciprocated, and many joined other business and professional groups who voted with suitcases and sought employment abroad.

Corruption has continued to flourish in the Fourth Republic. The 1995 Auditor General's report mentioned the squandering of one and a half billion cedis over the previous year, and of money being 'embezzled, misappropriated or diverted' (Abugri 1995: 3). Yet amidst all the tales of corruption, incompetence and politicisation (or even resistance to political authority), one can meet dedicated senior officials who work long hours and try to make sense of the often vague policy intentions of their political masters. There may have been few striking cases of successful bureaucratic policy initiation or implementation, but the sheer survival of the bureaucratic process might be regarded as an achievement when one compares Ghana with countries such as Benin or Sierra Leone where even the basic functions of collecting taxes and paying the wages of public employees have barely been performed. (The resettlement of 80 000 residents from areas flooded following the construction of the Volta Dam might be taken as one impressive case of bureaucratic policy implementation.

See Moxon 1984: 176–83.) Soldiers and party politicians have come and gone but budgets have been produced, roads have continued to be passable if imperfect, students have been educated, hospitals have been kept functioning and foreign aid has been solicited. A more honest, more competent and better motivated bureaucracy might perhaps have enabled elected governments to have achieved more, or even to have thwarted military intervention on the basis of their achievements, but this seems doubtful in view of the external constraints on the Ghanaian economy and the attitudes of the military. At worst it is difficult to see the Civil Service as a major reason for the inadequacy of democracy in Ghana, and at best it may have increased the feasibility of democracy by maintaining at least the skeleton of a political/administrative process on which democrats could build.

THE ARMY

The most obvious contribution that an African army can make to democracy is by removing authoritarian governments which cannot be removed by any other means, and then permitting competitive elections. This was the pattern between 1966 and 1969, even if one has reservations about the military's elitist conception of democracy. Since 1969 it has been much more difficult to see the army as a friend of democracy. Acheampong and Rawlings (strictly speaking an airman, but using the army as his power base) both overthrew democratically elected governments and, when they did belatedly concede the need for competitive elections, it was on a basis that the vast majority of political parties and leaders rejected.

Why should the army since 1969 be so different from the army that had previously sustained a relatively liberal military government? Explanations can be sought in terms of the characteristics of military personnel, the changing nature of civil–military relations and the state of the economy. Of the post-1969 military personnel, Acheampong himself was in the mould of British-trained officers who had been prominent in the first military government, but such officers were a dying breed. New generations were emerging who were trained locally and had little attachment to the liberal democratic values espoused by General Afrifa. Although they were not as keen on writing their memoirs as members of Afrifa's government had been, their behaviour suggests that they took a pragmatic view of Ghanaian politics and saw the army as a key actor in the struggle for power and resources, rather than as an arbiter of last resort in the event of democratic breakdown. The literature on the sociology of the Ghanaian military is sparse, but it seems likely that the very fact of an army seizing power will encourage new recruits to join in the expectation of sharing in that power and the benefits that go with it. No longer is the attraction of a military career simply the camaraderie and the outdoor life, or even the job security.

These changes of background and motivation, in turn, affected civil–military relations. Where the 1966 coup makers had been at pains to stress that their intervention was prompted by exceptional circumstances, and was a deviation from normally accepted military behaviour (Afrifa 1966: 107–8; Ocran 1968: 17–27), the 1972 coup makers could see nothing wrong in overthrowing a functioning democracy in order to restore officers' amenities which the government had taken away. Neither did they have any scruples about distributing the spoils of office to soldiers. Whereas the NLC had never contained more than four soldiers and four policemen, and had given most ministerial posts to civilians, Acheampong set up a National Redemption Council (NRC) of ten officers from the armed forces, and appointed a further ten to ministerial portfolios (Oquaye 1980: 15–16). This military patronage was subsequently extended to a range of state corporations. It was clear that military intervention was no longer seen as exceptional, short term or requiring elaborate moral justification.

Even the most minimal military government is likely to create tension between soldiers enjoying political office and soldiers confined to the more mundane everyday military tasks. In the case of the Acheampong government, the range of 'civilian' political offices given to soldiers and the wealth that these soldiers acquired, often corruptly as a result, was in stark contrast to the falling living standards suffered by soldiers outside this elite group, and by the bulk of the civilian population by the late 1970s. It was the combined effects of an army that now wanted a permanent place in the political power structure, and a deteriorating economy, that led to

Rawlings's intervention in 1979 which aimed to purge the army of its corrupt elements and to give a voice to the poor, inside and outside the army. The fulfilment of Rawlings's promise to allow the 1979 elections to go ahead, and then withdraw from government, might have suggested that democracy was secure and that the army would now revert to a non-political role, but Rawlings continued to regard himself, rather than the electorate, as the main judge of the government's performance, and he decided in December 1981 that the performance was inadequate.

Democracy was not a high priority within the army during the early years of the second Rawlings government, unless one equates democracy with populist attempts to mobilise the poor against the elite. As in 1979, attempts to apply egalitarian values to the army as well as society, including the appointment of other ranks to positions in the cabinet, contributed to a further weakening of military discipline and hierarchy, as did the indiscriminate distribution of arms to lower ranks. Whatever the merits of an egalitarian army, such policies gave a larger number of soldiers a vested interest in continuing military government and the benefits it bestowed on them, as well as reducing the ability of the military leadership to enforce any disengagement from politics which they might attempt.

We have already seen that the populist phase, in its most extreme form, gave way after 1983 to a more technocratic approach. Just as the scope of revolutionary committees was narrowed when it was realised that populist agitation could as easily be turned on the government as on the 'ruling class', so some degree of discipline and hierarchy were restored in the army in the realisation that freely-distributed guns could be trained on the government and not just on corrupt senior officers. The restoration of order within the army was supplemented by large wage and benefit increases, and the purchase of new military equipment, all of which helped to reduce the danger of rebellions in the ranks (Martin in Callaghy and Ravenhill 1993: 139).

There is even some doubt as to how far the PNDC was a 'military' government by the end of its reign, as most political offices were given to civilians, but if political decisions were taken by men in suits, they were often enforced by men with guns. It could hardly have been otherwise, given the range of enemies the government had made, including radicals who deplored the 'betrayal of the revolution', liberals who deplored the suspension of pluralist politics, and many ordinary citizens faced with the hardships created by the austerity which acceptance of IMF policies required. Faced with frequent attempted and alleged coup plots, and civilian demands ranging from wage increases to the restoration of party politics, the use and threat of military force were never far away.

It might still be argued that eleven years of authoritarian rule were necessary to establish a sound economy, without which any future democracy could not function, and that once the job had been completed the army could move to a more 'constitutional' role of defending the nation and serving the United Nations in whatever capacity the government deemed fit. But experience suggests that armies in countries which have experienced military intervention do not easily revert to such a role except in cases where the intervention was an aberration, out of keeping with the country's normal political processes, as in Greece and Uruguay, or where the country has undergone a major social transformation, as in Spain. Ghana does not fit either of these models. The army appears to have been kept at bay since the restoration of pluralist politics in 1992, partly through careful personal control of appointments by Rawlings and partly through being kept occupied on peace-keeping missions in other parts of Africa, but these are shaky foundations on which to build stable civil–military relations. We do not know how the army would respond to the election, or the prospect, of an anti-Rawlings government, or even to Busia-style budget cuts in the face of general austerity. There has been a military disengagement from politics in the formal sense, but one might still regard the current ruling party as the army's party. It evolved from a military regime, and the Government still contains six military men (Ghana Government Information Services Department, n/d), while it is difficult to think of any prominent soldier or ex-soldier who supports the opposition. One can envisage future military intervention to protect Rawlings, or to protect the army's interests. It is much more difficult to envisage such intervention in the cause of establishing or preserving a more democratic form of government.

CONSTITUTIONAL CHECKS AND BALANCES: THE LEGISLATURE AND THE JUDICIARY

We continue to be haunted by the question of whether pluralism, diversity and a willingness to challenge authority to the limits (or to ignore it altogether) are functional to democracy in Ghana or a recipe for chaos. While the Tanzanian Parliament has enjoyed a continuous existence since independence, the Ghana Parliament has suffered long periods of suspension by the military. But while commentators have noted the generally docile nature of parliamentary debate in Tanzania, Ghanaian MPs have seldom been afraid to embarrass the government. Not even when Nkrumah was at the height of his power could all the backbenchers be silenced, though some paid a heavy penalty for their outspokenness. Similarly the judiciary was not always willing to give the verdicts that Nkrumah wanted, notably when it acquitted men accused of attempting to assassinate him, and it challenged Busia's right to a wholesale dismissal of civil servants and Rawlings's attempts to curb protest demonstrations. In the Fourth Republic the Ghana Bar Association has continued to be active in seeking to modify legislation which it sees as bypassing the formal judicial process, notably over the Courts Act and the Serious Fraud Act. Such challenges have been unsuccessful as often as not, but they tell us something about a society which does not take kindly to subordination to the executive.

The resilience of Parliament serves as a reminder of the 'parochial' nature of much of Ghanaian politics, which we examine in more detail in the next section (see also Lee 1963: 380). Just as the chieftaincy always bounces back after attempts by authoritarian rulers to squash it, so local interests continue to assert themselves. Despite some pretences to the contrary, the CPP could never become a totalitarian party on the East European model, subordinating local interests to a general will, as defined by the leadership. Subsequent ruling parties have not even pretended to follow such a model, and have been little more than loose coalitions within which leaders, aspiring to win and hold power at the centre, have to offer the appropriate rewards in patronage and resources at the periphery. MPs are thus quick to use parliamentary debates to advance local interests. There has also been a healthy contempt for political structures at the centre, even if it has sometimes been prudent not to attack individual political leaders by name. We have noted the defeat of the Limann Government's budget proposals in the Third Republic, and the rulers of the Fourth Republic have had to yield to the combined pressures of backbench opinion inside Parliament, and public demonstrations outside, in withdrawing its proposals to introduce value-added tax in 1995. In interviews, ministers in this government appeared to respect the competence of Parliament to use question time and investigatory committees to provide effective scrutiny.

None of this is to suggest that a willingness to champion local interests in the face of official disapproval, or to deploy skills of parliamentary debate and investigation, are sufficient to guarantee the survival of democracy, but it should remind us that we are looking at more than a 'subject' political culture. A willingness to question authority runs through most levels of Ghanaian society. Once again Crook's notion of 'harnessing' potentially democratic forces comes to mind. Parliamentary dissent can run into a cul de sac of parochial demands, while key decisions on economic priorities go unchallenged, and perhaps unchallengeable, as in the First Republic. Or backbench dissent may reach the stage where few MPs are willing to accept the discipline of supporting unpopular, but possibly necessary, economic measures. Perhaps the problem for a sustainable democracy is not so much to find MPs of the right calibre as to develop a party system in which loyalty to one's party provides a balance between the extremes of subservience to authoritarian rule and the narrow pursuit of parochial and personal interests.

The judiciary has, if anything, been more of a thorn in the flesh of actual or aspiring authoritarian rulers than has the legislature. This is partly because the judiciary cannot be 'closed down' on the whim of a ruler in the way that Parliament can. Litigation continues, irrespective of who is in power. Some functions may be taken away from the judiciary by bodies such as Rawlings's people's tribunals, or governments may choose to ignore court rulings, but the existence of an institution making judgements on matters with political implications, whether on the innocence of alleged plotters against the president or the propriety of purging civil servants, means that there is some counterweight to the executive. This might be true in most parts of the world, but it is especially true in Ghana for two interrelated reasons. Firstly there is a long-standing tradition, going back to colonial times, of using the courts as a platform for challenging authority, in the absence of alternative channels such as the mass media or Parliament (which has functioned only intermittently). Secondly, and this may be a phenomenon more peculiar to Ghana, the legal profession has always been a powerful, well-organised interest group, rooted in a broader group of professional and, to a lesser extent, business interest which sees itself as having a major role in a pluralist political system where governments ought to be limited by checks and balances. Ghanaian governments, of course, have often seen matters differently, either rejecting pluralism altogether or rejecting manifestations of if which threaten their own freedom of action.

The contrast with Tanzania here is significant. While Tanzanian judges and lawyers tend to see politicians as errant schoolboys who sometimes need to be reminded to obey the rules, or perhaps to observe aspects of the rule of law which do not exist but ought to, the conflict between Ghanaian lawyers and the executive is much more deep-rooted. It is partly a matter of the lines of political cleavage. Just as there are relatively few prominent soldiers or ex-soldiers who support current opposition parties, so relatively few lawyers have supported Nkrumah, Acheampong or Rawlings. They belong, for the most part, to that side of the political divide which prescribes a limited role for governments and, by implication, a substantial role for judges. Nkrumah, Acheampong and Rawlings are not merely seen as straying occasionally from the correct path, but as governing illegitimately without regard for the rule of law. The venom with which the Ghana Bar Council attacks the government is very different from the more consensual dialogue between the Tanzanian Government and the Law Reform Commission (a government-appointed advisory body comprised mainly of lawyers).

Again we are left with the question of whether an apparently confrontational aspect of the Ghanaian political system is a sign of healthy democracy or of political deadlock. In challenging, and perhaps ultimately helping to undermine, undemocratic governments, few would question the major role played by the judiciary. In confronting elected governments which allegedly step beyond their powers, one might regard the judiciary as equally heroic, but one might question the mechanics of a political system which makes such confrontations necessary. As we shall see when we look at the 'transition to democracy' the problem is not just one of the nature of different political institutions, but of a 'top-down' democratisation process from which the government's main opponents were generally excluded. These opponents, including much of the judiciary as well as opposition parties, thus continue to challenge rules of the political game which they played no part in shaping.

LOCAL GOVERNMENT

> The primacy of economics is of course profoundly moderated by local social and political relationships which in some cases are independent of recent economic history. But essentially it remains true that Ghana has exhibited a degree of stability in such relationships over time. The toils at the centre have represented little more than political manoeuvres within an urban 'middle class' and have made for little, if any, significant structural change in Ghana.
> (Rathbone in Dunn, 1978: 34–5)

> In many areas of Africa, the authority of the village, town or ethnic group – frequently symbolised by the institution of chieftaincy – may be far more significant and influential than the 'far away' national or regional government.
> (Owusu 1992: 377)

Few people doubt the importance of local politics in Ghana. Conflicts over the enstoolment and destoolment of chiefs stimulate widespread, and sometimes violent, public involvement, with supporters of rival protagonists expecting to benefit from patronage from the chief's court if their man is successful. National politicians are often valued more for their ability to channel resources into local areas than for their policies on national issues. In competitive parliamentary elections much has depended on the ability of parties to win votes through the mediation of a variety of local and regional organisations, as well as local chiefs (see especially Twumasi, in Austin and Luckham 1975: 146–60, on the 1969 election). 'Tribalism' may not be the most important element in Ghanaian politics, but many votes have been won or lost on account of the ethnic background of party leaders. Thus the defeat of Gbedemah in 1969 was accentuated by an anti-Ewe vote in the Akan regions, and Limann's victory in 1979 was helped by the solid base he built in the North (Jeffries 1980: 413). But local 'politics' are not synonymous with local 'government'. When we come to look at the impact made by local government, in the sense of legally designated authorities which have been allocated distinctive functions within their boundaries, it is more difficult to see significant achievements.

In terms of policy outputs, local government in Ghana does not appear to have been particularly successful in building or maintaining adequate roads or schools, providing regular supplies of clean water or electricity, or stimulating agricultural production. It has not provided a model of democratic participation which might be translated into national politics, and it has not challenged the national government as an alternative focus of power, most local and legal challenges having occurred outside the formal local political structure. Local elections do not even provide a useful barometer of public opinion, since the ruling party, when one exists, normally ensures that most of its own nominees get elected by fair means or foul.

Why then has local government attracted academic attention? The answer may be that, just as local citizens and local activists try to exploit the national political system to benefit their own localities, so national politicians see local government as a means of advancing their interests or ideological preferences. At its crudest level this may mean no more than rewarding supporters through political patronage, and ensuring that a structure is in place that will at least leave the government's authority intact. But even the most authoritarian government will have some notion of what needs to be done to enhance its legitimacy, what sort of political mobilisation and participation are desirable and what sort of individuals and groups have the strongest claims to dominate the decision-making process. When an authoritarian government is either trying to bolster its own authority or to smooth the transition to democratic politics, local government can acquire a role out of all proportion to the mundane tasks that it performs. The CPP, as we have seen, tried to preserve the myth of single party hegemony while in practice conceding much autonomy to local 'notables', provided they were not openly hostile to the party. The first military government, having suspended the constitution, resorted to an almost colonial-style reliance on chiefs as the embodiment of local communities, and the Progress Party, with its elitist origins, did not depart vary far from this model. By the time Rawlings came to power in 1981, even central government had lost much of its capacity to govern, and local government was rendered still more incapable as a result of corruption and inadequate financial resources which, in turn, meant an inability to attract high-calibre staff (see especially Tordoff 1994: 557–79).

In keeping with his apparent belief that the state of the country was attributable more to the misbehaviour of individuals than to structural weaknesses, Rawlings paid little attention to structural reforms in his early years and relied on the revolutionary committees to mobilise local activity and punish wrongdoers, but as the committees fell foul of the government by questioning its policies, and failed to secure rural power bases on account of their antagonism to the chiefs, more formal structures had to be sought. But to what end? The objection that bourgeois democracy and party politics gave power to an unrepresentative elite seemed to have even greater force at the local level, but the alternative of a 'mobocracy' (Oquaye 1992: 62) seemed equally unattractive. How was the populist ideal of mass participation to be achieved while avoiding these evils? Ninsin suggests that the creation of district assemblies (DAs), elected in 1988 and 1989, reflected a compromise between radical mobilisation and liberal democracy (Ninsin in Gyimah-Boadi 1993: 105). Under PNDC Law 207 of 1988, substantial powers in promoting development were devolved to the DAs. Two-thirds of the members were to be elected on a non-party basis and one-third, together with the chief executives, were appointed by the central government. But was a compromise between radical mobilisation and liberal democracy possible, or was it a case of 'this town is not big enough for both of us'? Owusu quoted with approval the PNDC's plan 'to create a new kind of democracy that will bring about greater efficiency and productivity in the state machinery through involving the people at all levels' (Owusu 1992: 377). He went on to describe the working of the system:

> The CDRs are the bed-rock of Ghana's democratic transformation, being designed to organise the masses for participation in making and implementation decisions in local communities and workplaces. Their functions include checking exploitation, corruption and abuse of power, as well as mobilising the people, especially unemployed youths, and organising them into democratic co-operatives to raise the productivity of the countryside. In carrying out these functions, the CDRs liaise with DAs, local chiefs and as many action-oriented voluntary bodies as possible. The fact is that decentralisation has provided many important new avenues for community development. (Owusu 1992: 395)

Oquaye also emphasises the new opportunities for mass participation. With political parties banned, and rival candidates only permitted to address voters from a common platform, the cost of contesting elections was minimised, to the advantage of poorer candidates. They were also helped by the abolition of candidates' deposits and the illiteracy bar (Oquaye 1992: 425). But he offers a less harmonious picture of relations between the DAs and the revolutionary committees, as the latter saw themselves as 'overlords of the revolutionary process and resented their loss of status' (ibid.: 346). Not everyone took the government's rhetoric about decentralisation at its face value. Ayee suggests that the real reasons for decentralisation were a desire for greater legitimacy, pressure from chiefs and local elites, and a desire by national leaders to rid themselves of political problems. Decentralisation was less to encourage participation than to promote legitimacy, recentralise power and enhance patronage (Ayee 1994: 200–2).

Despite Owusu's optimism, the district assemblies do not appear to have been any more successful than earlier local authorities in promoting development. Oquaye reported that the assemblies had 'virtually come to a halt' by 1992, with the enthusiasm of members waning as the central government failed to ensure that their allowances were paid (Oquaye 1992: 353), and Ayee offers a similar picture, with assembly members unable to keep their election promises on the provision of electricity, water, feeder roads and schools, and with decentralisation superseded by decisions taken by the government (Ayee 1994: 202, 212). Both authors note the contributory weaknesses of rushed reforms at a time when the government faced a legitimacy crisis, and which did not take sufficient account of the problems of personnel, co-ordination, logistics, corruption and finance.

Not for the first time, expectations about the potential socialising powers of local government were at variance with the reality of life in Ghana. Local government may be seen as a means to achieving a variety of democratic objectives, including those in the populist version of democracy favoured by Rawlings. It may be seen as a training ground where voters and politicians can gain experience in deciding priorities in allocating resources between roads or health or water supply, before meeting the more national challenges of tackling unemployment or inflation, or responding to IMF demands for economic retrenchment. It may also be seen as the level at which real political choices are most readily available, given the constraints of global economic forces on national decision-making. There has also been the hope that standards of honesty, integrity and competence are more readily achievable at a local level, where tasks are less complex and people are less likely to want to cheat their immediate neighbours than a more impersonal state bureaucracy. The authoritarian nature of single-party politics and the confrontational style of multi-party politics may be avoided, as voters choose politicians, and politicians choose policies, on their local merits rather than on the basis of 'my party right or wrong'.

Few of these hopes have actually been realised. There is the immediate problem of the shortage of skilled personnel to translate voters' expressed preferences into policy outputs. Thus voting for greater priority for a supply of clean drinking water will have little effect if there is no manpower to construct dams or install pumping or filtering equipment. In a country where skilled manpower is scarce, most skilled workers tend to gravitate to the urban centres rather than serve the rural communities where the majority of the population live.

The unattractiveness of employment at the local level was worsened by the inability of district authorities to raise sufficient revenue. On North Tyneside Council, which administers a relatively poor area in North-East England, the rival political parties argued in 1995 about whether it was feasible to achieve a council tax collection rate of 95 per cent or 97 per cent. In contrast, a case study of seven district assemblies in Ashanti showed that no DA had managed to raise more than 62 per cent of the estimated revenue available, and that the worst figures were 11 per cent for the basic rate and 23 per cent for the property rate. This performance was attributed to 'poor management and inefficient methods of collection' (Aggrey-Finn 1995: 5). This is a common problem in Africa. Regular payment of taxes has not become the deeply-ingrained habit that it has become in the West where most people, the British poll tax notwithstanding, part with their money as a matter of course, with little regard for the equity of the tax or the wisdom with which the money is spent. In a country like Ghana, residents may be less willing to pay their taxes if they perceive that the money they pay is being used inefficiently or corruptly, with few signs of any benefit in return (Oquaye 1992: 329–37). To those who can offer rational justifications for not paying, must be added those who evade payment because evasion is relatively easy, given the limited means available for policing collection and the scope for bribing officials.

The spectre of corruption did not cease to haunt local government despite the ringing appeals of words like participation, decentralisation an development. An official report in the Central Region in 1995 revealed that most districts had misapplied grants, and most did not have development plans to specify where the money should go. 'In some cases funds were distributed to outspoken assembly members to carry out their own projects' (Sam 1995: 3). The cultural factors which shape attitudes to public property, which we noted in the previous chapter, cannot be changed merely by exhortation from political leaders. Yet again, a largely unchanging Ghanaian society had responded in its own way to another attempt at innovation by those at the centre.

We have, however, suggested that the significance of what happens in local government goes beyond the competence or honesty with which its functions are discharged. Had Ghana, as Ninsin suggests, arrived at a compromise between populism and liberal democracy, or was it more a cross-roads where a choice had to be made between one or the other? If local government was concerned not just with development and the provision of services, but with who had a legitimate right to participate in politics and in what ways, the election of district assemblies could have ramifications for the evolution of national politics. After seven years of authoritarian rule, this was the first time elections of any sort had been permitted, and their organisation and outcome could help to shape democratisation at higher levels, whether in sustaining a populist, no-party system or in moving closer to liberal democracy. Some of the early signs were that the populist element was winning. In the 1988–9 local elections, 89 per cent of those eligible registered, and 59 per cent of those on the register voted, as compared with 35 per cent in the previous general election in 1979 (Ninsin in Gyimah-Boadi 1993: 105). This might confirm not only the view that Ghanaians are more interested in local than national politics, but that the particular form of non-party politics, which took away the advantages previously enjoyed by wealthier candidates, was also popular. The occupational backgrounds of the successful candidates certainly suggested a defeat for the elite, and this was only partly because some members of the professions had boycotted the elections as a protest against continued authoritarian rule. 33 per cent of the successful candidates were farmers, 32 per cent teachers, and 12 per cent other public servants. Lawyers, who had previously been the dominant profession in Ghanaian politics, numbered only 0.6 per cent (Ninsin in Gyimah-Boadi 1993: 110). Were these assembly members dependable foot soldiers who would carry the 'revolution' in whatever direction Rawlings wanted, or were they more a fifth column, able to impose their own wishes? The occupational background of MPs, overwhelmingly from Rawlings's party, elected four years later, had some striking similarities. 31 per cent were teachers, 14 per cent other public servants and only 7 per cent lawyers (Ghana Parliament 1992). It is tempting to suggest that Rawlings had sidelined the old elite of lawyers, academics and other professionals, many of whom enjoyed the advantage of a secure income irrespective of who ruled the country, and had replaced them with people of lower social status who could be kept in line more easily because many of them were employed directly by the state. If one follows this hypothesis, the local elections were the first step along the road to a Rawlings-led elected civilian government. The next step was the election of a consultative assembly, which exhibited a similar social composition, to draft a new constitution, and the culmination was the parliamentary and presidential elections of 1992. At each stage many members of the professions chose to boycott the elections, on the grounds that they were not genuinely democratic, though there is no guarantee that they would have fared as well as in previous elections even if they had participated wholeheartedly, in view of the public disillusionment with the performance of the old 'political class'.

But is the hypothesis correct? Ninsin argues that the newly-elected district assembly members were comparable with the early CPP members: mainly lower middle class, but better educated, better endowed materially and more self-confident, and thus able to assert themselves as key power brokers between the state and civil society. They attempted to consolidate power either against government representatives in the district assemblies or against the PNDC itself, with no guarantee that the PNDC would be able to control them (Ninsin in Gyimah-Boadi 1993: 110–11). Ayee takes a different view with his emphasis on the extent to which the PNDC centralised control over local government to promote patronage or use it as a support base (Ayee 1995: 3), and Oquaye emphasises the extent to which control over the DAs has been monopolised by government nominees, generally technocrats or loyal supporters, who comprise a third of the membership (Oquaye 1992: 425).

One might also ask whether teachers, farmers and civil servants have sufficient interests in common to be seen as a 'group' pressing common demands, but they are clearly different from the professional people, wealthy business men and academics who had previously dominated Ghanaian politics. The lower-middle-class groups which now predominate in Parliament and local government are a far cry from both the common man idealised by Rawlings in his revolutionary phase and from the previously dominant elites. The populist conception of local government as a process of mobilising the masses had clearly subsided, but whether it had moved far along the alternative road towards liberal democracy was less clear.

CONCLUSION

How do the prospects for democracy look from this brief review of Ghana's political structures? The findings might suggest, though many would dispute this, that the Civil Service is on balance a help and the army a hindrance, while the legislature, the judiciary and local government present a fascinating range of possibilities. As with several other African states propelled from authoritarianism to pluralism by a mixture of internal and external pressure, Ghana now enjoys many of the trappings of liberal democracy. There is ample freedom of expression, no imprisonment without trial, and there are no apparent barriers to opposition parties winning people's votes if they can win the arguments, but this might also have been said in 1972 or 1981, and it did not prevent elected governments from being superseded by authoritarian ones which lasted for much longer than their democratic predecessors. Admittedly the ending of the Cold War has made the non-democratic alternatives less attractive and less achievable, with external aid increasingly dependent on democratic behaviour. Yet there is still the question of whether the political structures have enough of an autonomous life of their own to provide democratic checks and balances, or whether the lines of division in the Ghanaian polity have become drawn in such a way as to frustrate the democratic process.

The polarisation of Ghanaian politics between the pro- and anti-Rawlings parties would be frightening if the contest were a 'winner takes all' one in which the winners could dispense patronage freely and humiliate their opponents, but the NDC of the 1990s is not the CPP of the 1950s. While the CPP put down deep roots in society by spearheading the struggle for independence and winning three democratic elections, the NDC was formed barely six months before the 1992 election, partly as a Rawlings supporters' club and partly as a coalition of people who had obtained political offices, especially in local government, during the PNDC years and who now wanted to retain these offices. Here is a party with a much shallower base which cannot even pretend to perform a 'leading role'. There is also much less patronage to dispense than in the more prosperous 1950s, as retrenchment and adherence to the IMF guidelines contrasts with the profligacy of the 1950s.

While the ruling party is weaker, civil society now seems to be stronger after its apparent collapse in the early 1980s, with the professions, the church, the chiefly 'stool', the senior common room and the market all flourishing. Many local councillors enjoy the advantage of having won their seats before the return of party politics, and therefore have relatively few debts to the ruling party, and the size of the NDC majority in Parliament has militated against tight party discipline. The position of the public service may be precarious as retrenchment limits its capacity, and prolonged service to one leader blunts its autonomy, but there does not appear to be any attempt to purge 'disloyal' elements. (The impartiality of polling officials is another matter.)

None of these points detracts from the argument in the previous chapter that the nature of the party system continues to make the achievement of stable democracy difficult, but I suggest that, even if Ghana becomes subject to prolonged one-party rule, such rule will be subject to more structural checks and balances than was the case under the CPP. In searching for pluralist democracy, the pluralist part is relatively easy to achieve. It is the democratic part which may take rather longer to refine.

5 Tanzania: the Search for Socialism and Pluralism

There is a village museum on the outskirts of Dar es Salaam which contains life-size replicas of traditional buildings from different parts of Tanzania. In front of each building is a plaque containing a synopsis of the history and culture of the area concerned. To a newly-arrived visitor from Ghana the most striking feature of the descriptions is the absence of any references to the role of chiefs in that history and culture. As the institution of the chieftaincy was abolished in 1962, the omission may be partly an Orwellian attempt to blot out inconvenient historical facts, but it may also reflect a genuine belief that chiefs had never played a major role. In a country with over a hundred small ethnic groups, in which no one of these was ever strong enough to have had pretensions about dominating the others, and none was greatly feared as a potential dominator, chiefs had been, for the most part, small fish in a big pond. All this is in contrast to Ghana, where tribes such as the Asantes and the Ewes dominate whole regions. They may see themselves as groups which can unite to maximise their collective benefits from the political system, and may be seen by others as a potential threat. It is often the Ghanaian chiefs, rather than transient politicians, who are seen as leaders of their people, and a hierarchy with paramount chiefs above and sub-chiefs below helps to maintain a stratified society. Parties of commoners such as the CPP may sometimes win power, but the social structure remains intact and egalitarian ideas have had difficulty in making any headway.

The Tanzanian culture is a more egalitarian one. Berg-Schlosser and Siegler describe a tradition of 'egalitarian-segmented social structures' which existed at the turn of the century. The 1905–7 rebellion against the taxation and compulsory cotton cultivation imposed by the German colonial government, although unsuccessful, helped to create a greater sense of unity between diverse tribes (Berg-Schlosser and Siegler 1990: 67), and this continued when Tanganyika passed into British control after 1918. When the British gave immigrant Asians trading monopolies and privileges, especially over the wholesale trade in raw materials, Africans responded by establishing co-operative groups which united to form the Tanganyika African Association (TAA) in 1920. This developed as a political as well as an economic force, and Julius Nyerere, a graduate recently returned from Edinburgh University, was elected chairman in 1953. India had gained independence in 1947, Ghana did so in 1957 and most of French-speaking Africa followed in 1960. The time was ripe for a nationalist movement that could prove its ability to lead the country to independence with a solid bedrock of support, and the TAA transformed itself into a political party, the Tanganyika African National Union (Tanu), in 1954. With the advantages already mentioned of an ethnic structure of many small groups rather than a few large ones, and of the common Kiswahili language, the party quickly developed a nationwide organisation with a million members, and won all the available seats in the colonial parliament (Berg-Schlosser and Siegler 1990: 68; O'Neill in O'Neill and Mustapha 1990: 9–10). Able to exploit urban middle-class resentment at European and Asian domination, and peasant grievances over agricultural prices and marketing systems, as well as building links with trade unions, Tanu had no competitors in sight, and the only non-Tanu members elected to the pre-independence parliament were a few independents.

THE MAKING OF A SOCIALIST IDEOLOGY

Dominant parties can go in a variety of directions after leading their countries to independence. In Ghana the ruling party set about demolishing a strong, if regionally based, opposition, through a mixture of rewards for defectors and preventive detention for persistent opponents, but the party gradually disintegrated once there were no elections to contest and no coherent ideology to inspire. In Kenya the strategy fluctuated between outlawing, and attempting to absorb, the opposition, and in Zambia and parts of French-speaking Africa, ruling parties survived for many years as dispensers of patronage after the initial nationalist idealism had evaporated. Tanu was distinctive, if not unique, in Africa in both developing an ideology that bore some relation to actual political practice and in maintaining an effective party machine which could regulate, and set the limits to, political competition. It is with the former that we are immediately concerned. Why did Tanu adopt a socialist ideology, and what did it mean in practice?

There appear to have been two consistent influences, and two that became more important over time. Firstly there was the influence of Nyerere, who continued to lead both the party and the nation until 1985, and who had no serious challengers. Hyden suggests that he was influenced by his own puritanical personality, and a mixture of exposure to Fabianism in Britain and rural communes in China, together with a realisation of the political advantages of being able to control the economy. His socialism was concerned less with grandiose projects for industrialisation, and more with simple rural developments, and a belief, on which doubt was cast by subsequent events, that equality must precede growth and that people's needs must be satisfied in order to make them more productive (Hyden in Barkan 1994: 83). The ability of one man to impose his own ideological stamp arose not only on the morrow of independence in 1961 but again with the Arusha Declaration in 1967. This bore a superficial resemblance to Nkrumah's Dawn Broadcast in 1961, but whereas Nkrumah was fighting a losing battle to contain corruption in his party, with no effective strategy for controlling the excesses which he criticised, Nyerere's strictures did, as far as one can tell, impose some degree of moral discipline on his followers. The declaration, which was endorsed by the party national executive committee, laid down that no party or government 'leader' should be associated with capitalism or feudalism, and none should hold company shares or directorships, receive more than one salary or let houses to others. The term 'leader' included members of the party national executive committee, ministers, MPs, civil servants and senior members of organisations affiliated to Tanu (Cleary 1989: 16).

Nyerere's vision of the sort of society he wanted, however much one may question its desirability or feasibility, and his own personal integrity, put him in a class apart from most other African politicians, and perhaps from politicians in most other parts of the world, but we still have to explain why the political system and society were so receptive to his ideas. A second constant factor was the poverty of Tanzania. It lacks the mineral wealth of Ghana, and of its immediate neighbours, and Britain made little attempt to develop the country after gaining it from Germany, in view of the uncertainty of its future within the Empire and the virtual absence of British settlers (Berg-Schlosser and Siegler 1990: 68; Ake in Barkan 1984: 134). By the late 1980s, Tanzania was calculated to be the fourteenth poorest country in the world (Cleary 1989: 4). Socialism, based especially on rural development and self-reliance, might thus be seen as making a virtue out of a necessity, especially with falling export prices and a lack of funds for development in the two years after independence (Ake in Barkan 1984: 131–2), and there were few capitalists to offer any resistance. There was also the constant factor, already noted, of a society that was not only poor, but largely egalitarian with no 'traditional aristocracy' to resist the ideological incursions of an all-embracing party and its leader.

Of the variable influences, an important one was the perceived threat to national unity in the 1960s. Despite Tanzania's apparent cultural homogeneity and social equality, its political structures might still suffer a similar fragility to those in other parts of Africa. It was conceivable that a general strike in key urban areas, or a coup organised by a small group of soldiers, could have brought the government down even if the perpetrators had lacked the support of the bulk of the population. The general strike never materialised, though there were ample signs of discontent as workers sought wage increases to maintain their meagre living standards, but an army mutiny occurred in 1964 and was only put down with the aid of British troops. A few days before the mutiny there had been a revolution in Zanzibar, in which Africans overthrew the old Arab elite whose party had 'won' the independence election despite polling fewer votes than their opponents. This revolution in turn led to the merger of Tanganyika and Zanzibar into the new United Republic of Tanzania, with the potential advantages to Zanzibar of the infusion of resources from its mainland neighbour, and to Tanganyika of damping down, through weight of numbers, the violent revolutionary forces

Tanzania: the Search for Socialism and Pluralism

of Zanzibar which might otherwise have encouraged similar uprisings on the mainland.

The government's authority survived intact, but it could no longer be taken for granted that the advantages with which Tanganyika had begun its independent life would guarantee its survival as a stable entity in its new incarnation as Tanzania. Part of the perceived solution lay in strengthening the ruling party, which we shall consider in the next section, but it also lay in giving greater prominence to an ideology which would both strengthen national unity and offer a practical guide to, and rationalisation of, action. Hyden and Leys noted that in the early 1960s

> Ideological guidelines were lacking and decisions were influenced by pragmatic and *ad hoc* considerations. Nyerere, though fundamentally a socialist since his student days, in the first years of independence showed no immediate concern with class differences and paid little attention to how these could be solved.... A more deep-seated contradiction in the post-independence period, however, began coming to the fore: the contradiction between Tanzania's ambition to be a socialist state with non-aligned foreign policies and the basically Western orientation of her actual economic development strategy with its heavy reliance on private foreign investment and Western aid.
> (Hyden and Leys 1972: 407)

By 1965 the problem was not merely the incongruity of domestic and foreign policy, but their incompatibility. This brings us on to the fourth influence on the evolution of the socialist ideology – the alienation of Tanzania from the West. Tanzania had already upset Britain and the United States by its recognition of East Germany and a 'non-aligned' foreign policy which some critics regarded as pro-Eastern, and the union with Zanzibar suggested a further lurch to the East, as much of the aid to Zanzibar came from the Communist Bloc. Then, with the coming of the unilateral declaration of independence by the rebel government representing a small European minority in Rhodesia (now Zimbabwe), Tanzania was one of the most outspoken critics of the British government's failure to attempt to crush the rebellion. Tanzania had now antagonised Western governments to such an extent that much of the anticipated Western aid for the 1964–9 development plan was withheld (Hyden and Leys 1972: 407; O'Neill and Mustafa 1990: 13). Expediency as well as ideology pointed to the need for an alternative to economic policy, and especially to greater emphasis on rural development based on self-reliance. This led to the attempt to move peasants from scattered settlements into *ujamaa* (collective) villages, through compulsion if necessary, with the expected benefits of such external economies as communal water supplies, schools, health centres and transport, as well as increased productivity.

What did the adoption of socialist policies mean in terms of specific policy outcomes and the distribution of power between different groups in society, and how did this in turn affect the extent to which the political system acquired democratic features? Most manufacturing came under state control, and attempts were made, though often unsuccessfully, to carry out collective agricultural production in the ujamaa villages, but the most striking advances were in social provision and reduced social inequality. The ratio between the highest and lowest government salaries was reduced from 70: 1 in 1961 to 15: 1 by 1975. By 1978, 7.7 million rural dwellers enjoyed access to piped water, half the 8000 villages had dispensaries, and the number of children in primary schools doubled from half a million to one million (Berg-Schlosser and Siegler 1990: 69; Yeager 1989: 77). The initial enthusiasm for these developments may have helped to strengthen the legitimacy of the government, but there were longer term questions as to what socialism really meant and who had the right to interpret it and shape its implementation. In addition to Nyerere himself there were at least three groups whose different interests and beliefs led them to take up conflicting positions: party leaders, ministers and state bureaucrats. The position of each group is suggested in Table 5.1.

As a president with widespread public support, Nyerere had no great interest in building up a vast bureaucratic structure, and appeared not be to be attracted to joining in any race for industrialisation and economic growth in the way that Nkrumah had been. He was interested in the ends of equality and social justice, especially as they related to eliminating poverty and hardship in the rural areas where most of

Table 5.1 The interests, ideologies and policy positions of the Tanzanian President, party leaders, ministers and state bureaucrats

	President	Party Leaders	Ministers	Bureaucrats
Interests	National unity, stability, continued legitimacy of authority.	Strengthening of positions through patronage in public appointments.	Short-term payoffs, especially in economic growth, to ensure survival in office.	Expansion of the size and role of bureaucracy. Recognition of the superior expertise of bureaucrats and technocrats.
Ideology	Equality, social justice.	'Scientific socialism', with development through an expanded public sector supervised by the party.	Largely pragmatic. Party ideology interpreted flexibly.	Orderly economic expansion, based on 'rational' criteria.
Policy Objectives	Rural development, self-reliance.	Party penetration of state bureaucracy, control over appointments; containment of bureaucratic power.	Economic growth by whatever means seemed most appropriate, not precluding foreign aid or investment.	Centralised state control of development. Minimal local participation.

the population lived, but he appeared to have rather less interest in the details of building a socialist administrative structure. Of the three groups outside the presidency, overgeneralisation is dangerous if only because there was considerable movement between them. Some ministers reached their positions by working their way up through the party, generally via Parliament, while others were recruited from the Civil Service on account of their bureaucratic and technocratic skills. The Civil Service itself was hardly likely to develop in the 'politically neutral' mould of Whitehall mythology when faced with indefinite one-party rule, and career advancement was likely to be helped by some acceptance of the objectives of the political masters. Each group did, nonetheless, depend on different circumstances for its survival, and therefore tended to rationalise the nature, interpretation and execution of socialism in its own ways, even if Table 5.1 implies unrealistic homogeneity within each group.

> Socialism to [the bureaucratic] class was synonymous with the intervention of the state in economic affairs. It meant that the state was the only agent that could bring modernisation and development to the 'backward' elements of society. It set the state as an organ apart from and above the direct producers. In this strategy, the interest of the state became paramount. All possible sources of opposition were removed. Due to its central self-appointed role in development, the bureaucracy's major preoccupation became the simple and expanded reproduction of the state. Development in the country became synonymous with the burgeoning of the state. The major asset of the bureaucratic class was its ownership of the expertise to organise production under the aegis of the state. (Stein 1985: 113)

All this was a far cry from Nyerere's simple faith in equality and self-reliance. While even Nyerere might be accused of fostering mobilisation from above rather than democratic participation, with his emphasis on moving peasants into ujamaa villages, the bureaucratic approach left still less room for democracy. If Stein's account is correct, bureaucrats believed that they knew best what served the public interest. In a system which largely rejected any role for the private sector, bureaucrats had ample scope for expanding their own 'empire' as long as they could keep the politicians at bay.

Party leaders, and especially those who were sufficiently skilful and articulate to obtain a place on the party's national executive committee, might be expected to occupy a position closer to Nyerere, and to see socialism more in terms of equality and social justice rather than bureaucratic rationality, but party leaders also had certain interests to defend which may have led them to adopt certain ideological and policy positions. Sundet suggests that party leaders favoured a more 'scientific' form of socialism, and were successful in persuading Nyerere to put more emphasis on nationalisation as opposed, presumably, to mere self-reliance (Sundet 1994: 46). As in most parts of the world where one party enjoys a prolonged monopoly, Tanu accumulated layers of ideology to justify its own role and to distinguish it from its enemies at home and abroad. It broadly accepted both Nyerere's ideals and the bureaucratic belief that a strong state structure was necessary to achieve them, but it had to be a state structure with the correct political orientations, and this required party control over appointments and party supervision of activities within the public sector. Yeager describes a system in which the party became more centralised and isolated from the grass roots. It used intimidation and payoffs as instruments of national policy, and subverted Civil Service hiring and performance standards. Party connections were often used to prevent incompetent officials from being dismissed (Yeager 1989: 86). As in the case of bureaucrats, it seems that party leaders were able to make a necessity out of a virtue, and to find ideological justifications for consolidating their own positions.

As to ministers, their positions were perhaps the least secure of all the groups. Although the average Tanzanian minister's tenure of office is longer than that in most other countries (Van Donge and Liviga 1986: 626–7), the job is in the gift of the President and is less secure than those of civil servants, or even party officers. Ministers' horizons may thus be shorter than those of party leaders, bureaucrats or the President, and their interests lay more in short-term payoffs to ensure their survival in office, rather than the search for some long-term goal of party or bureaucratic domination. This is likely to lead to a pragmatic interpretation of ideology, so that self-reliance was interpreted so as not to preclude foreign investment, and socialism so as not to preclude accepting IMF constraints on economic policy, if the means achieved the ends of enhancing governmental performance and the delivery of material benefits (see especially Sundet 1994: 47; Yeager 1989: 86).

Where did all this leave the development of democracy? One could acknowledge that voters had chosen a *de facto* one-party state, and that the creation of a *de jure* one-party state with intra-party competition extended the rights of voters by offering them a choice of Tanu candidates, when there would otherwise have been a large number of unopposed returns in the absence of any opposition. But the scope for democratic participation between elections was constrained not only by the party's monopolisation of virtually all political activity, to which we shall return presently, but by the forces which we have just examined which led bureaucrats, party leaders and ministers to seek to strengthen their own positions. Each may have sought to do this largely at the expense of the other groups, but all had an interest, and presumably a belief, in controlling the allocation of resources from above rather than encouraging citizens to articulate their own priorities or to execute policies in their own way. The socialist ideology may thus have helped to provide Tanzanian citizens with better water supply, health standards and education, but its contribution to democratic development is less clear.

A PARTY OF THE REVOLUTION?

Why a single party?

In 1977 Tanu merged with the Zanzibar ruling party to form Chama Cha Mapinduzi (CCM) – 'the party of the revolution'. What sort of party was this and its antecedents, and what sort of revolution was it upholding? In the case of Zanzibar, the revolution had been unambiguous: a ruling elite had been overthrown violently and the revolutionaries had captured the spoils of office. In mainland Tanganyika, any 'revolution' that had occurred appeared to be more a series of historical accidents. We have seen how a socialist ideology had developed as an official guide to action largely as a result of Tanzania's impoverished and isolated position in the world, and the establishment in 1965 of a *de jure* one-party state similarly owed as much to particular circumstances as to any Leninist belief in the need for a vanguard party. The failure of opposition parties to win any seats in free competitive elections would have made any attempt to emulate the Westminster model look incongruous, so there was nothing illogical, still less revolutionary, about attempting to institutionalise competition within the ruling party. But the perceived threats to national unity in 1964, with the army mutiny, labour disputes and fears over the fallout from the Zanzibar revolution, all created a desire among political leaders to close off any alternative route for dissidents. There seems to be a paradox that a country often has the greatest fear of an eventuality that is least likely within its own frontiers. Thus Americans developed a paranoiac fear of communism in the 1940s, when there were no preconditions for a proletarian revolution, the West Germans feared the collapse of democracy when they had one of the world's most effective working democracies, and the Tanzanians have a curious fear of national disintegration, which resurfaced in the 1995 elections, despite the virtual absence of potentially powerful divisive groups, as compared with most of Africa. The fear was perhaps not so much of a Biafra, a Buganda or an Ashanti, demanding independence or autonomy, but of a general fragmentation into the various local, ethnic and religious groups that had been brought together by Tanu. This would not necessarily have produced rebel governments, but the Tanzanian government's writ would have run less effectively and its authority might have been undermined. In this atmosphere, both Hyden and Leys and Mmuya and Chaligha suggest that the desire for national integration was a stronger reason than socialist, let alone revolutionary, ideology for establishing a one-party state (Hyden and Leys 1972: 405–6; Mmuya and Chaligha 1992: 4).

Electoral choice

The party's decision to allow voters to choose between two of its candidates in each constituency offered more democratic opportunities than the East European model, and it has to be seen in the context of an Africa where the vast majority of governments were denying their citizens any electoral choice at all. At the risk of being patronising, one might argue that the Tanzanian peasant was more interested in choosing a good constituency representative who would bring resources into the constituency than in choosing between national party programmes. (Whether the peasants should have been more interested in national politics, or should have been encouraged to take more interest, is another matter.) Barkan reported that peasants were skilled in evaluating whether the performance of MPs served their interests. They saw the MP's role as initiating small scale development projects and representing local interests at the centre. A higher proportion of voters than in industrial societies knew who their MP was and what he had done for the local community (Barkan 1984: 91). Mvungi and Mhina's case study of Dodoma reinforces this view, with success going to the candidate who demonstrated his understanding of the constituency, especially in relation to its economic problems and essential social services, and who exposed the incumbent MP's neglect of these matters (Mvungi and Mhina in Othman, Bavu and Okema 1990: 103–20).

As in the Ghanaian local elections of 1988–9, electoral rules restricted campaigning to rival candidates speaking and answering questions from a common platform and, as in Ghana, this advanced equality at the expense of liberty, with no candidate handicapped by the cost of electioneering but none able, within the rules, to exercise freedom of expression through canvassing, meeting influential individuals or pressure groups, or organising independent rallies. Local studies suggest, however, that the rules could not always be enforced, and Munishi and Mtengeti-Migiro describe how over-bureaucratisation and central control led voters and candidates in Rombo to innovate to express their wishes, so that 'parallel campaigns' were carried out with candidates building up a group of supporters, and one candidate allegedly winning the support of church congregations by ensuring that permits were obtained for corrugated iron sheets for the churches (Munushi and Mtengeti-Migiro in Othman, Bavu and Okema 1990: 182–201). Berg-Schlosser and Siegler, too, detected the growth of unofficial election campaigns, with candidates accumulating large sums of money and building up clientelistic relationships (Berg-Schlosser and Siegler 1990: 83).

The freedom for voters to replace representatives who did not serve their interests adequately, with representatives who did, should not be underrated and, as several observers have noted, there was at least a replenishment of elites, subject to some popular control, if not a circulation of elites, but freedom of choice was largely on the party's terms. It was the party national executive committee that selected the two candidates to contest each constituency from the nominations received from below, and there was, at least on paper, a tighter scrutiny of the ideological credentials of candidates by 1970 (Okema in Othman, Bavu and Okema 1990: 40). The party's first choice might still be rejected by the voters, as was the case in 42 per cent of the constituencies in 1985 (Van Donge and Liviga 1988: 51), but the party could also reject the voters' first choice. At Mbozi in 1985 a popular sitting MP was de-selected, apparently on account of a speech in Parliament attacking nepotism in the government and party. Nearly 19 per cent of the voters responded to the exclusion of their preferred candidate from the ballot paper by spoiling their papers – a remarkable show of defiance but one that did nothing to affect the outcome of the election (Mwakyembe in Othman, Bavu and Okema 1990: 134–49).

Other controls over elections ranged from the ideological to the pedantic. Election meetings were not permitted to applaud or jeer the candidates, and the chairman decided which questions were permissible, and all candidates were expected to endorse the party's national manifesto, although this was of so little interest to most voters, especially in the absence of any alternative manifestos, that it was something of an empty ritual. Yet these restrictions did serve as a reminder of who was in command. It was not simply a case of elections without formal opposition, for which there might have been a strong case, but of elections on terms set by the national leadership which could generally filter out anyone who might present a serious threat to that leadership. And the Parliament, to which voters were electing centrally-approved candidates, was severely limited in its scope, with most power in the hands of the party national executive committee and the President. Election to the former was restricted to the minority of the population who belonged to the party, and elections to the latter office remained uncontested until the multi-party elections of 1995. Voters could vote on the merits of corrugated iron sheeting or local development projects, but national and international policies remained beyond their control.

Citizen participation

A single party might have provided a framework for citizen participation between elections, but most of the evidence suggests that it did not. Such participation might have been feasible if either the party had opened its doors to anyone who wanted to join, or if it had permitted large areas of participation outside its own structures, but it did neither. After the fear of national disunity in the mid-1960s, the army, trade unions and co-operatives were integrated into the party and, with the economy under the extensive control of the state, which the party in turn controlled, there were few autonomous centres of power, and few areas of political activity outside the party. Dissent was further hampered by a virtual party monopoly of the mass media by 1970. Yet within the party the 1982 constitution made membership more restrictive. In theory this was to prevent infiltration by people who did not subscribe to the socialist ideology, but in practice it facilitated the blocking of any potential members who might constitute a threat to the leadership. After the merger of the Tanganyikan and Zanzibari ruling parties, membership actually fell from three million to two million (in a country with a population of over 20 million), and Berg-Schclosser and Siegler suggest that this was only partly the result of stricter conditions for membership (Berg-Schlosser and Siegler 1990: 81). The other major factor was presumably a belief that party membership did not provide many opportunities for political influence. They went on to suggest that the party's functions had extended so much that it was doubtful in the long run 'whether it can exist as a democratic participatory institution intended to represent the interests of the population' (ibid.: 82). Yeager offers a similar picture. In the early 1960s Village Development Committees and ten-house party cells had provided links between the centre and the periphery, but mainly to strengthen central access. By the 1980s local initiative had been virtually eliminated, and replaced by party domination and corporatism. The party had become more centralised and isolated from the grass roots (Yeager 1989: 65, 85–6). And McHenry argued that mass organs had become mechanisms for party policy implementation rather than popular representation (McHenry 1994: 53).

In view of experience in Eastern Europe and other parts of Africa, there is nothing remarkable about a party with a monopoly of power becoming increasingly centralised and intolerant, if not fearful, of dissent. No doubt the self-interest and personal vanity of those at the top played a part in the process, but there was also a genuine fear, which was echoed later by Rawlings in Ghana, that free competition in politics, like free competition in economics, would benefit the few at the expense of the many. Okumu and Holmquist remind us that the party had been very responsive to such basic needs as primary education, health and water, and that 'subordinate classes' were protected by the party's socialist ideology, despite the lack of evidence of mass participation: 'The rise of the party and its ideological thrust has diminished the "free wheeling" and clientelistic character of politicians as constituency representatives' (Okumu and Holmquist in Barkan 1984: 67).

Writing a decade later, Sundet noted the justification for central party organs denying people the right to stand for election was to defend popular democracy and avoid 'the subversion of the population by the few', but he was more doubtful about the diminution of clientism. The selection of candidates on the basis of ideological purity had declined and there had been a growth of patron–client relationships 'in which party leaders and their ideas were given support in return for the clients' opportunity to compete for office' (Sundet 1994: 54). It may be that, in the intervening decade, economic liberalisation had provided more scope for clientelism, yet political liberalisation lagged behind. For the first 20 years after independence, once could perceive a deliberate trade-off between liberty and equality, with restrictions on both private enterprise and private political entrepreneurship enabling the relatively poor to benefit from social provision and to stand for political office on equal terms with their social superiors, but in reality relatively few sons of the soil were elected to Parliament. Of the MPs elected in 1985, only 1.7 per cent were peasants, as compared with 21.8 per cent from 'administration', 10.9 per cent 'workers' and 48.7 per cent 'professional politicians' (Van Donge and Liviga 1989: 57). The freer rein given to private enterprise from the mid-1980s gave a head-start to people near the top of the party and bureaucratic hierarchies who had more strings to pull in gaining economic resources and, the relatively egalitarian distribution of income notwithstanding, more wealth than the average peasant with which to acquire a stake in the capitalist economy. When a more pluralist political system did emerge in Tanzania in the 1990s, the elites which had emerged within and around the ruling party appeared to enjoy substantial resources, in both political and economic terms, to fend off any opposition challenge.

A one-party state or a state party?

'By 1965 the party had settled into an honourable retirement as a kind of minor government department ruled over by a civil servant' (Barker 1969: 57). This was a description of the ruling party in Ghana by a British writer, but it can easily become the fate of any ruling party, which sets out to do everything, to end up by becoming nothing. If opposition is eliminated and elections are uncontested, as they were in Ghana between 1960 and 1966, there is little left for the party to do, and any authority that party officers wield may owe more to their positions in the state structure than in the party structure. It was never quite that simple in Tanzania, where the party continued to have a role in overseeing elections and in propagating an ideology that bore more relation to political reality than the ideology of the ruling party in Ghana. Yet there was a fear that the party could become redundant and, like many who suffer redundancy, become dependent on the state. The desire to re-invigorate the party was one of the reasons for eventually permitting multi-party politics. The reforms of the party constitution in 1982, with their stricter ideological controls over entry into the party, the abandonment of the practice of automatically appointing local and regional party functionaries to corresponding administrative positions, and the reintroduction of elected district councils, were interpreted as attempts to keep party and state separate (Berg-Schlosser and Siegler 1990: 82).

Yet the suspicion that the party was becoming, or had become, an arm of the state did not abate. Hyden wrote of a party that had become wholly associated with the state, and had marginalised civil society (Hyden in Barkan 1994: 94), and Okumu and Holmquist noted that 'tendencies of the party to become the state have been ever present' (Okumu and Holmquist in Barkan 1984: 67). Baregu suggested that, with the merger to form the CCM in 1977, party supremacy was more apparent than real. The CCM as a party was stillborn, with no real voluntary or loyal members, and the distinction between party and state had become so blurred that party and government positions were held by the same people, usually authoritarian bureaucrats. The party was now one of the state's coercive instruments (Baregu in Widner 1994: 165). One could argue that the movement was not all one way. Public officials, including soldiers and directors of parastatals, are not likely to serve under one set of political masters for more than 30 years without either absorbing many of the values and interests of their masters, or being replaced by other officials who are more pliant. It is difficult to believe that the party was merely serving the interests of bureaucrats, or of the elite from which bureaucrats were drawn, especially when there was considerable interchange of personal between party and Civil Service. Several ministers, including the incumbent prime minister on the eve of the first multi-party elections, had begun their careers as administrators and had then brought their skills into the party, while appointments to the bureaucracy came to depend increasingly on loyalty to the party.

A nation in which there is a fusion of party and state, with no permitted opposition, does not appear to be very attractive for supporters of liberty or democracy. Are we looking at a country which set up nominally democratic structures but fell short of the democratic ideal, or are we, as Baregu implies, looking at a more blatantly authoritarian political structure not very different from those found in most of Africa, but which was given an air of respectability by the idealism and integrity of Nyerere, and by the generosity of social provision in the early years? An authoritarian element undoubtedly existed, and was most obviously manifested in the suppression of autonomous trade union activity in the 1960s and the movement of peasants into ujamaa villages in the 1970s, though Legum suggests that only 800 000 were moved by force as compared with 13 million who had moved 'voluntarily' (Legum in Legum and Mmari 1995: 189). There was also the special case of Zanzibar, where a government which had won power by force of arms needed to use considerable coercion to retain power. Preventive detention existed in Tanzania, as in Nkrumah's Ghana, as a last resort to silence any dissidents, and to remove any criminals who could not be caught in the judicial net. Amnesty International estimated that over a thousand people were in detention on the mainland in 1977, but the estimate was reduced to 'some hundreds' in 1978, most of whom were thought to be alleged criminals, but there were no official figures against which to check these estimates (Read in Legum and Mmari 1995: 139). The judiciary did not suffer the humiliations that its counterpart in Ghana had suffered under Nkrumah and Rawlings, though there was growing party control over judicial appointments, and lay assessors with voting rights were appointed to magistrates' courts (ibid.: 134).

To an innocent detainee, a trade unionist denied the right to strike, a peasant forcibly moved from his home, an opposition politician denied the right to offer an alternative party programme, or a journalist denied the right to produce a newspaper critical of the government, any restriction on civil liberties or democratic participation is one restriction too many. But to anyone familiar with events in Africa as a whole since the 1960s (or indeed earlier, when most Africans were denied the right to self-determination) the Tanzanian government and party appeared to rule their citizens with a lighter touch than most. There were no executions of political opponents, no obvious discrimination against, or punishment of, particular ethnic or religious groups, and if corruption and exploitation of the advantages enjoyed by party and state officials was not absent, it never revealed itself on the same scale as in Ghana or Nigeria.

THEORY INTO PRACTICE?

In terms of immediate policy outputs, the socialist policies espoused by Nyerere appeared to be more successful than those of Nkrumah. The infant mortality rate was reduced by a third between 1975 and 1980, average life expectancy increased by 15 years between 1960 and 1980, literacy rose to 79 per cent of the population, and primary education was made free and compulsory (Berg-Schlosser and Siegler 1990: 90–3). Tanzania overtook Kenya in terms of the level of literacy, the proportion of the population supplied with piped water and the number of dispensaries in proportion to the population (Barkan 1984: 27). Economic growth was not spectacular, but there was a modest annual rise of 1.1 per cent in the gross domestic product (GDP) per capita between 1965 and 1980, followed by a fall of 2.4 per cent between 1981 and 1985 (Barkan 1994: 22). This compared favourably with Ghana's performance, where the rate of growth was negative in 12 of the 20 years between 1964 and 1983, and by margins of between –5 per cent and –15 per cent in five of those years (Frimpong-Ansah 1991: 95).

The egalitarianism implicit in the increased social provision was enhanced by the party's leadership code which followed the Arusha Declaration. The code may not always have been followed to the letter, but politicians did not have the same opportunities as their Ghanaian counterparts to use public office to enrich themselves. There is no record of any Tanzanian politician's wife buying a gold bed. Berg-Schlosser and Siegler suggest that, quite apart from the benefits that the egalitarian policies conferred on the population, they reflected the values of a long-standing culture (in a society where there had been few powerful chiefs or wealthy indigenous businessmen) and thus helped to reinforce the legitimacy of the political order (Berg-Schlosser and Siegler 1990: 94).

One major attempt to improve social provision was the establishment of the ujamaa villages, which made it easier to provide communal services such as water, schools, roads and medical facilities. Here the benefits were less clear cut. The desired policy outputs were achieved, but not the desired outcomes. Between 1973 and 1980 the proportion of the rural population living in these villages rose from 15 per cent to 91 per cent (Berg-Schlosser and Siegler 1990: 70), but agricultural production fell considerably, partly on account of the unsuitability of some of the areas to which the peasants had been moved, partly because of the disruption caused by the movement of population, and partly because peasants were often unwilling to perform on the terms laid down by the government. The artificially low prices which they received for their produce led many to turn to the black market. Of the 5000 villages created by the mid-1970s, O'Neill estimates that only 400 had developed sufficiently to the stage where co-operative farming was economically significant (O'Neill in O'Neill and Mustafa 1990: 13–14). In addition to the economic failure, we need to consider the political damage done by the compulsory movement of people from their homes. Estimates of the extent of compulsion vary widely. Legum puts the figure at 800 000 people being moved by force out of a total of 13 million (Legum in Legum and Mmari 1995: 189) whereas Barkan speaks of 80 per cent of the rural population being 'forcibly moved' (Barkan 1994: 20). We are never likely to know the truth, and it is difficult to distinguish between cases where people moved as a result of physical violence, or having their homes destroyed, and others who moved under protest for fear of suffering a similar fate.

In immediate political terms, the movement of peasants did not seem to do any harm, especially when the government could blame over-zealous regional commissioners for exceeding their authority while the commissioners could claim that they were only implementing government policy, but it did mean that any claims that Tanzania was operating a system based on democratic participation, with formal opposition absent only because voters did not want it, looked increasingly threadbare. Villagisation, like most economic policies, had not been adopted as a result of widespread national debate, but by the decision of a narrow elite. Some individual members of that elite could be removed through the ballot box, but not the elite as a whole or the policies it represented.

Economic policy in general was no more successful than villagisation. Much of the story of Tanzania was a microcosm of the story of Tropical Africa as a whole. The international economic climate was generally hostile, with worsening terms of trade and rapidly increasing oil prices after 1973, and the situation was worsened by African governments fixing artificially low prices for farm produce, thus lowering the peasants' already low living standards still further, and by putting such manufacturing as existed in the hands of inefficient, and sometimes corrupt, state corporations. Nationalisation went further in Tanzania than in most other African countries, covering all banks and insurance companies, the wholesale trade and many plantations (Berg-Schlosser and Siegler 1990: 70). Hardship was mitigated to some extent by the ability of peasants to resort to the black market and, in the case of Tanzania, Hyden suggests that most people could engage in private sector activity and take advantage of the ample land available. As with villagisation, a stoical acceptance of one's lot was more common than rebellion, and Tanzanians 'had been indoctrinated to believe that the cause of their difficulties was external, not domestic' (Hyden in Barkan 1994: 88). This may be a difficult argument to substantiate, but we return to the nature of a political culture which, while it might expect an equitable distribution of the wealth available, did not appear to have much expectation of influencing national political decision-making. This again may be true of much of Africa, but it is especially true of a country where most people have traditionally lived in small rural settlements. In Ghana the intrigues of the chiefs' courts gave some grounding in political skills, or at least an awareness of the existence of politics, which might eventually be transferred to the national level. In Tanzania, improvisation in the face of adversity was a more common response than political protest.

Another effect of economic decline was seen in the shift in power from politicians to officials. In the parastatals, managers were given more authority in relation to party functionaries, in an attempt to improve performance (Berg-Schlosser and Siegler 1990: 72), and the moves towards economic orthodoxy in the 1980s were made possible by a greater reliance on technocrats than party ideologues. This was partly a question of expertise, but it may also reflect the general tendency for politicians to enjoy the limelight when they are the bringers of good news but to leave the bringing of bad news to others. From an economic point of view, the greater technocratic role may have been beneficial, but it made the process of government even more remote from the people. 'Bureaucratic authoritarianism' might be an apt description of what evolved, although it was much less brutal than the Latin American version.

Like so many political changes in Tanzania, the shift from socialism to economic orthodoxy was an incremental one, in contrast to the more abrupt turnabouts in Ghana after changes of government in 1966, 1972 and 1981. Nyerere fought a rearguard action against devaluation, privatisation and cuts in welfare spending, but Western-trained economists at the University of Dar es Salaam and technocrats at the Bank of Tanzania and the Ministry of Finance eventually won the day. In 1981 Tanzania accepted IMF demands which required doubling the share of development expenditure on agriculture, imposing a wage freeze, raising interest rates, removing many subsidies and price controls, and imposing charges for secondary education. After the negative economic growth of the early 1980s, the annual rate of GDP growth rose by 1.4 per cent between 1986 and 1990 (Barkan 1994: 22, 28; O'Neill in O'Neill and Mustafa 1990: 17–19). When the more pragmatic Ali Mwinyi succeeded Nyerere as President in 1985, economic liberalisation became the accepted creed, and not just an alternative that might be pursued if the right coalition of party, government and administrative forces could be brought into play.

Economic liberalisation might be seen as the prelude to the establishment of pluralist politics in the 1990s, but it was not as simple as that. The emergence of business and professional groups autonomous from the party and state was a necessary condition for pluralist democracy, but hardly a sufficient one. The grip of the party was still substantial, and much depended on whether it was willing to recognise the legitimacy of inter-party competition. On this issue, Mwinyi the economic liberaliser turned out to be a political conservative, wanting to retain the CCM's hegemony, while Nyerere the opponent of capitalist competition became a convert to political liberalisation. Nyerere was by now a retired elder statesman, and the democratic outcome depended as much on the balance of political forces as on economic changes. We shall return to this delicate balance in Chapter 9.

SOCIALISM AND PLURALISM: ALLIES OR ENEMIES?

By the mid-1990s Tanzania had demolished both the political and the economic structures created under Nyerere's leadership. Most of the economy had been returned to the private sector, a lively free press had emerged, and any political party that could recruit the necessary members was free to enter the political arena. On the face of it, socialism had left the country poorer than it had been before independence, and attempts to regulate the political system to protect the people from exploitation or ideological impurity had at best made for bureaucratic stagnation, and at worst for repression. Socialism, if it was feasible at all, appeared to require constrictions on pluralist politics to the point where they ceased to be pluralist, and where political choice was reduced to seeking the best local ombudsman to do battle for constituents against the state bureaucracy.

Yet if the type of socialism practised in Tanzania until the 1980s left limited room for pluralist politics, one might argue that it still provided opportunities for democratic participation which were rare in Africa, and placed fewer barriers in the way of a more pluralist order when conditions were more conducive to this. McHenry makes a distinction between liberal democracy's concern with 'means', such as civil liberties, majority rule, political equality and elections, and the concern of 'popular democracy' with 'ends' in terms of ultimate decisions reflecting the wishes of the people. Nyerere claimed to support both types of democracy, and appeared to see the exclusion of any legal opposition as a matter of practicality, in the absence of fundamental disagreements, rather than an article of faith (McHenry 1994: 47). Liberal democracy was not so much rejected as held in abeyance while a more practical form of democracy, which seemed to satisfy the majority of the population, was operated. Mmuya and Chaligha also note that the Tanzanian political structure combined socialist with liberal democratic elements, including the separation of powers (though one might query the extent of legislative autonomy), a bill of rights, an independent judiciary, an ombudsman and elections, together with party organs which facilitated some interest articulation (Mmuya and Chaligha 1992: 4–5).

The East Germans built some impressive multi-storey flats in Zanzibar shortly after the revolution. These flats appeared to meet most of their tenants' needs, except that the water pressure was often insufficient to reach the higher storeys, and the tenants were thus deprived of a basic necessity. This might provide a crude metaphor for the Tanzanian political system. The electoral and party channels appeared to provide opportunities for upward political communication and participation, yet the pressures often failed to reach the crucial organs at the top. The ruling party, as we have seen, decayed in terms of membership and activity, and the free market policies adopted, when all the alternatives appeared to have been exhausted, left the party as an increasingly powerless bystander as technocrats took the decisions. This growth of bureaucratic control did not begin with economic liberalisation, and there were earlier accounts of bureaucrats taking control of development projects, co-operatives, parastatals and marketing schemes, when community and party participation had been the objective (see especially Siddiqui in O'Neill and Mustafa 1994: 50; Sundet 1994: 43; Mmuya and Chaligha 1992: 4–5). The party had, perhaps, created an over-ambitious command economy, which its members ultimately lacked the expertise to command, and still less the expertise to dismantle when it failed to function adequately. The ideological justification for a single party looked increasingly dubious if the party no longer had a clear role, and the pragmatic justification on the grounds that there was no disagreement over fundamental issues became less sustainable. The right of a single party to monopolise political recruitment and patronage was becoming a fundamental issue in itself. As Mmuya and Chaligha point out, people with independent positions or alternative views were often left out of the political process (Mmuya and Chaligha 1992: 4–5), and the number of such people was growing with the growth of increasingly autonomous business and professional groups.

The one-party, socialist state might thus be condemned on a variety of grounds, and there is no doubt that it was often sustained through coercion, corruption and patronage, but it is by no means certain that most Tanzanians would have preferred any alternative political order during the first twenty years of independence. Nearly 80 per cent of the Nyalali Commission's respondents in 1990s still favoured a one-party system. For all its limitations, the economic and political systems established in the 1960s provided wider opportunities for political debate and participation, more curbs on corruption and the extraction of wealth by the privileged few, and more social benefits for ordinary citizens, than were found in most of Africa. These achievements helped to endow the political order with a legitimacy which helped it to survive in the leaner years, and ultimately to adapt to a more pluralist order, in first the economic and then the political sphere. This peaceful transition might be attributed partly to a political culture within which there is little tradition of challenging authority, but it may also owe a lot to the influence of a political order which emphasised equity as well as accountability.

6 Tanzania: Political Structures, Civil Society and Democracy

THE STATE AND CIVIL SOCIETY

In Ghana we noted that the strength of civil society had fluctuated, but that there had been, for most of the post-independence years, an abundance of flourishing groups built especially on ethnic, religious, professional and cultural bases. These groups had frequently believed in, and practised, democratic principles, yet their interaction with the state had not led to sustained democratic government. The ruling party had proclaimed that 'The CPP is Ghana and Ghana is the CPP' but this claim had always been a hollow one, with the party doing little more than scratching the surface of civil society. The ruling party in Tanzania did not make a comparable boast, yet it might have had more justification for doing so.

While the viability of democracy in Ghana may depend on the ability of a strong (if not always effective) state, and a strong civil society, to achieve a consensus on their respective roles, a major problem in Tanzania appears to be the weakness of civil society in the face of a state that has been dominated by the same elite for over thirty years. Indeed it is not always clear to an outsider where one should begin looking for civil society. Tribal chiefs have long since been abolished, so there are no obvious channels for articulating the demands of 'traditional' groups, and religious groups have remained largely aloof from politics. As in much of the Third World, religious groups which have accepted the existing political order, and have been partly co-opted into it, have faced competition from more 'fundamentalist' churches which offer a spiritual alternative to failed political gods, but these churches tend to offer an exit from politics rather than alternative political paths. There have been sporadic Christian-Muslim clashes, notably over the proposed return of nationalised schools to church ownership and over Zanzibar's short-lived membership of the Organisation of Islamic Conference, but in each case the situation was defused with a return to the status quo ante. (Ludwig in Westerlund, 1996: 216–36) For the most part, religious groups have been neither a major source of institutional support for, or opposition to, the government. An unspoken understanding of mutual non-interference may have developed between church (or mosque) and state. The churches have not had to suffer the near-deification of the head of state, with party ideology being presented almost as a pseudo-religion, in the way that they did in Ghana under Nkrumah, with the ever-present possibility of a criticism of this cult producing political retaliation, which would in turn drive the churches further into the realm of opposition and resistance. Neither was there any obvious scope for the churches in Tanzania to take up the injustices suffered by the poor, as in Latin America, given Tanzania's record of social provision. As for Islam, Muslims are in a minority except in Zanzibar, and there is therefore no possibility of establishing an Islamic state. The practice of nominating a Zanzibari (and invariably Muslim) vice-president whenever there is a Tanganyikan president, and vice versa, has probably helped the process of integration.

Where, then, does one look for autonomous groups beyond the state which might help to devise and police the unwritten rules of political conflict, and which might thus provide counterweights to the power of the state? One obvious role for such groups would be in encouraging people to register as electors, and ultimately to vote, thus preventing a monopolisation of these processes by party and state officials who might have a more direct interest. Maliyamkono suggests some of the 'opinion leaders' whose services were sought.

> Opinion leaders are people of influence who can motivate others to register and later to vote. In most cases they are primary school teachers, co-operative workers, youth leaders, religious leaders, elders and influential workers or business people. (Maliyamkono 1995: 19)

Insofar as these people belonged to organised groups, many of the groups were, or had recently been, wings of the ruling party or employees of the state. Or, in the case of religious leaders, they represented groups which had chosen to avoid entanglements with the state. If these groups were the most easily identifiable elements in civil society, it was a society which enjoyed little autonomy in relation to the state. The relationship between state and society appeared to be a clearer, zero-sum relationship than in Ghana. Whereas in Ghana there were arguments (though sometimes disputed) that increased state power sometimes provoked groups in society into organising more effectively, and that the decline of the state in the late 1970s and early 1980s may have been paralleled by a decline in civil society as increased poverty made personal survival a higher priority than communal action, in Tanzania the strength of the state contributed to the subordination of society from the 1960s to the 1980s, and it was only as the state began to relax its grip in the 1990s that society began to show some renaissance.

We have already noted that the predominant political culture and the power structures in society put few barriers in the way of state domination. There were few, if any, ethnic groups or regions which attempted to assert their autonomy, and there was little tradition of independent political activity outside the nationalist movement, which eventually became the ruling party. It is generally agreed in the academic literature that it was the ruling party that was the main instrument for subordinating society, or keeping it subordinate. Hyden speaks of the party 'marginalising' civil society and of the CCM becoming a party wholly associated with the state; Berg-Schlosser and Siegler of the intermediate groups, especially trade unions, being largely subordinated to the party; Okema of state building through a strong party, with little need for violence and little resistance (the culture of passivity again); and Barkan refers to the 'crushing' of civil institutions (Hyden in Barkan 1994: 94; Berg-Schlosser and Siegler 1990: 138; Okema in Othman et al. 1990: 37–8; Barkan 1994: 20).

If the state was the winner of an uneven contest with civil society, how could this outcome be translated into victories or defeats for particular groups or policies within the polity? In a socialist economy which eliminated most of the private sector and offered only limited scope for political participation in national policy making, the most obvious winners were the people at the top of the party hierarchy and the state bureaucracy. There was some overlap between these two groups, but the bureaucrats' superior expertise, and control over the day-to-day process of administration, appeared to give them the major role once the broad party guidelines had been set. How far this made for self-enrichment, in the way that membership of a capitalist ruling class makes for wealth as well as power, is not entirely clear, though the command economy obviously created a range of well-paid jobs in the public sector, and Shivji reported that, in 1971, nine principal secretaries in government departments together held 89 directorships and 26 chairmanships in the parastatals (Shivji 1976: 89). He also hinted that their control over policy implementation had a major bearing on who participated (or not) in politics, and thus on the nature of political decisions themselves. In the emerging bureaucratic bourgeois ideology, problems were seen 'as the problems of administering things rather than the involvement of the people', and the technocratic implementation of decisions required the correct expert advice, efficient expert organisation of planning and the use of qualified manpower, with little interest in self-help (Shivji 1976: 96–7).

The immediate 'losers' in this consolidation of state power appeared to be ordinary citizens. They may have gained in terms of the provision of amenities such as schools, roads, medical facilities and water supply, but they forewent the political power and influence which national independence had appeared to offer. In the longer term, socialist ideologues in the ruling party were also losers, although one can argue about whether they represented a larger constituency or were merely isolated individuals pursuing an intellectual fad. The preservation of the policies espoused by Nyerere would have been difficult in any event, with the worsening of economic conditions from the early 1970s, but the bureaucratic domination of the state tipped the balance of power further away from idealistic politicians and towards more pragmatic technocrats. In the previous chapter we traced the ways in which the loss of power from society to the party developed into a loss of power from the party to the state. The extent of the retreat from socialism in the 1980s was as remarkable as its initial advance.

The economy, in the early 1980s, was strictly controlled; the movement and sale of many crops and consumer goods were restricted and roadblocks covered the country to enforce the controls. Essential commodities were supposed to be sold only through co-operative shops. Imports were minimal and strictly licensed. By the end of the period (1980–5), trade was liberalised, food prices were determined in a free market and shops were full of imported commodities. Provided the importer secured his or her own foreign exchange, virtually all imports were allowed in. Accumulation of property and wealth was no longer condemned and was openly displayed in an unprecedented manner. (Van Donge and Liviga 1989: 48)

Van Donge and Liviga go on to suggest that it was difficult to locate the initiative of these policy changes, although 'liberalisation was carried by a consensus in society. Government gave in to popular pressure' (ibid.: 49). It is not clear how one can gauge popular opinion in such matters if one cannot even locate sources of policy making. It seems plausible to suggest that people were dissatisfied with policies that both kept them in poverty and imposed restrictions on their everyday economic freedom, but it is not clear whether there was any popular demand for, or awareness of, the free market alternatives. The authors note that

[The policy changes] were never presented as diverging from the road to socialism that Tanzania had taken. There was very little public debate about them nor any recriminations about what had happened in the past. These major changes were made in a political culture of consensus that is so typical in Tanzania. (ibid.: 49)

The points about lack of public debate, and the pretence that the new policies were not a divergence from the old (or at least that the new policies were based on the same principles as the old), was also true of the economic liberalisation in Ghana initiated by Rawlings after 1983, though in Ghana several radicals left, or were dismissed from, the government and some, such as Hansen and Yeebo, continued an ideological war of words from the safety of exile. Ghana could never be accused of having a 'political culture of consensus'. If Tanzania had one, it was more a consensus that economic policy should be left to decision-makers at the centre rather than a consensus about the nature of the policy. Even the existence of this 'blank cheque' consensus might be challenged by writers like Baregu who see a more coercive hand behind the policy process (Baregu in Widner 1994: 159–63). If, as we suggested in the previous chapter, much power had slipped from the party to the state bureaucracy as the party decayed and decisions increasingly required technical expertise, the reality of the distribution of political power had much to do with the pace and extent, if not the direction, of policy change.

Technocrats were 'winners' in the sense that tilts in the balance of power between state and party helped them to get their own way. Whether they were also winners in terms of the distribution of material wealth is more difficult to establish, but people such as these, who were among the best paid in the country, would presumably have been in the best position to enjoy the 'accumulation of property and wealth' which economic liberalisation facilitated, especially as the disciplines imposed by the Arusha Declaration were abandoned. Among the losers, in addition to party ideologues after 1980, we should also note that in the early years, while the party was still gaining power from the rest of civil society before losing much of it to the state, such organised groups as existed, other than religious groups, became incorporated as 'wings of the party', and much more effectively and more durably than in Nkrumah's Ghana. The army and trade unions were both threats in the early 1960s, and their subsequent subordination to the party reduced the likelihood of the removal of the government by means of a coup or general strike.

The zero-sum game between state and society continued in the late 1980s and 1990s with a weakening of the state making for modest increases in the strength of civil society. Barkan refers to the re-emergence of civil society generally (Barkan 1994: 21) and Tripp examines the increased opportunities for women to participate, though many of the forces she mentions would presumably have had some effect on men as well. Cuts in welfare and social security encouraged greater attempts at self-help, and the legalisation of opposition parties in 1992 was accompanied by a process of starting to disengage affiliated mass organisations from the ruling party, including those concerned with women, youth, trade unions, co-operatives and parents (Tripp in Harbeson, Rothchild and Chazan 1994: 155, 157–8). These changes have not produced any startling challenges to the state but, together with the emergence of a free press and an opposition electoral challenge, there are at least the foundations of a more autonomous society. The significant contrast with Ghana is in the more 'controlled' way in which the Tanzanian state has retreated in both the economic and the political spheres, so that there were structures and activities available which autonomous groups could take over, whereas in Ghana the state's loss of resources and authority in the late 1970s and early 1980s looked more like an abandonment than a retreat, and civil society had greater difficulty in picking up the pieces. Tanzania's relatively orderly economic and political liberalisation appears to provide ample opportunities for the building of participative, democratic structures in society, but the underlying political culture may continue to be a handicap. The culture that made for only token resistance to authoritarianism in the early years of independence does not appear to have changed radically. A small minority of the population, mainly the more educated and urbanised, demanded liberalisation, many members of the ruling party itself felt that it could benefit from competition, and external donors demanded structural adjustment and 'good government', but pressures from below were much less evident. The wider society has yet to put the assets it has obtained to politically profitable use.

CIVIL AND MILITARY BUREAUCRACIES

The Tanzanian civil bureaucracy was much more a master of its own fate than its Ghanaian counterpart. While the latter had to cope with unconstitutional changes of government, rulers who frequently despised its members' backgrounds and values, and purges of personnel in the prosecution of party and ethnic conflicts, the Tanzanian bureaucracy was much more integrated into the political process. It evolved simultaneously with the ruling party, but its interests, its ideology and its power base often conflicted with those of the party. We suggested in the previous chapter that the interests included a continued expansion of the size and role of the bureaucracy, the ideology an orderly economic expansion based on 'rational' criteria, and the power base a body of personnel claiming a near-monopoly of the skills necessary to maintain the command economy. This contrasted with the party's concerns with expanding patronage on its own terms, and pursuing socialist aims which, at least on paper, gave greater prominence to social equality and popular participation, while keeping both the state bureaucracy and Parliament under party supervision.

Tanzanian history from the early 1980s onwards suggests that the bureaucracy fared rather better than the party. Samoff's claim that the bureaucracy became the governing class, as its empire grew with the growth of state corporations, was disputed by Mukandala, who argued that civil servants were generally underpaid and had become less efficient as their duties had grown (Samoff 1982–3: 117. See also Yeager 1989: 76, on the growth of the parastatals from 64 in 1967 to over 400 by the 1980s; Mukandala 1983: 19), but there is little dispute over the extent of bureaucratic power. Yeager mentions increasing reliance on bureaucratic command techniques to impose policies from above, Shivji refers to the emphasis on the expert advice and efficient planning at the expense of encouraging self-help, and Samoff noted that the views of technocrats 'dominate decision-making and policy' (Yeager 1989: 76; Shivji 1976: 97; Samoff 1983–3: 122). In the heyday of a socialist state, once the party's initial enthusiasm for deciding the direction of policy has worn off, it may take a lot to prevent the bureaucrat from becoming king. The pretensions to efficiency, as Mukandela suggests, may be exaggerated, and not all bureaucrats will be well paid, but those at the top can survey a political scene in which there are few autonomous centres of power in civil society, and in which the ruling party has lost much of its will and ability to control the political process.

What is less clear is the role of the bureaucracy once the command economy has been dismantled, or even its role in dismantling it. We noted that the pressures for economic liberalisation came largely from technocrats, in the face of resistance from the party. Why should they want to dismantle a system that had apparently served them so well? Part of the answer may be that the term 'technocrat' includes people such as directors of state banks, academics and members of the professions, as well as regular civil servants, and that the former groups saw an extended role for themselves in a liberalised economy. It may also be a common feature of the 'rolling back of the state' in many countries that the most senior bureaucrats (those who presumably have most influence over the direction of policy) emerge unscathed. Mrs Thatcher's distaste for the public sector in Britain did not seem to damage the careers of her senior mandarins, many of whom were able to devise means of economising on the employment of their subordinates rather than themselves. And for those senior officials who do become surplus to requirements, whether in Britain or Tanzania, the newly-privatised sectors of the economy may provide lucrative new job opportunities.

This still leaves us with the question of how far the bureaucracy has been, or is likely to become, a significant contributor to the process of democratisation. The outline offered so far does not appear to offer many grounds for hope, with a bureaucracy confident of its own superior knowledge and expertise, and sceptical of the value or legitimacy of any wider community participation. There is also the long record of inter-penetration with the ruling party, which continues to create a suspicion among opposition politicians that the bureaucracy is not dedicated to serving the whole nation, and that it might not co-operate willingly with any alternative government. The actual administration of the 1995 elections did little to allay the suspicions. If public officials cannot or will not cope with the logistics of a relatively simple exercise such as administering an election, it raises questions about their administrative competence in the context of a mixed economy and a pluralist political system. For all its complexity, the command economy allowed bureaucrats to operate a chain of command within which giving and conveying orders was more important than the art of persuading, or negotiating with, autonomous groups which might be pursuing objectives that conflicted with either the bureaucracy or with one another. The new political and economic order is likely to require an increasing amount of policy making and implementation involving groups from outside the Civil Service (governments 'steering rather than rowing'), and the ability of the Tanzanian Civil Service to work within such an environment has yet to be proved.

The Tanzanian army, like the civil bureaucracy, was always a potential threat to the ruling party's quest for a monopoly of power, despite attempts to integrate it into the party, and to ensure that key posts were held by loyal party members. Having never actually captured power, the army has not been exposed to as much journalistic or academic investigation as the Ghanaian army, but the denial of the fruits of political office appear to have spared it from much of the jealousy, corruption and internal conflict associated with tasting forbidden fruit. The attempted mutiny in 1964 had more to do with internal army matters, such as pay and conditions of service, than with challenging the competence of the government, but the mutiny served as a warning that the army might be strong enough to take power, and it thus led to a purge of personnel and the integration of the army into the ruling party.

One-party rule may have been benign by East European standards but, in the absence of peaceful means of removing the ruling elite, there was always the possibility of illegal resistance, whether passive or violent, which could engulf the army. It intervened as the servant of the government to break resistance to resettlement in ujamaa villages (Berg-Schlosser and Siegler 1990: 95), and some of its leaders intervened against the government in an attempted coup in 1982–3. The government responded by extending army–party inter-penetration still further, with more ideological training for soldiers and more military appointments to political positions (Zirker in Danopoulos 1992: 113–14). There is no guarantee that such a model of civil–military relations will keep the army at bay, but the government did enjoy the fortuitous advantage of having 'real' military tasks to occupy the army, and thus avoided the Devil making work for idle hands. General Amin's invasion of Tanzania from Uganda in 1979, during his final attempt to demonstrate his authority to the world, required substantial military resources to repulse the attack and ultimately drive Amin into exile, and the liberation struggles in Southern Africa also involved a substantial Tanzanian contribution. Partly to meet these commitments, and partly, presumably, to minimise military discontent, the percentage of the budget allocated to the military grew from 4 per cent in 1979 to 14 per cent in 1990, with 'special political perquisites for senior military officers' (Zirker in Danopoulos 1992: 115, 117).

The ending of the Cold War, including its offshoots in Southern Africa, and the ending of single-party monopoly, raised questions as to the future role of the military. While the disaffiliation of trade unions or youth movements from the ruling party might create some teething troubles as they seek a new role, the casting adrift of an army previously integrated into a ruling party may have more serious repercussions. Can one assume that a move away from the, 'apparat control' model of one-party domination will necessarily imply a move to the 'objective control' model of liberal democracy (on this typology see Luckham 1971: 22)? Perhaps the army should be grateful to the CCM for its generous defence budgets, especially in a poor country where other priorities might have higher claims, but there is no law in political science to suggest that generosity is necessarily reciprocated with support, as witness the political pressures from already-pampered Latin American armies. It is possible that external pressures for 'good government', and threats to withhold aid, make military intervention less likely today, but events in Rwanda, Nigeria and Sierra Leone suggest limitations to external pressure. If a peaceful change of government is now constitutionally possible, but deemed to be impracticable on account of the weakness of the opposition, how can the army be constrained if it sees the government as inadequate, and is no longer socialised into loyalty to the ruling party? The optimistic answer may be that Tanzania has become a sufficiently mature nation to resolve its conflicts peacefully, but optimism may have to be supplemented with thinking about means of consolidating 'objective control'. An alternative fear is of an actual or anticipated opposition election victory, or perhaps an opposition revolt against an allegedly rigged election, with the army intervening out of anticipation of a less generous budgetary provision or a purge of personnel thought to be too close to the CCM, or simply out of fear of disorder. There were hints that this might happen when opposition parties questioned the legitimacy of the 1995 election results, but the actual outcome was nothing worse than a few scuffles outside the High Court when the judges ruled against the opposition.

If Tanzania has survived periods of severe shortages, increasing poverty and authoritarian rule with minimal violence and disorder, certainly compared with most of its immediate neighbours, one might argue that administrative inefficiency and military lack of a sense of role are problems which the country can take in its stride. The Civil Service may continue to improvise as best it can, and soldiers may be kept occupied in useful public works or in policing the political conflicts of other

African states, but we return to the problem that the relatively smooth dismantling of the one-party state may prove easier than the inculcation of pluralist values and structures. The civil and military services may yet prove their ability to contribute to a democratic polity, but the elimination of their more negative qualities is easier to detect than the creation of positive ones.

CONSTITUTIONAL CHECKS AND BALANCES: THE LEGISLATURE AND JUDICIARY

The Tanzanian Parliament has produced fewer martyrs to the cause of democracy than its Ghanaian counterpart. While Ghanaian MPs might make speeches of defiance before disappearing into exile or preventive detention, Tanzanian MPs have generally confined themselves to safer, more parochial issues. The small minority who have criticised corruption, and the growth of state bureaucracy or authoritarianism, have generally suffered nothing worse than de-selection or expulsion from Parliament. The less confrontational nature of society, as compared with Ghana, is evident here as at so many other points in the Tanzanian political system, but the alternative to confrontation may not be so much consensus as subordination. Article 51(4) of the 1977 constitution referred to Parliament's role as ensuring that the government implemented party policy, and there was never much doubt about Parliament's subordination to the ruling party in theory or practice. Okema speaks of Parliament being reduced to 'a committee of the national conference of the party' (Okema in Othman et al. 1990: 51) and Tordoff suggests that it was safer to raise constituency issues than to criticise the fundamentals of government policy such as ujamaa villages, foreign policy or relations with Zanzibar. Yet Parliament was able to retain an air of legitimacy by allowing MPs to attack inconsequential legislation (Tordoff 1977: 238, 243). It could also be useful from the point of view of the President or the party in scrutinising ministers or the bureaucracy, especially when there were few other fora available from which the government could be criticised (Tordoff 1977: 243; Van Donge and Liviga 1989: 47). An obvious advantage of this from the point of view of the President and party was that criticism was deflected from the merits or feasibility of policies to the often thankless task of implementing them.

There were parallels with Lee's description of Ghanaian MPs representing the government in their constituencies rather than their constituencies in Parliament, though some of the literature speaks of representing 'the party' or even 'Parliament' rather than the government (Okema in Othman et al. 1990: 50; Barkan 1984: 78; Marmo 1989: 70). The ideal MP from the party's point of view would have been one who assiduously explained party policy to constituents and ensured that executive decisions were implemented locally, but survival in Parliament in a system of intra-party competition required MPs to ensure that resources were brought into their constituencies. We saw in the previous chapter that MPs who failed to do this might face electoral defeat, so that any bureaucratic allocation of resources was tempered by pressures through an elected, if not a pluralist, Parliament.

Parliament also enjoyed some advantages in terms of its actual capacity, as compared with the party, to scrutinise policy, so that some functions which nominally belonged to the party were left to Parliament (Okumu and Holmquist in Barkan 1984: 57). Even in a one-party state, the mere existence of a parliament which is required to examine draft legislation and executive documents will give it an advantage over 'amateur' party activists, who may anyway feel that they should concentrate on higher matters while legislative drudgery is better left to MPs. But the division of labour appeared to become less clear cut once members of the party executive were paid salaries comparable with those of MPs, and more able activists were thus attracted. The impression of MPs as 'below stairs' members of the political household could never be completely eradicated, and those who got ideas above their station could easily be de-selected. In 1968 seven MPs were actually expelled from Parliament for challenging the party's superiority (Okumu and Holmquist in Barkan 1984: 55), and this proved a sufficient deterrent against any other potential rebels.

If MPs' place was below stairs, the position of judges was more ambiguous. Perhaps it was more like that of the butler who emphasises his humble position but ensures that correct standards are observed. There have been few, if any, of the unseemly clashes between executive and judiciary comparable with those which have occurred in Ghana, with politicians criticising not only the rulings but the right of judges to take decisions which constitutional and common law would have suggested were within their remit. The Tanzanian judiciary may have had to pay a price, which purists might regard as too high, for being able to participate in decisions where politics and the law overlap. Judges appointed to high office appear to be people were broadly sympathetic to the ideals, if not always the actual behaviour, of the ruling party, and in this they were not very different from the vast majority of the population. There was thus much less of an ideological gulf between executive and judiciary that there has been in Ghana for much of its history, where most of the legal profession belong to an elite which is hostile to radical governments (though the situation has become more complicated with a prolonged period in which senior judicial appointments have been in the gift of Rawlings). Tanzanian judges might, at the risk of over-simplification, be regarded as belonging to the 'libertarian left', and in such a position they had a potential ally in Nyerere himself, who deplored some of the ruling party's authoritarian tendencies and became one of the first converts to multi-party competition.

Legal reforms could be seen as attempts to fine-tune the political system rather than as a crusade by the upholders of the rule of law against authoritarians. Read notes that the Bill of Rights passed in 1984 was the result of 'influential opinion', and that the courts have 'repeatedly shown their active commitment to the enforcement of these new guarantees' (Read in Legum and Mmari 1995: 130). In 1987 citizens were permitted, for the first time, to challenge the constitutionality of government actions, and a large number of cases have come before the courts as a result. Conflicts over sensitive political issues can go either way. Judges criticised the government for using its parliamentary majority to reverse a High Court ruling over the right of independent candidates to stand for Parliament and local councils once one-party rule ended, but such reversals are not unknown in other countries where the final decision lies with the ruling party in Parliament. An important decision that went against the government was the ruling that it was unconstitutional for the executive to prohibit public meetings, thus preventing the undue harassment of opposition parties in the approach to the 1995 elections.

Opposition parties complained of political bias over the High Court ruling that the election results could not be nullified, following allegations of a range of irregularities, but the case would have been a difficult one to prove before any court. There had been ample cases of incompetence and individual misconduct, but it would have required a very strong case to persuade any court that the results were legally void, whatever moral judgements one might make over what had happened.

As a footnote on the judiciary, one should also mention the work of the Law Reform Commission. This is a body comprised mainly, but not exclusively, of lawyers which is appointed by the government, keeps the law under continuous review and makes recommendations for modifications. This is another area in which a genuine search for consensus appears to have been made, rather than politicians deciding the law is whatever they want it to be, or judges entrenching themselves in positions that are too inflexible to cope with political reality.

LOCAL GOVERNMENT

There have been obvious similarities between local government in Ghana and Tanzania. Not the least of them was the limited capacity of local authorities to perform their basic functions in the face of expensive statutory tasks, inadequate sources of revenue, inadequately qualified staff, corruption and embezzlement (Berg-Schlosser and Siegler 1990: 86; Tordoff 1994: 571). But in both countries interest in local government goes beyond the efficiency with which local authorities dealt with blocked drains or potholed roads, or any other specific function, to the question of what sort of structures and functions central governments were attempting to put in place, and with what anticipated and actual consequences for the working of the political system as a whole. In Ghana the patterns were more varied over time, with abrupt changes of government leading to changed perceptions of the role of local government. In each case local government was designed not merely to serve local needs, but to give expression to the current ideology and to secure the government's power base in a political system where the means of coercion were inadequate, yet popular legitimacy was difficult to secure.

In Tanzania one might have expected the task to be easier, with the same party in power continuously, but the power wielded by those at the centre was slippery, and not always in the hands of the same individuals. And when it came to allocating power to actors at a local level, the outcomes were not necessarily those which the central power holders had sought. As in Ghana, words such as 'decentralisation' and 'participation' recur frequently, yet Ayee's assertion that decentralisation in Ghana was less to encourage participation than to promote legitimacy, re-centralise power and enhance patronage (Ayee 1994: 200–2) sounds a warning note for the student of Tanzanian local government seeking to discover a participatory utopia hidden somewhere off the beaten track of authoritarian politics.

A participatory society might appear to be a more consistent ideal among Nyerere and his followers than it had ever been in Ghana. Here were politicians who saw economic and political salvation in co-operation at village level to improve the lot of the peasants, rather than through any attempt at industrialisation under the guidance of a Leninist party, yet the results were generally disappointing. Berg-Schlosser and Siegler describe the 'disintegration' of district councils in the 1960s in the face of falling tax revenues and the burden of expensive tasks (Berg-Schlosser and Siegler 1990: 86), and the elected councils were abolished in 1969, with many major functions, such as control of primary education, larger health centres and district roads, transferred to central departments. This obviously reduced the scope for community participation, leaving residents as supplicants making requests and supplying information, rather than shaping decisions. In Samoff's words, this transformation favoured expertise over participation and administration over politics (Samoff 1982–3: 114; see also Berg-Schlosser and Siegler 1990: 86; Yeager 1989: 75; Tordoff 1994: 562, 571). Such changes might not normally be of much concern to politicians firmly entrenched at the centre but, in the Tanzanian context, it raised two major problems. One was that the legitimacy of the whole political edifice depended heavily on the premise that citizens exercised substantial political control where it really mattered to them – at the local level – even if high politics, in which they were allegedly less interested, were dominated by a non-elected

President and a party which carefully restricted entry into the national political arena. If it was seen to be untrue that there was local participation, the legitimacy of the whole system might come into question. Secondly, there was the 'party versus bureaucracy' conflict which we have already noted. Reduced community participation implied increased bureaucratic power, and there was the ever-present fear that increased bureaucratic power could ultimately reduce the party to an appendage of the state. Largely for these reasons, elected district councils were restored in 1982, and at the same time the practice of appointing individuals to party and state posts concurrently was ended. Yet, according to Tordoff, the same centralising trends recurred (Tordoff 1994: 571).

The advance of the bureaucracy at the expense of the party at national level in the 1980s thus appears to have been replicated at the local level. It was, however, a retreat for the party rather than a surrender. It still had the advantage of vast powers of patronage in overseeing the election of councillors and, when the *de jure* one-party system came to an end, the party was careful to ensure that it retained its monopoly by other means. Parliament decreed that no independent candidates should be permitted to contest elections, locally or nationally (in contrast to Ghana, where local candidates were not permitted to be anything other than independent), and this meant that any challenge to the CCM in the 1994 local elections had to come from a registered opposition party. As the existence of such parties had only just been legalised, the logistics of forming a party and building up any serious local organisation was considerable, and the ruling party won 97 per cent of the seats (though only 74 per cent of the votes) on a low turnout.

To the extent that the objective of manipulating local government was to reinforce single-party domination, the ruling party was very successful. It might now be a long way from the democratic socialist party envisaged by Nyerere in the early 1960s, but it had been sharp enough to turn internal and external demands for democratisation to its own advantage by holding local elections before opposition parties had had any time to develop, and without the programme of 'civic education' in democratic rights demanded by the opposition parties. A democratic local structure now exists on paper but, if we use Dahl's dimensions of 'participation' and 'contestation' in assessing the strength of democracy (Dahl 1971: 203), the participatory element has already been blunted by increased centralisation and bureaucratisation, and such contestation as has occurred has been on very unequal terms.

TRADE UNIONS AND INDUSTRIAL RELATIONS

It may seem incongruous to include trade unions in a chapter on formal political structures but, if the ruling party in its early years envisaged a more participant society, workplaces as well as local government might offer scope for ordinary citizens to participate in decisions important to their everyday lives. There were certainly indications that the government saw industrial relations as something more than a private battleground between workers and employers, or a means of imposing centralised state control over production. A 'workers' participation programme' was introduced in 1970 which, according to Masanja, assumed a harmonious relationship between workers and management (Masanja in O'Neill and Mustafa 1990: 218), and legislation required the establishment of workers' committees and workers' councils in all establishments employing more than ten trade union members.

Difficulties arose, however, when the ideal of democratic participation conflicted with other objectives. As in other areas of political activity, different actors had different interests and, while they did not necessarily reject worker participation as an ideal, it might have a lower priority than more immediate concerns. The trade unions, like most other groups in society, were incorporated into the ruling party and, while this compromised their autonomy, it did give them representation at the highest levels in the political system which could be used to articulate their demands. This structure was based on the assumption that workers should be more than mere employees in a socialist state. In the parliamentary debate on the 1967 Permanent Labour Tribunals Bill, some trade union MPs criticised the limitations which it imposed on collective bargaining, and demanded the right of workers to discuss the economic performance of their factories 'and thus create industrial democracy' (Masanja in O'Neill and Mustafa 1990: 224). The government and party leadership took a different view of industrial relations, bearing in mind the threat of labour disputes to political stability in the early 1960s. They favoured worker participation only within a tightly controlled structure which left little room for independent union action. As for state technocrats, and especially those running state corporations, there were parallels with their attitudes towards participation in local politics. There might be a genuine belief in the virtues of participation, but not if it conflicted with applying the expertise of those who were best qualified to take decisions.

Legislation during the years of one-party rule more frequently reflected the interests of senior politicians and technocrats than those of the workers. The 1962 Trade Disputes Act made strikes illegal unless the negotiating machinery had been exhausted, thus making legal strikes virtually impossible, and as a result the number of strikes was halved over the next two years (Shivji 1976: 134). The Permanent Labour Tribunals Act of 1967 further restricted workers' capacity to bargain over wages and working conditions (Masanja in O'Neill and Mustafa 1990: 224). The National Union of Tanganyika Workers (Nuta) was made the only legal trade union, affiliated to the ruling party and with little independence from the government. Its general secretary and his deputy were appointed by the President of the Republic, and top officers were appointed rather than elected (Shivji 1976: 128). On a more positive note, the statutory workers' committees had the right to advise employers on matters such as welfare, work rules and redundancy, and had to be consulted by employers before an employee was punished for a breach of discipline. The statutory works councils, which were required in every public corporation, enterprise, firm or parastatal organisation, included all members of workers' committees, and advised the board of directors on wages policies, productivity, marketing and planning. But both Masanja and Shivji argue that, while these structures occasionally provided opportunities for workers to organise themselves and influence decisions, most power remained with the management. The workers' committees had the right to be consulted rather than to take decisions and had 'responsibility without power' (Shivji 1976: 129. See also Masanja in O'Neill and Mustafa 1990: 218), while the workers' councils were said to be dominated by bureaucrats, and allowed little effective worker participation in decision-making (Shivji 1976: 131–3).

The actual course of industrial conflict highlighted the limited powers and resources of the workers. Shivji suggests that they started off from a position of weakness, with limited experience, a tradition of leadership from the top and a separation of trade unions from Tanu before independence, which was designed to give the party greater legitimacy as a nationalist movement (Shivji in O'Neill and Mustafa 1990: 196). When the unions were subsequently affiliated to the party, it was very much on the party's terms. On the other side of the divide, Masonja emphasises the way in which managers were able to treat publicly owned resources as their own in the absence of local level political monitoring, leaving workers with very limited ability to influence political decisions despite occasional appeals to the party's sense of justice (Masanja in O'Neill and Mustafa 1990: 228–9). Sporadic strikes continued to occur during the 1970s, in spite of the constraints imposed on the workers, often organised outside the formal trade union channels and involving factory takeovers, but the government response was generally harsh, with workers frequently dismissed (Shivji 1976: 136).

Any philosophical conflict there may have been between Tanzania as an egalitarian country in which workers were recognised as co-partners with managers, as envisaged in the 1970 workers' participation programme, and Tanzania as a state where the role of workers was to implement party policy decided from on high, was resolved in favour of the latter (McHenry 1994: 53; Masanja in O'Neill and Mustafa 1990: 219–20). Shivji points out that worker participation, like the citizen participation in local government which we considered earlier, was much more limited than had been envisaged by the more idealistic Tanzanians, and did not compensate for the lack of political competition (Shivji 1976: 134). Once again, in Dahl's terminology, any measure of democracy revealed very poor score on the 'contestation' axis, while one party monopolised the political process, and only a modest score on the 'participation' axis. Industrial relations during the years of economic liberalisation are not so well documented, but there is no reason to believe that private employers, and especially foreign ones, would be any more sympathetic towards industrial democracy than the party and state had been previously.

Yet one is left with questions about the standards by which we should be judging the quality and quantity of democracy in Tanzania. It may be true that the government took little notice of parliamentary debate, that the ruling party sometimes imposed candidates whom constituencies did not want, and that bureaucrats frequently got the better of peasants in local decision-making, as did managers in relation to workers, but is there anything unusual about this in Africa, or even in many parts of Europe? The workers' participation programme may not have worked well, but how many countries generally regarded as democratic have even attempted to establish such programmes? Whether it is Baregu on civil liberties or Shivji on industrial relations, Tanzanians are often rigorous critics of their own political system, demanding standards which may be admirable but which would demand a lot of any country, and especially a country that is one of the world's poorest, with little tradition of pluralist politics and little tradition of standing up to authority. In terms of expectations in the early years of independence, there may have been disappointments. Compared with the fortunes of democracy in most other parts of Africa since the 1960s, there may be room for a little self-congratulation.

CONCLUSION

Our search for political structures which might contribute to the consolidation of democracy does not appear to have revealed a great wealth of assets. Parliament has never been more than a worthy forum that sometimes facilitates the articulation of local demands more effectively than other means. The competence of the state bureaucracy to cope with a mixed economy and a pluralist political system has yet to be demonstrated, and a prolonged period of one-party rule may lead people to question the political neutrality of the bureaucratic personnel, though they do appear to be less corrupt than many state bureaucrats in Africa. The army has the advantage, from the point of view of democratic consolidation, of never having tasted power directly, so that the 'veto power' exercised to topple elected governments in Ghana and Nigeria may be less of a threat in Tanzania, though it is conceivable that any future attempt by the ruling party to cling to power by rigging elections, or any militant response to such rigging by opposition parties, might bring in the army rather than the judiciary. As in Ghana, the prospects of military intervention to promote authoritarianism may be a remote one, but the prospect of such intervention to maintain or advance democracy is even more difficult to imagine, especially while the army is still led by men socialised in the ways of a one-party state. Local government might yet prove a useful training ground in democratic politics, especially if opposition parties can build up their strength in areas where they performed well in the national elections in 1995, but for the immediate future the one-party stranglehold is greater than in Ghana, where all the district authority members are nominally independents, and many of those who are not independent in practice are opposition sympathisers, or even members. For a time industrial democracy offered the possibility of strengthening the 'participatory' axis of democracy even when the 'contestation' axis was weak, but technocratic domination stifled much of the participation, and privatisation may have extinguished it altogether. The judiciary may offer rather more hope to aspiring democrats, as an institution that is not in the pocket of the ruling party or bureaucracy, but the judicial role may be more important in dealing with conflicts between well-established institutions in a relatively mature democracy, rather than in fostering the growth of democracy in its early years.

This assessment would suggest an unhealthy deficit on any democratic balance sheet, but much depends on whether one expects democracy to grow out of political structures that are basically democratic, or whether a more important precondition might not be a relatively orderly society in which power can be transferred or transformed. Would anyone looking at Spanish political structures, on the eve of the death of General Franco, have found many indicators of democratic potential? No doubt any subsequent democracy would have been enhanced if such indicators had existed, but what may have been at least as important was the relative stability of the political system, alongside a realisation that the system could not stand still as an authoritarian outpost in a predominantly democratic Western Europe. To try to draw exact parallels between Spain and Tanzania would be foolish, but a basic stability did exist in Tanzania, in contrast to neighbouring countries such as Rwanda, Uganda, Zaire and even Kenya, as did the realisation that the one-party state was an anachronism and would have to be replaced by something new. It is tempting to follow Huntington's argument that stable authoritarian systems may provide better antecedents for stable democracy than do nominally pluralist systems which are unstable.

> Countries that have had relatively stable authoritarian rule (such as Spain and Portugal) are more likely to evolve into relatively stable democracies than countries which have regularly oscillated between despotism and democracy .... A broad consensus accepting authoritarian norms is displaced by a broad consensus on acceptance of democratic ones.
> (Huntington 1984: 210)

Our brief survey of Tanzanian political structures may thus throw light on the prospects for democratic development in an indirect way. These structures did have some democratic features, certainly compared with structures in most other parts of Africa, and the myth and the ideal of a participatory democratic society never faded completely, even though everyday politics took on a largely authoritarian form. If there was, in Huntington's words, 'relatively stable authoritarian rule', the stability (again an unusual feature of African politics) has still to be explained. A long-standing cult of compliance and a strong army undoubtedly helped, though it hardly compared with the coercive forces at Franco's disposal, but it is arguable that the democratic myth was also important. There was little circulation of elites, but there was circulation within the elite, with incumbent MPs frequently defeated or de-selected, and even the all-powerful party national executive was subject to election. It is certainly an unusual authoritarian system in which ministers in the government can be humbled by a simple vote of their constituents. Similarly in areas such as local government and industrial relations, we saw that everyday practice was frequently authoritarian, but that too blatant a closure of democratic avenues or aspirations might undermine legitimacy, and thus threaten the stability of the existing structure. Hence the restoration of elected local councils after a long period of suspension, and the language of workers' participation programmes. The democratic myth was buttressed by the egalitarian myth, so that the legitimacy of political structures, especially in the early years, was strengthened by their redistributive policies.

One could, of course, argue that some of the most brutal totalitarian regimes in the world have also described themselves as 'democratic', but these were regimes which had many more coercive forces at their disposal, and their survival depend ultimately on incarcerating and executing large numbers of people. The rulers of Tanzania never had the resources for that sort of coercion. Neither did they have the power, which many African military governments have possessed, to terrorise relatively small numbers of people and thus frighten the rest of the population into submission. This is something that can be done when it is soldiers who wield power, not party officers and bureaucrats. If the government could not use the levers available to totalitarians or military rulers, it had to resort to more subtle forms of authoritarianism which at least had democratic (and egalitarian) undertones and some democratic safety valves, such as intra-party elections and workers' councils. It is difficult to envisage the stable political structures surviving without this subtle blend. Indeed the ultimate acceptance of the need to end single-party rule, albeit influenced also by external pressures and resisted by many within the party, could be seen as a recognition that, as the party's effectiveness was declining, political reality must be brought more into line with democratic mythology.

To sum up, the hypothesis offered is that the transition to democracy was helped by an environment in which political structures enjoyed relative stability and that, although many of these structures were not 'democratic' in the normally accepted sense, their stability rested on a belief that political outcomes should ultimately be determined by democratic means, and should produce a redistribution of resources that would benefit the majority of the population. In the absence of totalitarian power or the power of a military junta, the survival of these relatively stable structures depended on not departing too far or too obviously from the democratic myth. When such departures did seem imminent, the structures had to be brought more into line with the myth, eventually to the extent of rejecting the legitimacy of continued single-party rule once the party was seen as inimical to democracy. The stability of the structures facilitated a relatively orderly retreat of the state and party from many areas of society, so that civil society could grow in strength, if only modestly, in a similarly orderly manner, in contrast to other countries where the state has 'abandoned' much of its role, rather than retreated, and left civil society with less solid ground on which to build. The emerging groups in Tanzanian civil society contributed to this orderly process because, in contrast to Ghana, there was not a long history of antagonistic relations between them. None of this guarantees a secure future for democracy, but impediments in its way may be fewer than in countries where political and economic liberalisation have been carried out in a less controlled manner.

7 The Politics of Democratic Transition and Consolidation: Some Preliminary Thoughts

We have already touched on some of the factors which contributed to the ending authoritarian rule, and on the prospects for democratic development. The aim of this chapter is to look more systematically at the concepts of democratic transition and consolidation, and at explanations of the extent and limitations of these processes. We shall then go on to examine the specific cases of Ghana and Tanzania in subsequent chapters.

A 'transition to democracy' is a less easily recognisable phenomenon than many other political events. A change of regime through a revolution, a royal succession, a foreign conquest or an election can be observed as an objective fact and be assigned a specific date on the calendar, but the beginning and end of a democratic transition are much more difficult to plot, and are more likely to be a subject of controversy. Should we take our bearings from the formal political process, and give prominence to such events as the lifting of a ban on opposition parties or the holding of a constitutional conference at the beginning of a transition and the holding of a free election at the end, or do we need to look more at the subtle processes that undermine an authoritarian regime? Does the transition begin with the first expressions of dissent within the cabinet, the first illegal public demonstration against the authoritarian government or the first hints at a withdrawal of foreign aid if human rights are not respected? Does transition necessarily end with the holding of an election, the conduct or results of which may be a matter of dispute and which may be boycotted by the opposition, or with the evolution of broadly accepted conventions on the means of resolving political conflict? As to democracy itself, philosophers and political scientists have argued for centuries about its nature and about whether particular political systems qualify for inclusion within the democratic camp. Of more immediate importance is the fact that the political actors participating in any 'transition to democracy' are likely to disagree on the nature of the democratic destination and the point at which it has been reached.

'Democratic consolidation' presents similar problems. It is normally taken to mean the process by which a system which is democratic in the formal sense of having free elections, the rule of law, and freedom of expression and association, develops into a system in which the spirit, as well as the letter, of democracy is accepted. A range of groups are thus encouraged to participate in the political process and are given access to those in authority; rulers become accountable to the ruled for their actions, and accepted channels develop for opposition and dissent. Even if different actors and observers could agree on which of these features were most important in consolidation, there might be difficulties in agreeing on the extent to which the features actually existed in any given political system. A system that looked 'consolidated' to one person might be seen by another as a system in which the ruling party enjoyed the use of state resources while opposition parties were harassed by the police, in which access to authority was confined to the privileged few, and in which governmental accountability was limited because the sanction of voting out the government was a remote possibility while the ruling party enjoyed a privileged position.

THE ELEMENTS IN A TRANSITION

A transition to democracy can be viewed from at least three perspectives: the unfolding of events which undermine the initial authoritarian system; the varied interests and demands of groups, including formal political structures, within the political arena; and the processes by which the conflicts thus emerging are resolved. The perspectives are offered not as a chronological sequence of events, but as different ways of viewing processes that can occur continuously from the moment that the legitimacy of the authoritarian regime is first challenged to the establishment of a pluralist political system. Thus challenges to the authoritarian system may occur at an early stage when there is a serious split in the ruling junta or party politburo, or at a late stage when public pressure prevents the legitimation of the current rulers through a no-party election, while conflict resolution may begin with the release of a few political prisoners on condition of good behaviour, and end with the adoption of constitution by a representative assembly.

THE SEEDS OF CHALLENGE TO AUTHORITARIANISM

There appear to be two 'common sense' explanations of the undermining of recent authoritarian governments: strong external powers are unwilling to support them in their current form and political actors, by design or misadventure, undermine confidence in the status quo. On the external front, the collapse of the Communist Bloc has had profound effects on Third World authoritarians. Governments, such as the Tanzanian, which had previously benefited from aid from the East were now deprived of that support, and found that new donors might demand changes in both the economic and political spheres. At the same time as losing economic support, they found it more difficult to justify the preservation of monolithic political systems, modelled on foreign systems which were now disintegrating rapidly. For governments which were already heavily dependent on aid from the West, this aid was no longer given in the hope of keeping them out of the Soviet sphere of influence, or without looking too closely at the ways in which they treated their citizens. Not only was authoritarian rule no longer seen as a necessary evil to be viewed with a blind eye, as it had been while the Cold War raged, it was increasingly seen as an inefficient form of government as resources were channelled to unaccountable politicians and their clients rather than towards national development. Aid began to depend increasingly to move towards political pluralism.

It also seems axiomatic that the pace and extent, if any, of democratisation depends in any country on the choices made by politicians. Ex-President Nyerere's conversion to the virtues of multi-party competition helped to set the wheels rolling in Tanzania, with this conversion followed by the appointment of the Nyalali Commission and the acceptance of its main recommendations, while the incompetence and corruption of General Acheampong's regime in Ghana effectively destroyed his attempt to remain in power as head of a no-party state, and intensified public pressure for his replacement by an elected government. Conversely the skills of anti-democratic leaders in countries such as Nigeria and Zaire have so far obstructed any transition to democracy.

While the ending of the Cold War and the choices made by individual politicians provided important elements in the democratisation process, we need also to look at the social and economic contexts within which recent transitions have taken place, and the constraints which these place on political actors. Libya and Saudi Arabia are wealthy enough to forego offers of foreign aid, and do not even have to pretend to be undergoing a process of democratisation to please Western donors. Singapore and Taiwan have been wealthy enough to relax authoritarian rule at their own leisurely pace without any foreign powers telling them how to do it. It is the poorer countries that have to make concessions to external pressure, but a democratic structure could hardly be built solely on a compact between an indigenous government and foreign donors and lenders. There must be forces within society which undermine the strength of the authoritarian government and which lead to a perception that a democratic alternative would be preferable, and worth striving for. Traditional explanations of democracy used to emphasise the importance of economic development, and the effects that it had on urbanisation, education, communications, the growth of civil society and the reduction in the intensity of political conflict, as political decisions became less matters of life and death (see especially Lipset 1959: 69–105). A few Third World countries, such as South Korea, approximate to this model, with industrialisation producing a more articulate population which demands an end to authoritarianism, but the vast majority were already poor and becoming poorer at the time when the challenge to authoritarianism was greatest. Why should this be?

The way in which authoritarianism is undermined will depend largely on the intensity of economic decline. In extreme cases, such as Benin and other parts of French-speaking Africa, the economies have collapsed altogether due to a combination of governmental ineptitude, worsening terms of trade and natural disasters such as drought or crop failure (see especially Allen 1992 on Benin). Governments which already enjoyed little legitimacy, having come to power through coups or fraudulent elections, no longer had the resources to survive through coercion or dispensing patronage, and sometimes even lacked the resources to pay the wages of their own employees. Such governments had little alternative but to surrender to demands for competitive elections, though whether democracy can be 'consolidated' on such a fragile economic base is another matter.

More common than economic collapse are cases of economic decline, where governments do not lose their grip on the political system altogether but face economic constraints which are severe enough to push them into policies which ultimately weaken their authority. The causes of the economic decline, like those of economic collapse, are generally a mixture of uncontrollable circumstances, such as crop failure or increased oil prices, together with political factors such as bureaucratic inefficiency and economically harmful policies. We have touched on bureaucratic inefficiency in previous chapters, looking at cases such as the failure to repair roads or to control smuggling in Ghana, attempts by Tanzanian civil servants to direct agricultural production, and the general practice of siphoning off resources through corruption. The problem is partly one of a lack of accountability, given the inadequacy or absence of representative institutions, partly lack of political will, since there are few rewards for keeping a tight administrative ship and many rewards for permitting or encouraging corruption and wasteful bureaucratic growth. Larger bureaucracy means more scope for political patronage, directly by putting more appointments in the gift of politicians and indirectly by awarding contracts for servicing the bureaucracy. The creation of a state hotels corporation thus creates new bureaucratic posts, and lucrative contracts for firms building new hotels.

In addition to facilitating the expansion of bureaucracy, politicians may choose a range of policies which place a strain on the economy. Heavy defence expenditure may be incurred in the hope of keeping the army happy and forestalling military intervention or counter coups; technically inappropriate decisions may be made in purchasing expensive capital equipment such as cocoa silos which are incapable of storing cocoa in the tropical heat, or locating hydroelectric dams at the wrong sites; and agricultural export earnings may be curtailed drastically through state marketing boards paying unrealistically low prices to farmers who then switch to other crops, or abandon agriculture altogether. None of this is to argue that an interventionist economic policy is intrinsically inferior to a free market policy, and the experience of East Asian countries indicates the benefits that prudent state intervention can bring, but intervention which leads to a less productive use of resources in already poor countries is likely to have serious repercussions. If these self-inflicted wounds are then accompanied by worsening terms of trade and by foreign lenders and donors imposing more rigorous conditions for granting assistance, indigenous governments are likely to be pushed into retrenchment.

Retrenchment is likely to weaken at least three of the government's key power bases. Firstly, the previous beneficiaries of government patronage, such as public servants and contractors, will suffer as jobs are lost. Secondly, the urban poor will suffer as social provision is reduced, unemployment rises and the prices of imported goods are increased as a result of a devaluation of the currency, designed to increase export earnings. This increase in deprivation, coupled with reduced government ability to mitigate its effects, may lead to the formation of a variety of self-help and protest groups which may ultimately provide fertile ground for opposition parties. Thirdly, the productive sector of the economy which was previously susceptible to substantial government control through compulsory marketing boards, import licensing, exchange control and, in many cases, extensive state ownership, will now depend more on market forces than on favourable government treatment. Constituents of the first two of these power bases may now become more reluctant to support a government which is bringing them fewer benefits. The position of the third group is more complex. In the short term, privatisation may create new opportunities for government patronage if state enterprises are sold to government supporters, and businesses which have benefited from free market initiatives may renew their loyalty to the government, but in the longer run greater autonomy for the private sector may help economic pluralism to generate political pluralism. Businesses will become freer to forge links with foreign investors, and their interests may move closer to the interests of the latter than to their own government. Some businesses, if only a minority, may begin to look to opposition parties to serve their interests rather than to rulers who have traditionally favoured state control.

Our model assumes economic decline rather than economic collapse. Complete collapse may be averted because the government retains some legitimacy, possibly on account of its earlier achievements, and is thus able to preserve some political and economic order, or because the economic decline was less severe or abrupt than in the countries reduced to collapse, or because it was possible to produce enough 'winners', as well as losers, in the process of retrenchment. Not only may many private businesses benefit, but devaluation, and the ending of compulsory marketing boards buying agricultural produce at artificially low prices, will increase the earnings of farmers and their dependants, who frequently make up the majority of the population. More remote from the sources of opposition propaganda, on account of illiteracy, limited radio and television ownership and the logistical problems of opposition politicians penetrating scattered communities, rural citizens are often among the last people to turn against the incumbent rulers, unless political divisions run along ethnic or religious lines. The risk of electoral defeat, should the government contemplate holding elections, is thus reduced, though there is still the possibility of a military coup, supported by the urban poor, the intelligentsia and possibly the business community, if no other means of removing the government are available.

What, then, is the relationship between economic decline and the challenge to authoritarianism? To begin with, governments are frequently blamed, rightly or wrongly, for economic hardship, and the especially authoritarian governments which stake their legitimacy more on competence than on any democratic mandate. Discontent may then manifest itself in the form of public protest, and the government may placate this at least partly by promising greater political liberalisation, even though coercion will also play a role. The remedy for decline will be sought in economic liberalisation, in the absence of any alternative that appears either practicable or acceptable to foreign donors. For many groups, the cure is more painful than the disease, especially in the short term. People now receiving fewer benefits from state aid will now turn to mutual self-help, and the self-help groups may turn their attention to challenging the government's authority. Businesses are less obvious losers in the process of economic liberalisation, and business people themselves often fight shy of direct political involvement, for fear of its effects on their enterprises, but behind the scenes they enjoy more influence as the public sector contracts and they may provide the support for, if not the leadership of, opposition parties which will have fewer commitments to what is left of the public sector.

If we view these processes through the eyes of the government, it has a diminished capacity to dispense political rewards and punishments, and to control economic events, and it faces sections of society that are increasingly hostile to it, yet it may enjoy a relatively secure rural base, with the benefits of rising agricultural prices. What strategies should it pursue? The ideal might be to try to regulate, infiltrate or at least build good relationships with the emerging, potentially autonomous groups, whether they be lorry drivers' cooperatives, manufacturing businesses or unemployed youths who might be diverted into public works projects. Such attempts may meet with only partial success, so greater pluralism and diversity will probably have to be acknowledged, together with greater freedom of expression for these groups.

The need for the government to create new economic and political openings, which it had previously rejected, will strengthen the arguments of its long-standing opponents amongst intellectuals, such as academics and lawyers, who question the competence of rulers who are now having to renounce their previous policies. These opponents demand a wider-ranging debate on the government's performance, and of the alternatives, and demand multi-party elections as a means of resolving the debate. In this they are supported by foreign donors whose assistance may be indispensable. Again the government can hardly avoid travelling along a more pluralist road, but again it can try to control the pace and direction. If a pluralist election is unavoidable, it can still try to wrong-foot the opposition, possibly by calling it before the opposition has built up too strong a base, and it can try to mobilise those groups, especially in the countryside, which are still in its debt. Given such prospects, democratisation may prove a better alternative than blatant repression.

THE CONFIGURATION OF INTERESTS

We now look at democratisation as a process which may emerge not merely through a series of chronological events but because of the interaction between a variety of groups in society with varied interests, beliefs and resources, all of which may change over time. These groups will include the formal state structures, such as the cabinet, the bureaucracy and the army, opposition parties, whether legal or underground; the variety of 'secondary' groups to which citizens belong, including churches, mosques, universities, professional bodies, trade unions, co-operatives and business organisations; external bodies such as foreign governments and businesses, and largely unorganised groups such as protesting mobs.

Each group will have recognisable resources. Trade unions can organise strikes, authoritarian governments can impose new laws, bureaucrats can claim expertise, mobs can riot and soldiers can turn their guns on either dissidents or on their superiors. But the ways in which these resources are deployed will be influenced by certain unwritten rules of political conflict which vary between different times and places. Democratic and authoritarian governments may come and go, and written constitutions, where they exist at all, may provide only a limited guide to political behaviour, but accepted political and social practices may prove more durable. To take some obvious examples, no government in Ghana would be able to survive for long without coming to terms with the chieftaincy, few governments in Thailand have threatened the monarchy, and few in Latin America would want to go too far in alienating the church. This is partly a reflection of the recognition of the strength of enduring institutions and partly a reflection of political cultures which value these institutions and the beliefs and customs which they symbolise. Tropical Africa's shorter experience of nationhood and independence may make the unwritten rules less clear and less binding than in Asia and Latin America, but some outlines are visible. A degree of ethnic balance, and not merely weight of numbers, is generally important for any group attempting to win or consolidate power, whether it is a political party or a military junta; technocrats tend to be respected to a greater extent in the Third World than in the West, where party politicians are more confident of their own prescriptions, and technocrats are frequently co-opted into high positions by authoritarian governments. At the same time, various niceties may be observed by authoritarian governments in relation to actual and potential opponents, even though the governments have the physical ability to crush them. Despite the horrors that have occurred in countries such as Burundi, Liberia and Rwanda, where authoritarian government merged into near anarchy, or praetorianism in the language of political science, many African governments have imprisoned rather than executed their opponents, and have tried to avoid confrontations with religious groups or universities even when these have been major sources of opposition. There have been exceptions, but generally it seems that respect for religion and education outweigh the politician's desire for conformity, while the non-execution of opponents may reflect a code of 'do as you would be done by' in relation to past, present and future rulers and dissidents, which tends to break down mainly when government ceases to be a regularised process, as in Ghana in 1979.

Having established that a variety of groups exist with varied resources, but subject to the constraints imposed by political culture and custom and practice, we now want to plot their positions in relation to attempts at, or resistance to, democratisation. An outline is suggested in Figure 7.1. The horizontal axis suggests a continuum which groups may occupy between membership of, or support for, the government, and support for the opposition, while the vertical axis suggests their positions on an elite–mass continuum. The latter continuum is important on account of the different resources which different

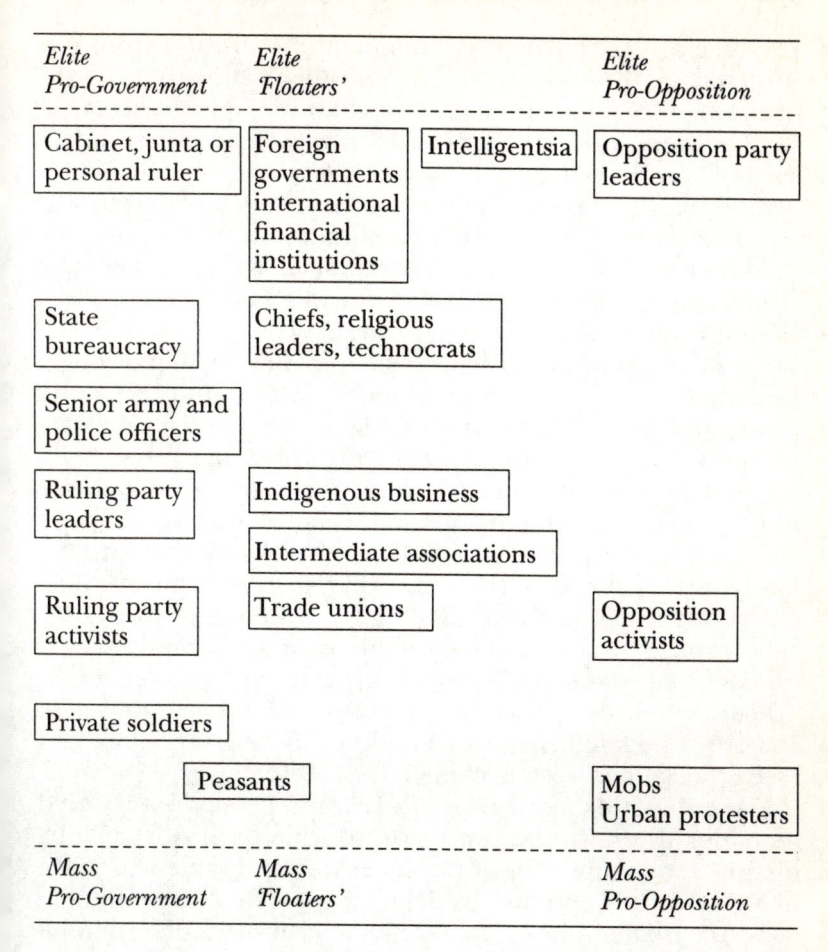

Elite Pro-Government	Elite 'Floaters'		Elite Pro-Opposition
Cabinet, junta or personal ruler	Foreign governments international financial institutions	Intelligentsia	Opposition party leaders
State bureaucracy	Chiefs, religious leaders, technocrats		
Senior army and police officers			
Ruling party leaders	Indigenous business		
	Intermediate associations		
Ruling party activists	Trade unions		Opposition activists
Private soldiers			
	Peasants		Mobs Urban protesters
Mass Pro-Government	Mass 'Floaters'		Mass Pro-Opposition

Figure 7.1 Sources of initiative for democratisation: government and opposition; elites and masses
Source: Adapted from Pinkney (1993): 131.

groups will be able to deploy in pursuit of their demands. Elites may be able to use formal authority, control over the machinery of state or manipulation of their followers, while the masses will be more dependent on weight of numbers, whether in casting votes, violence or civil disobedience. The use, or threatened use, of such resources, might therefore produce a different type of democratic transition from one initiated at the elite level. The positions plotted for each group in Figure 7.1 are merely suggestive, and will obviously vary between different times and places. The Figure might suggest the layout of a battlefield, but is a field in which several battles may be going on simultaneously, with the contestants not necessarily remaining on the same side throughout. There is a configuration of issues as well as a configuration of interests, and democracy may be only one of several outcomes that is being sought. The more immediate interests of groups may be with such matters as higher wages for trade unionists, better equipment for soldiers, more foreign exchange for businesses, higher commodity prices for co-operatives, or adequate roads for farmers marketing their crops. The government may be under pressure, but people are not necessarily seeking its removal. Even where they are, they are not necessarily demanding democracy. Members of tribe A may want to displace the authoritarian government dominated by tribe B, to ensure that more of the benefits of political patronage are diverted to them, or middle-ranking army officers may want to displace a government run by senior officers, in order to enjoy the spoils of office, but these changes would not necessarily imply any shift to democracy (see especially Herbst in Widner 1994: 190).

Yet within this kaleidoscope of varied groups with varied demands there will be some groups which can normally be identified as supporters of the status quo and some which are likely to be proponents of democracy, with a large middle band of 'floaters' whose role may be crucial in determining the outcome. Thus members of a ruling party or state bureaucracy are unlikely to turn against the incumbent government, while students and academics are seldom enthusiastic supporters of authoritarian rule. The position of soldiers is slightly more problematic, but the plotting of coups is generally a minority activity occupying a minority of the time, in contrast to the long periods during which the military sustain authoritarian governments. Businesses, we have already suggested, prefer not to be too openly involved in politics and prefer to be on good terms with whoever is in power, but they may begin to look to opposition groups if these appear to offer a better deal without creating instability.

These different positions are more frequently taken for granted than explained. We are used to the peasant dutifully supporting the government no matter what hardships it imposes, the sociology professor and the lawyer demanding democratic rights despite their apparently privileged positions in the existing order, and the opportunist business man changing sides when it seems expedient to do so. Bates offers an explanation in terms of people with 'fixed and specific human capital' who have invested in skills which are imperfectly transferable elsewhere, such as the Ghanaian lawyer who cannot easily ply his trade abroad or the politician in exile who is a nonentity outside his own country (Bates in Widner 1994: 21), but this still leaves out the question of political conviction. Lawyers are presumably still in demand in authoritarian countries, unless justice is handed over to people's tribunals, and it was often the outspokenness of politicians that initially drove them into exile. And academics, who are often among the greatest thorns in the flesh of authoritarian governments, appear to have readily transferable skills which many take to European and American universities.

Nyong'o explains 'African bourgeois' demands for democracy in terms of expectations of less corruption and a more efficient allocation of resources (Nyong'o 1992: 99), and it may well be that the longer authoritarian government lasts the more corruption and inefficiency are exposed, so that there is a general bourgeois stampede towards democracy. But even here a rational calculation of what is best in terms of value for money may merge into broader ideological or even philosophical, considerations about what form of government is socially desirable. Once again we may be underplaying the importance of political conviction, and the way in which it may gather momentum. Alternative explanations might be sought in terms of the disciplines which an occupation highlights, though at the risk of creating rigid stereotypes. Academics and lawyers expect the truth to emerge through allowing a free flow of conflicting evidence, whereas technocrats and soldiers perceive incontrovertible solutions and are less tolerant of dissent, while business men seek a 'best buy' with less concern for the processes by which the policies they favour have emerged. But again we need to be careful to distinguish between the pursuit of democracy as a desirable end, and actions which have the effect of easing the transition to democracy even if that is not necessarily the intention. Technocrats, and even soldiers, may turn against an authoritarian government if they feel that it is straying from the correct path, and may make common cause with opposition groups concerned more specifically with democracy.

We are still left with the 'floaters' whose position may be crucial in achieving or blocking the transition. Religious groups, tribal chiefs, trade unions and self-help groups are not primarily concerned with the advancement of democracy, although individuals within all these categories will have their own preferences. Like businesses, they may be more concerned with the impact of individual policies than on when whether the government is democratically elected but, unlike businesses, they are more likely to be adversely affected by the policies of retrenchment and economic liberalisation which are the government's response to economic decline, as employment, real wages and social provision are reduced. The effects on churches are less obvious than on the other groups, but they may be used as vehicles for protest if political parties and other formal means of protest are prohibited. Embryonic opposition parties will want to incorporate these floaters in a broader challenge to authoritarianism, but the government will be equally eager to contain them within its sphere of influence. Many will already exist as 'wings of the party' in a one-party state, and a military government may try to bring them under its umbrella as 'revolutionary committees' or as bodies dependent on state patronage, or at least subject to state dismissal, as was the case of chiefs in Ghana.

On the face of it, a government with powers of patronage, coercion and financial inducements holds the advantages in winning this middle ground but, if the groups are hostile to the policies which have affected them adversely, the government may have to pay a price for their allegiance in terms of a greater willingness to consult, and to permit a greater degree of criticism and autonomous activity. The government may ultimately retain enough support from the key groups to win a competitive election, but the fact that democratisation has advanced to a point where it is deemed necessary to hold an election is a reflection of the ability of the floaters to create new openings.

THE RESOLUTION OF CONFLICTS AND THE CONSOLIDATION OF DEMOCRACY

The interaction between our different groups may be resolved in a variety of ways, and the paths followed will have an important bearing on the nature and durability of the democracy that ultimately emerges. (For a fuller discussion of these points, and a review of some of the relevant literature, see Pinkney 1993: 136–51.) Among the questions which it is important to ask are:

1. WHO dominates the process of transition?
   (a) THE GOVERNMENT? GHANA, TANZANIA.
   (b) The opposition? Argentina, Greece.
   (c) A balance between government and opposition? Uruguay, El Salvador.
   (d) External powers? Axis powers, 1945.
2. HOW is the transition achieved?
   (a) Pact? Uruguay, Chile.
   (b) IMPOSITION? GHANA, TANZANIA, Brazil, Ecuador, Greece.
   (c) Reform or revolution? Bolivia, Nicaragua.
3. And subject to HOW MUCH DISSENT?
   (a) Consensus? Spain, Uruguay.
   (b) Conflict? Nicaragua, Nigeria.
4. At WHAT PACE and to WHAT MAGNITUDE?
   (a) MODERATE? GHANA, TANZANIA, Nigeria, Uruguay.
   (b) Radical? Spain, Nicaragua.
   (c) GRADUAL? GHANA, TANZANIA, Brazil.
   (d) Rapid? Argentina, Greece, Nicaragua, Spain.

The answers shown in capital letters are those that approximate most closely to the cases of Ghana and Tanzania, with an agnostic position adopted towards Question 3 on the extent of conflict and consensus. There was consensus to the extent that both government and opposition in each country favoured a multi-party system (though reluctantly in the case of the Ghana government), an elected president and a largely capitalist economy, but in both countries opposition groups were virtually excluded from any participation in the formulation of proposals for the new order, and in both the opposition protested against the preservation of undemocratic elements, including revolutionary committees and extra-judicial tribunals in Ghana, and a constitution in Tanzania which was an amended version of the one-party model rather than one specifically designed for a liberal democratic era.

As regards the process of consolidation of democracy, some of the obvious questions to ask are:

1. How wide a degree of *consensus* exists over the processes of resolving political conflict?
2. How *stable* is the system?
3. How *extensive* is democracy in terms of scope for *political participation* This may in turn rest on the resources available to citizens, and thus on *social equality*.
4. How far is there an *elite veto* on democratic activity?
5. How far is there a *military* or *external veto*?

One could construct a wide variety of permutations of different processes of democratisation, and of the relationship between these and the nature of democratic consolidation (see especially Pinkney 1993: 136–51). For our purposes we can advance the hypothesis that transitions, such as those in Ghana and Tanzania, based on government imposition, and moderate and gradual change, are more likely to lead to a relatively stable democratic system, but subject to an elite veto and with only limited scope for broadening public participation. This is in contrast to Opposition-initiated transitions which are more likely to break elite vetoes, and radical or rapid transitions which may stimulate participation but reduce stability.

The elite which devised the system has presumably ensured that its interests are safeguarded adequately and that the democratic dog is only let off the leash when the elite is satisfied that it will not be able to stray into unacceptable areas, such as threatening the liberty or property of the elite. The possibility of an elite veto remains present, whether through the manipulation of state resources through the bureaucracy, if the old rulers win a competitive election, or through the possibility of using contacts in the army if they lose. The prospects for democratic participation beyond the electoral process, or for a more egalitarian system, would not appear to be so bright, though Ghana and Tanzania are different from many African states in that democratisation emerged from what had initially been left-wing governments which had based their legitimacy on popular participation and the quest for a more just society. The reality was rather different by the time the governments began to consider the transition to a pluralist system, but the preservation of socialist and populist myths may at least mitigate moves towards 'one dollar, one vote' rather than 'one citizen, one vote'. There is also a question mark over the extent to which the threat of an external veto might check undemocratic tendencies, especially after years of Western pressure for African states to democratise. The experiences of Kenya and Zimbabwe suggest that the foreign powers are not too hard to please when it comes to going through the motions of a competitive election, but a desire to keep foreign aid flowing might impose some checks on any potential authoritarians.

There remains the question of whether the refusal of the Ghanaian and Tanzanian governments to seek a consensus with their opponents will prove a threat to stability and consensus in the new order, especially when government control of the administration of the elections in both countries led to opposition parties rejecting the legitimacy of the outcome. Opposition parties may pose little threat to stability while governments continue to control the means of coercion and patronage, unless these opposition parties forge links with any groups that are less concerned with constitutional niceties when protesting about their lot, but consensus on the rules of the political game may prove elusive, especially in Ghana where the animosity stretches back over many years.

These hypotheses about the future shape of democracy are, of course, based on the assumption that other things remain equal. In particular, we assume that there is not any serious economic deterioration, which would make any sort of democracy difficult to sustain; that the behaviour of political actors, whether through violence, corruption or incompetence, does not provoke reactions that create a general downward spiral; and that the international climate does not lead to foreign powers supporting authoritarians rather than democrats, as was the case for much of the 1970s.

Beyond the specific variations in the transition process in individual countries, there are more general variables that affect the nature and limitations of any democracy emerging in the modern world.

> It is difficult to identify and analyse ... what I propose to call *unconsolidated* democracies. Regimes trapped in this category are, in a sense, condemned to democracy without enjoying the consequences and advantages that it offers. They are stuck in a situation in which all the minimal procedural criteria for democracy are respected. Elections are held more or less frequently and more or less honestly. The various liberal freedoms exist – multiple political parties, independent interest associations, active social movements, and so on – but without mutually acceptable rules of the game to regulate the competition between the political forces. The actors do not manage to agree on the basic principles of co-operation and competition in the formation of governments and policies. Each party considers itself uniquely qualified to govern the country and does what it can to perpetuate itself in power. Each group acts only in the furtherance of its own immediate interests, without taking into consideration its impact upon the polity as a whole. Whatever formal rules have been enunciated (in the constitution or basic statutes) are treated as contingent arrangements to be bent or dismissed when the opportunity presents itself.
> (Schmitter in Tulchin and Romero 1995: 16)

Why should many Third World countries have democratic constitutions but day-to-day political processes that frequently fall short of democracy? The 'traditional' road to understanding the existence of democracy was via a search for 'preconditions' such as economic development and a civic culture which embraced democratic values. The more modern road has often been via a search for scope for favourable 'transitions', where authoritarianism can be undermined and judicious political behaviour can achieve democratic outcomes. The road to democracy travelled by Britain, if we take the revolution of 1688 as the starting point and the 1884 Reform Act as the culmination, required a journey of nearly two centuries in which the various preconditions gradually nurtured democracy. In Ghana and Tanzania the transition to democracy lasted less than a decade. These countries had apparently followed the bypass while Britain had followed the packhorse route, but perhaps the African countries failed to pick up some of the necessary baggage on the way.

It is not simply a matter of arguing that democracy, like whisky, improves with age. Japan developed a relatively successful pluralist system from a standing start in 1945, while South American countries which began their first attempts at democracy much earlier have had more chequered careers. Spain was an even later starter, and had had only limited democratic experience before 1975. No doubt greater democratic maturity is an additional asset, but Japan and Spain did appear to enjoy many of the generally accepted social and economic preconditions which Ghana and Tanzania do not. While indigenous intellectuals and external powers may continue to insist on preserving the freedoms which Schmitter describes, the establishment or enforcement of his 'mutually acceptable rules of the game' remains a difficult task. At an abstract level, most significant political actors would probably prefer democracy, however loosely defined, to any other set of political arrangements, but the immediately 'rational' course of action in preserving or advancing one's interests may lead to behaviour which is detrimental to democracy, yet such behaviour is not subject to the sanctions which it would be likely to face in the West. Bribery, patronage, election rigging, and voting for politicians who are more interested in trading benefits for votes than in observing democratic norms, are all manifestations of such behaviour. This can be attributed partly to the 'immaturity' of democracy, but also to conditions in which poverty makes for a more desperate struggle for power, and in which civil society provides inadequate counterweights to 'undemocratic' political behaviour. There may also be sins of omission, as well commission, that inhibit the growth of democracy. These include a reluctance to jeopardise one's career or wealth by criticising authority, and a reluctance to devote one's energies to building up pressure groups or opposition parties if their prospects of power or influence seem remote in the face of a government that controls the key resources.

If the culmination of democratic transition in Britain was 1884 (though some people might prefer 1928), the 'democratic consolidation' over the following century can be seen in an acceptance of the legitimacy of participation in the political process by business, trade union, professional and later environmental groups, and in the responsiveness of the state to public demands for extensive social provision, especially in relation to education, health, housing, working conditions and social security. At the same time, new avenues were opened up, through such devices as administrative tribunals, public inquiries and ombudsmen, to enable the aggrieved citizen to seek redress against the state. This is not to suggest that perfection was achieved, but that the legitimacy which the state enjoyed, in the eyes of the newly-enfranchised population, owed much to its willingness and ability to respond to the demands of society. Civil society attracted more adherents largely because it could be seen to be shaping the political environment and, as it grew, it became better able to impose checks and balances on the state. What is the relevance of this to Africa? There are clearly few immediate prospects of any great expansion of social provision, and states seem ill-equipped to improve channels of redress. In the face of economic constraints and a tenuous hold on the administrative process, mere survival might be regarded as an achievement, without any attempts to build a welfare state or a participatory democracy. As Schmitter points out, democratic transition and consolidation often occur at times when there are pressing parallel problems such as civil control over the military, the efficiency of the fiscal system, the fate of inefficient state enterprises and the stabilisation of the currency (Schmitter in Tulchin and Romero 1995: 27).

It is not for any outsider to prescribe which policies should be followed to ensure an effective consolidation of democracy, even assuming one believes that such consolidation is possible, though there are obvious policies to avoid, such as corruption, election rigging, use of the army for political ends and undue favouritism towards particular sections of society. If consolidation is taken to imply working towards a situation in which governments are held accountable not merely through periodic elections but through the constraints imposed by civil society, and in which political decision-making involves the participation of a variety of groups in society, much depends not just on specific policies but on an atmosphere of mutual trust. It may be that such trust is unattainable, as citizens continue to expect more of their rulers than the rulers can deliver, and that rulers will therefore have to continue to seek means of retaining power other than through public consent, but this may be placing undue emphasis on material resources as the key to democracy. Whitehead speaks of 'consensual public morality' as an important factor in developing democracy in the West (Whitehead 1993: 1248), and this may depend less on any grand political achievement than on public perceptions of politicians and officials attempting to achieve feasible goals with reasonable competence and honesty. Such a world seems remote from the current reality of African politics, but any tentative moves towards it will need to be scrutinised carefully if we are searching for steps in the direction of democratic consolidation.

8 Ghana: Democratic Transition and Consolidation

A LONG MARCH OR TRENCH WARFARE?

'Democratic transition' was not a new experience for Ghana. The 1966 coup against Nkrumah, supported by the opposition parties, could be seen as marking the beginning of the first transition. This was completed with the 1969 election which offered electoral choice for the first time since independence, though with many members of the former regime disqualified from standing. The ensuing regime was criticised for arrogance and economic ineptitude, but on the whole it observed the letter of the constitution. The military government which overthrew it in 1972 met with relatively few pressures for democratisation during its first three years in office, possibly on account of its populist policies, improved economic conditions and a feeling that both the main political parties had now been tried and found wanting. With a deterioration in economic conditions after 1975, the greater visibility of corruption, and the attempts by the military to stay in power indefinitely by seeking public approval for a no-party state, the challenge to authoritarianism grew rapidly. The combined effects of mass discontent with falling living standards, dissent within the army and the challenge from the ousted politicians, were sufficient to bring about the establishment of the Third Republic in 1979. The new regime was generally even more scrupulous in upholding democratic standards, but even more economically inept, than the government of the Second Republic, and survived for barely two years before the military extinguished democracy again.

Put alongside the experiences of Eastern European countries which achieved liberation after over 40 years of communism, or even Tanzania with its elections after 34 years of one-party rule, one could ask whether the concept of 'democratic transition' is an appropriate one to describe events in Ghana. It might have been more a case of alternations between authoritarianism and democracy, with democratic elections used as an occasional safety valve when public dissent forced authoritarians to seek an exit, or when authoritarians sought to legitimise their own rule or that of their nominees. 'Transition' might be taken to imply a move from one state of being to another, rather than a form of trench warfare in which democracy advances a few miles, is then forced to retreat abruptly and then advances again, without being able to claim any real hold on the terrain it is trying to conquer. Transition could perhaps be seen as a longer-term process beginning with the struggle for independence, with Nkrumah's suppression of opposition in the early 1960s, and the coups of 1972 and 1981, as setbacks which halted the long march to democratisation temporarily without preventing its ultimate triumph. Such a perception could be reinforced by the fact that the Danquah/Busia political tendency was at the heart of struggles to maintain or restore democracy in the face of all three authoritarian regimes, with the underground United Party, the People's Movement for Freedom and Justice, and the Movement for Freedom and Justice respectively providing a thread of continuity in personnel and ideology. But if the pro-democracy activists were frequently the same people, or at least members of similar social and ideological groups, during the three periods of authoritarian rule, the metaphor of the long march to democracy still seems less satisfactory than that of the advances and retreats of trench warfare. There is little evidence that the emergence of pluralist democracy in 1969 and 1979 produced any achievements which might have made subsequent attempts at democratisation more effective or long lasting. Indeed the insensitivity of one democratic government, and the corruption and ineffectiveness of the other, may have helped to discredit the whole idea of democracy in the public mind, and thus made the third attempt slower and less complete than it might otherwise have been.

It therefore seems sensible to speak of democratisations in Ghana in the plural, with three discrete phases occurring approximately from 1966 to 1969, 1975 to 1979 and 1983 to 1992. The first two democratisations were relatively easy, although the subsequent consolidation was not. There was little resistance to the 1966 coup which ousted Nkrumah and, once his erstwhile party had been disbanded, there were few groups in society which resisted moves towards a pluralist system. Western powers provided tacit support for the coup and the subsequent government which oversaw the transition, but their role was not a crucial one. Far more important were the military and bureaucratic elites which were committed to re-establishing what they saw as the Westminster model of democracy, supported by the business, professional and traditional elites. The transition between 1975 and 1979 was much less smooth, with the authoritarian government attempting to legitimise its rule through a referendum which, in the event, provided a rallying point for its opponents. In contrast to the more common pattern in transitions, where the early seeds of challenge come from mass protests but the initiative then passes to elite-dominated opposition parties, the early challengers were the displaced party leaders demanding political rights, as they feared that the no-party state proposed in the referendum would freeze them out of the political process indefinitely. But their demands were followed by mass demands for an adequate standard of living as the economy deteriorated rapidly. These demands were paralleled by dissent among junior officers and other ranks in the armed forces who resented the privileged enjoyed by their superiors. The moral victory of the government's opponents in the referendum, in which they secured a 45 per cent 'No' vote despite blatant rigging by the government, led to concessions to demands for multi-party elections, while discontent in the armed forces led to Rawlings's first coup. The coup was concerned more with ensuring that senior members of the army were punished, instead of being able to take their ill-gotten gains into retirement, than with influencing the timing or outcome of the democratisation process. There were thus 'bottom-up' elements in the transition, unlike that of 1966–9, with a government having to concede democracy on terms that it did not want (multi-party politics, rather than a no-party state with a major role for the military hierarchy) in response to pressures from not only the leaders of the previous regime, but from the urban poor and private soldiers.

The consolidation of democracy after 1969 was hampered by the intolerance of the new Busia government towards members and supporters of the previous Nkrumah government, though it also managed to alienate such groups as judges, civil servants and students which would normally have been seen as its obvious allies. Its apparent rejection of not only Nkrumaism but of the broader African nationalism to which most politically-aware Ghanaians had always subscribed, as exemplified in its attempted dialogue with South Africa, made for still more enemies. The coup which displaced the government may have had less to do with such matters as with the adequacy of the amenities enjoyed by army officers but, like the previous civilian government, the Busia government had so few friends left in civil society that there was little resistance to its removal and little mourning of its passing.

The democracy established in 1979 was even more difficult to consolidate. In the terminology of the previous chapter, it owed its existence more to economic collapse than economic decline. The way in which Rawlings had staged his first coup and removed most of the top military hierarchy, before permitting elections to take place, made the existence of a power behind the throne – a power of military veto – all too apparent. Within its own narrow confines the democratic process may not have worked badly, with continued freedom of expression and association, and mutual tolerance in Parliament, but the democratic process was something of a side-show in the larger circus of politics where a continuation of economic decline, corruption, and unrest in the army, did little to arouse the enthusiasm of the Ghanaian citizen for defending the new order.

The third transition was the longest and, in many ways, the most fiercely contested. Nkrumah's regime had seemed impregnable for a time but, once army officers of a different political persuasion had removed him, there were few obvious barriers to democratisation. Acheampong had seemed secure in the early years of economic growth, but had few secure power bases left by 1978, as both mass and elite groups turned against him. Unable to find any solutions to economic decline, and unable to find backing for his no-party state, he could only depart and leave his colleagues to extricate themselves from government as best they could. The Rawlings regime established in 1981 was different. Not only did Rawlings deny the desirability of multi-party politics, but he appeared in the early years to reject even non-party elections, preferring the unstructured 'democracy' of revolutionary committees of citizens and workers. Even when Rawlings modified his views, there remained two obstacles to democratisation which had been much less apparent under the previous authoritarian regimes. One was the position of soldiers who were now treated not just as subordinates whose superiors happened to be in government, but as part of the 'revolution'. Other ranks and junior officers served alongside senior officers in the ruling PNDC, and soldiers had a more positive role in the execution of government policy, whether in encouraging the development of revolutionary committees or in the suppression of anti-government demonstrations. They were not therefore likely to be keen on a transition to a new order which would diminish their role. Secondly, the PNDC presided over a period of growing GNP from 1983 onwards, rather than decline. Although this growth brought few immediate benefits to the ordinary citizen, the government was more a master of its own destiny than its predecessors had been, and could seek to persuade key sectors of public opinion at home and abroad that any hasty handover to elected politicians would destroy the emerging economic benefits.

THE SEEDS OF CHALLENGE TO AUTHORITARIANISM

In the immediate aftermath of the 1981 coup, there seemed to be little reason to expect any clamour for democratisation. Both the main political parties had proved inadequate, the economy was in tatters and the country was now ruled by a man who had already established a reputation as a friend of the underprivileged, and as a decisive actor against the corrupt and the exploiters. Here was an almost de Gaulle-type figure, appealing to the common people over the heads of established political and social structures, in this case over political parties, the officer corps, the bureaucracy, business, the professions and the chieftaincy. They were all easy targets for attack, not only verbally but often physically through the activities of revolutionary committees, having been held responsible for the hardships and injustices which the nation had endured. But while it may be possible to rule a country without the support of some these structures, a ruler who alienates too many of them may find himself dangerously exposed. The government's immediate internal power bases were the Marxist intellectuals (who provided both the ideological rationale for the policies of national self-reliance and much of the personnel of government) the army (though this had lost much of its coherence as insubordination in the ranks had been encouraged and weapons had been dispersed widely in pursuit of the idea of an armed revolutionary citizenry), and the revolutionary committees based on local communities and workplaces, while external support came from countries such as Cuba and Libya which were sympathetic to the government's objectives. By 1983 it was clear that economic policies hostile to private enterprise and foreign capital were not working, and a sharp reversal was made in the direction of economic liberalisation. This immediately alienated many of the Marxist intellectuals. Some were dismissed from the government, some resigned and some fled the country, from whence they demanded not only the restoration of socialist economic policies but liberal political rights. As such rights were unlikely to be granted in the foreseeable future, authoritarianism was challenged by a series of unsuccessful coup attempts.

Economic liberalisation had implications for the challenge to authoritarianism beyond the Marxist left. Increased unemployment resulting from retrenchment, and increased import prices resulting from devaluation, struck at the weak and underprivileged citizens to whom Rawlings had pitched many of his earlier appeals, and the revolutionary committees were used increasingly as vehicles of protest rather than auxiliary arms of the government. Their immediate concerns were with bread rather than democracy, but the government could no longer count on them as allies in striving to retain its power. If the revolutionary committees were now a less reliable power base, there remained the time-honoured alternative of building better relations with the chiefs. Here was another group which did not necessarily put liberal democracy high on its list of priorities, but which did at least expect a form of government in which co-operation was conditional on the granting of favours in return, rather than on blind obedience to authority.

At the centre of government, the departure of the Marxists created further cracks in the authoritarian edifice. Technocrats, who had previously been perceived as part of the exploitative bourgeoisie, were now sought to provide expertise in the new economic order, while senior army officers, who had also been out of favour, were now required to bring order to an army whose revolutionary ambitions might now differ from those envisaged by the government. These developments might not have any obvious relevance to challenges to authoritarianism, but there was likely to be an unspoken price to be paid for seeking the co-operation of groups which did not share the government's political vision, and which in some cases had been closely linked to the political parties that were demanding the restoration of what they regarded as their rightful position. At the very least, some softening of the government's coercive style and some promise of future democratic openings might help to mend fences.

The government was not entirely passive in the face of actual or potential challenges. As early as 1983 Rawlings appointed a National Council for Democracy which was to engage in political education, advise the government on the removal of obstacles to 'true democracy', and assess the extent to which the government was carrying out the wishes of the people (Shillington 1992: 157–9). The fact that the Council did not report until 1987 might suggest that the government was in no great hurry, but at least it no longer equated democracy with impromptu meetings of revolutionary committees and, as Haynes suggests, there is evidence that democratisation was not merely a reaction to external pressure, most of which was exerted somewhat later (Haynes 1992: 53). Much of the external pressure was implicit rather than explicit, with foreign governments and international financial institutions (IFIs) dropping hints about the virtues of 'good government' rather than specifying how much democratisation was required in return for any aid package, but the message was clear that countries which failed to make progress towards democratisation might lose aid to those which succeeded. On the internal front, discontent with particular policies eventually crystallised into demands for democratisation. While it had appeared to be an advantage in the early years that the government was against all political parties, and not merely the one it had displaced, and thus had a 'clean' image, this asset turned into a liability as politicians right across the political spectrum came to realise that they had no chance of winning power unless they united to demand multi-party elections.

Unlike the previous democratic transition in the late 1970s, when much of the rump of the CPP had campaigned on the side of the government in the hope of sharing power in a no-party state, leaders of virtually all political tendencies united under the umbrella of the Movement for Freedom and Justice (MFJ) in 1990. Although the Danquah/Busia group, which had gone through different incarnations as the UP, PP, and PFP, had generally provided the nucleus of the resistance, it was now joined by the right-wing Nkrumaists who had made up the bulk of the government overthrown by Rawlings in 1981, and by the radical Kwame Nkrumah Revolutionary Guard which was led by radicals who had abandoned Rawlings when his government moved to the right in 1983 (see especially Shillington 1992: 169–70). With the government still insisting on a no-party state, with the implication that its members would continue to have a role after the restoration of an elected civilian government while the party politicians would not, it is tempting to envisage a replay of the 1978 no-party referendum, but Rawlings and his supporters had learnt their lessons from that experience. In a sense the anti-authoritarian challenge was stronger in the 1980s in that it embraced a broader coalition, and enjoyed the advantages of the impact of the collapse of authoritarian rule in Eastern Europe and the growing belief, not least among foreign donors, that only multi-party democracy was the genuine article. But against that, Rawlings in 1990 enjoyed much more public support than Acheampong in 1978, having reversed the economic decline and governed with relative honesty and competence. While much of the urban population had suffered as a result of economic liberalisation, rural areas producing for the export market had benefited from devaluation. Rawlings therefore had more room for manoeuvre, and still had the possibility of getting most of what he wanted even if he had to make some timely concessions to his challengers.

THE CONFIGURATION OF INTERESTS

The main groups involved in shaping the process of transition are indicated in Figure 8.1. At the elite level there was a wide gulf between a government hostile to the restoration of multi-party politics and opposition leaders who would settle for nothing less. The government's power bases included a somewhat demoralised civil bureaucracy, many of whose members had fled the country in search of better conditions of employment but which was not explicitly disloyal, the army,

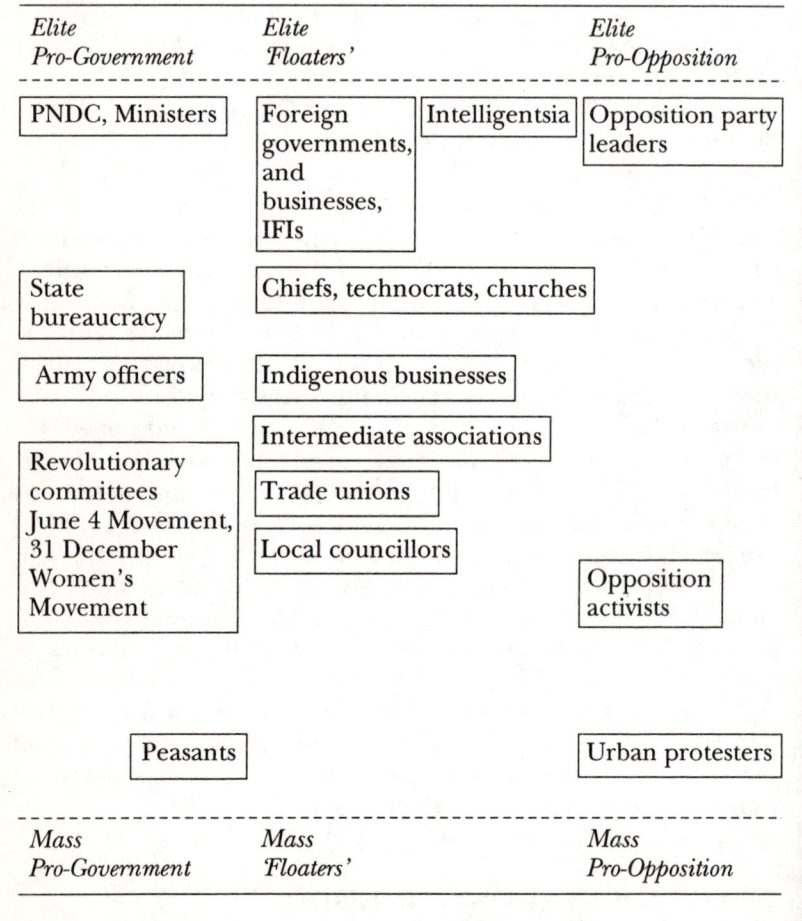

Elite Pro-Government	Elite 'Floaters'	Elite Pro-Opposition
PNDC, Ministers	Foreign governments, and businesses, IFIs	Intelligentsia	Opposition party leaders
State bureaucracy	Chiefs, technocrats, churches	
Army officers	Indigenous businesses	
Revolutionary committees June 4 Movement, 31 December Women's Movement	Intermediate associations	
	Trade unions	
	Local councillors	Opposition activists
Peasants		Urban protesters

| Mass Pro-Government | Mass 'Floaters' | Mass Pro-Opposition |

Figure 8.1 Sources of initiative for democratisation in Ghana: government and opposition, elites and masses
Source: Adapted from Pinkney (1993): 131.

the revolutionary committees and supporting groups of citizens such as the June 4 Movement, the 31 December Women's Movement and, in the early days, the Kwame Nkrumah Revolutionary Guard. (The informal nature of these groups made their behaviour unpredictable, but they had more to gain by supporting Rawlings than by supporting a multi-party system which would almost certainly diminish their role.) The opposition's power bases were necessarily less clearly structured while opposition remained illegal, but each political party retained a network of contacts, including activists in exile, and there were protest activities which the opposition might seek to exploit, whether at the elite level of lawyers wanting to curb the powers of people's tribunals or at the mass level of urban workers demanding increased wages to compensate for the effects of devaluation.

The power bases of both government and opposition might be eroded at the margins, with some middle-class opponents of the government attracted into public office when populism gave way to economic orthodoxy, or some revolutionary committees becoming more like protest groups as the poor were further impoverished by this orthodoxy, but the main battle was for the middle ground of 'floaters'. On the margins of the middle ground were some floaters who had a broad affinity to the government, such as peasants who generally accepted whatever was the current source of authority, and other groups which were more likely to see opposition as their natural habitat, such as academics and lawyers who disliked the erosion of civil liberties, but the allegiances of these groups were less secure than those mentioned in the previous paragraph. Peasants might switch to opposition if their incomes fell or if their leaders were won over by opposition politicians building bases in local communities, and intellectuals might decide that the credentials of opposition politicians were not adequate for them to be trusted with power. It is when we move further into the middle that we find groups that were more clearly agnostic, and which might form the crucial battleground, like marginal constituencies in a parliamentary election. Foreign governments and business, IFIs, technocrats, chiefs, religious leaders, indigenous businesses, co-operatives, self-help groups and trade unions might all 'support' the government to the extent that they recognised its legitimacy and generally observed the law of the land, but any of them might decide their interests or beliefs would be served better by democratisation.

These groups were not, for the most part, monolithic bodies which thought and acted in unison, and different individual 'members' might move in different directions, but government and opposition could both act in ways that might influence the degree of support they enjoyed. This in turn could influence the pace and extent of the democratisation, and the extent to which the process benefited the government or its adversaries. On the government side, the military power base was shored up as a more disciplined hierarchy was restored in place of the less dependable 'revolutionary' army of the early post-coup days. The absence of a successful counter coup always owes a certain amount to luck as well as judgement, but the government had taken reasonable precautions to make a palace revolution less likely. Its civilian bases seemed less secure after 1983, as radical members of the government such as Hansen and Yeebo went into opposition and some revolutionary committees turned their attention to unpopular government policies rather than to capitalist exploiters. The people's tribunals, too, became a source of embarrassment as they began to question Rawlings's associates rather than his enemies (Yeebo 1991: 61). The government's immediate responses were to replace the departing radicals with more technocrats, and to transform the People's Defence Committees and Workers' Defence Committees into Committees for the Defence of the Revolution (CDRs) which were more concerned with administration and local development than political mobilisation. Enough willing technocrats were found to fill the necessary public offices, but the middle class and professional groups as a whole remained suspicious of the government, if not openly hostile, having only recently been the targets of physical and verbal attack.

The transformation of the revolutionary committees turned out to be a much more successful move, and perhaps the crucial one in ensuring that democratic transition was achieved largely on the terms that the government wanted. The original committees had not only threatened the stability of the government but had, by giving an impression of mob rule, been an embarrassment in seeking Western aid (Ninsin in Gyimah-Boadi 1993: 104). As the committees came under tighter control, it became easier to attract resources from such 'floaters' as foreign governments, foreign investors and IFIs. The weakening of the revolutionary committees required a search for new power bases to enforce the government's authority at a local level, hence the need to make peace with the chiefs. In the longer term the government accepted the need for elected district assemblies (DAs). Although Ninsin suggests that there was no guarantee that the government would be able to control these authorities (ibid.: 111), their creation generally seemed to strengthen its position. A third of the DA members were government nominees, thus giving it an opportunity to extend patronage while claiming a more legitimate base in local government, and the government-appointed chief executives and district electoral committees are said to have been key figures in influencing constituency results in the 1992 election. As for the elected members, they may not always have been in the government's pocket but they were, for the most part, a new intake of political recruits with no previous political allegiances, and drawn largely from lower-middle-class groups which had been remote from the earlier political parties. (The decision of the underground opposition to boycott the local elections in many areas did nothing to strengthen their own hold on local government.) When Rawlings eventually formed his own party, it became the obvious home for many of these councillors and their supporters, with the prospect of consolidating the political advances they had already made. We noted in Chapter 4 the striking similarity between the social backgrounds of the councillors and the MPs elected in 1992.

It may be difficult to assign the district authority members to a specific group of 'floaters', but Ninsin's description of them as 'lower middle class' suggests that here was another key group won over by the government. Revolutionary committees (drawn largely from the bottom of the social scale) had been tamed, foreign sources of aid and investment had been attracted by an appearance of financial rectitude, chiefs had been pacified by being given greater deference and an enhanced role, and soldiers and their arms were subject to tighter control. A price had to be paid for obtaining such support, including the abandonment of the ideals of a more egalitarian, participant, self-sufficient society, and what sometimes amounted to apologies to the more privileged sections of society for previous harassment. For supporters of the 'revolution', the Rawlings regime had ended in failure, but for students of democratic transitions it had showed remarkable skill in winning over the key groups which Rawlings required in order to retain power on his own terms.

We can deal only briefly with the remaining floaters. The government alienated the churches with its Religious Bodies (Registration) Law of 1989, which compelled all denominations to register, and empowered the government to prohibit any religious body, but the churches resisted and refused to register, the government beat a retreat and churches played little subsequent role in the democratisation process (Drah in Ninsin and Drah 1993: 104). Trade unions were frequently at loggerheads with the government but, like their counterparts over much of the world, they had little bargaining power in the face of retrenchment and rising unemployment. Cooperatives, self-help groups and small businesses expanded as the role of the state contracted but, as we noted in Chapter 4, they appeared to be more concerned with survival than with any broad political objectives.

THE RESOLUTION OF CONFLICTS

The Rawlings government did not appear to have any master plan for democratisation. Insofar as there was any coherence or consistency, the populist idea of facilitating participation by, and ensuring that government served the interests of, 'ordinary people' was probably more important than specific constitutional blueprints. Political parties were seen as vehicles through which elites had exploited the masses, in contrast to revolutionary committees and tribunals which articulated the interests of the masses, but if the revolutionary committees became an encumbrance and parties (or at least a party) could carry forward whatever was now perceived as the 'revolution', then there was room for flexibility. It is anyway difficult to speak of a 'government' view, since Rawlings was the only member of the government established in 1982 who was still in office by 1992. The Marxists had gone, but the people who replaced them were not comparable with the technocrats who served the military governments of the 1960s and 1970s. Interviews with them suggested that they had a strong commitment not just to competent administration but to the ideals of serving the underprivileged who had allegedly been neglected by previous governments. It is difficult to think of any ideological label other than 'populist'. There was an almost apolitical belief that one should pursue the ends of greater equality and social justice without undue concern with the means adopted. These were individuals who, for the most part, had probably never done anyone any physical harm in their lives, yet they saw the arbitrary violence of the early Rawlings years as unavoidable means to desirable ends. The observation of any rule of law would have allowed too much crime to go unpunished, and too much injustice within the bounds of the law. Even after the regime had transformed itself into an elected government (though with nearly half of the PNDC ministers still in place) there were still some ministers who seemed genuinely puzzled by all the fuss about democracy, and who wanted to carry on with the business of serving the people with a minimum of distraction from parliamentary questions, party meetings or hostile press criticisms. All this was in contrast to opposition politicians who saw competition between parties as the only means of enabling voters to choose between rival programmes, and the only means of ensuring governmental accountability to the people. As this perspective was shared increasingly by the external donors on whom the government was dependent, a wide gulf had somehow to be bridged between political actors with widely differing notions of good government.

Whether either side saw the solution in terms of bridging a gap is another matter. The opposition might have hoped that eventually a coup attempt would succeed, and that they would then be restored to their rightful place. The government might have hoped that non-party local elections would provide a model for non-party parliamentary elections which would be controlled sufficiently to filter out most enemies of the revolution – perhaps something approximating to Tanzanian intra-party competition. Any 'pact' between the government and its opponents was ruled out by the distance between them, so attempts at democratic transition were a matter of trial and error on each side.

> The two sides talked a great deal at each other ... but not once did they talk to each other. In consequence, no real consensus on observing the rules of the game, or even on what those rules were, was developed. The mutual antipathy was clearly informed by more than just keen political rivalry. On the one side, Rawlings viewed opposition leaders not as *bona fide* advocates of democracy but rather as would-be deceivers and exploiters of the common people, as rascals who had sought to obstruct 'the revolutionary process' and were intent on attaining power in order to reverse its achievements. On the other, opposition leaders saw Rawlings as a brutal dictator, with the worst human rights record in Ghanaian history, determined not to relinquish power. (Jeffries and Thomas 1993: 334)

The government's attempts to establish a more regularised form of populist democracy had already led to the election of district authorities in 1988 and 1989, and the next step was the establishment of regional seminars in 1990 to consider national constitutional arrangements. These seminars included representatives of the DAs, the revolutionary committees, the 31 December Women's Movement, chiefs, nurses, farmers and trade unions. The basis of appointing representatives to the seminars put the middle-class groups, which generally supported the opposition, in a minority, and the minority was diminished further by the refusal of some groups, such as the Ghana Bar Association, to attend (Shillington 1992: 166–8). The majority at the seminars favoured a no-party state, but the Movement for Freedom and Justice was quick to point to the parallels with General Acheampong's unpopular proposals in 1978, and memories of the fate that ultimately befell Acheampong may have had some influence on Rawlings. When the National Commission for Democracy, which he had appointed, came out in favour of a multi-party system in 1991, this gave him an opportunity to reverse his original position with a minimal loss of face. While he had appeared to strengthen his control over the transition process by winning a variety of key groups to his side, a refusal to back down on the question of party competition would have left open the possibility of opposition groups mobilising public opinion as they had in 1978, probably supported by external donors threatening implicitly to cut off aid. (The process of transition between 1990 and 1992 is covered well by Jeffries and Thomas 1993: 334–66, and Haynes 1993: 451–67. Much of the material here is taken from these sources.)

If multi-party politics had to be conceded, the next task for the government was to ensure that there was at least one party which would uphold the spirit of the revolution, as now interpreted, and to ensure that that party won a competitive election without the election appearing to be rigged to such an extent that the outside world would reject the legitimacy of the result. The government bowed to opposition pressure to release political prisoners and extend freedom of the press, but it also appointed a Consultative Assembly to consider a draft constitution, and ensured that the Assembly, like the regional seminars, was dominated by people likely to support Rawlings. 117 of its members were elected by the district assemblies, 22 were appointed by the government and 121 were elected by 'established organisations'. The latter were, for the most part, 'mass' rather than 'elite' groups, with market women, bakers, hairdressers and canoe fishermen gaining a platform, in contrast to the 1969 Constituent Assembly which had been dominated by lawyers, business men, technocrats and academics. Multi-party politics were duly approved, but with a ban on finance from foreign sources, and on individual donations of more than £200, which would handicap opposition parties, while any party supporting the government would be likely to be backed by thinly-disguised state aid. The decision to recommend an American-style president also seemed tailor-made for Rawlings, should he decide to stand, since he could yet again appeal to public opinion over the heads of intermediate political structures. The constitution was approved in a referendum in April 1992 with a 92 per cent 'yes' vote. Any other outcome would have delayed the restoration of democracy indefinitely, so the opposition had little alternative but to support a constitution which conceded the principle of multi-party democracy, but on terms which largely suited the government.

The question of whether the 1992 election was 'free and fair' is probably as unanswerable as it is for many other recent

African elections. Opposition parties presumably believed that they had a chance of winning, or they would not have taken part, but the advantages enjoyed by the government were considerable. Political parties were legalised barely six months before the election, after 11 years underground, and the opposition faced an administration and a propaganda machine which made little distinction between the long-standing government and the newly created party led by Rawlings. Its title, the National Democratic Congress(NDC), indicated continuity with the PNDC regime. Like governments about to face the electorate the world over, the government ensured that the right 'goodies' were distributed to target voters at the right time, with a national electrification scheme reaching a hundred towns and villages in 1992, new feeder roads and secondary schools constructed, and generous help given to district assemblies (see especially Green 1995: 578–9). Such activities might be regarded as imposing handicaps which most opposition parties have to bear, and need to be distinguished from the actual administration of the election. Rothchild estimates that 'hundreds of thousands' of opposition supporters were unable to vote because Rawlings refused to open the voting list to those who had not registered to vote in the referendum or the district elections of 1987–8 (Rothchild in Widner 1994: 212). Opposition politicians complained in interviews of harassment by members of the revolutionary committees, which now formed a key element in the NDC, including the illegal arrest of opposition party agents and other party officials on polling day, and of the bias of bureaucrats employed as election officials. One journalist complained of two million 'ghost voters' giving' Rawlings his majority (Duodu 1992: 20).

Rawlings won 58.3 per cent of the vote in the November 1992 presidential election, with his nearest rival, Professor Adu Boahen, obtaining 30.4 per cent, so any rigging would have to have been on a substantial scale to have determined the outcome. While opposition parties were quick to condemn the result as fraudulent, the Commonwealth Observer Group took a more moderate view. The election was managed in the interests of the incumbents, especially the failure to consult opposition parties over the transitional process, but the election as a whole was fair.

Although there were aspects relating to the 'playing field' that were unsatisfactory, they were not such as to provide an impediment to the point where it challenged the process as a whole. (Commonwealth Observer Group 1992: 63)

This verdict effectively removed the fear of outside donors cutting off aid, so the government had achieved its twin objectives of securing re-election without alienating the outside world, but it left any emerging democracy in a precarious position. Most of the opposition parties boycotted the subsequent parliamentary election in December 1992, with the result that the NDC won 191 of the 200 seats (Ghana Parliament 1993). 17 of the 36 members of the previous non-elected government were re-appointed to the new government (Ghana Information Services Department n/d), which made it easier for opposition politicians to portray the new order as a continuation of an authoritarian regime which had survived through holding a bogus election, rather than a new government elected at the culmination of a transition to democracy.

THE CONSOLIDATION OF DEMOCRACY

Even if one puts the worst interpretation on events, Ghana after 1992 was a very different place from Ghana before 1990. People who believed that the government was authoritarian were at least free to say so without being locked up, and a lively independent press kept its readers entertained with salacious stories about ruling politicians and their associates. President Rawlings's wife was alleged to have acquired a £20 000 Jacuzzi (*Insight* 1995: 1–2), and the activities of opposition groups abroad were reported when the President visited London. 'Rawlings's car had been pelted with eggs, fruits and paper bottles in British tradition on occasions [sic]' (*Free Press* 1995: 1).

Lecturers at the University of Ghana took part in a prolonged strike and, when students became restless over their lack of tuition, they rampaged around the Ministry of Education in a style that was also reminiscent of British traditions. Mass public protests in May 1995 against the proposed imposition of value-added tax were marred by the killing of five demonstrators, apparently by ruling-party thugs, but the demonstrations had the effect of getting the tax proposals withdrawn.

At the more formal level of politics, the prospects for democracy looked mixed. One commentator drew attention to Article 164 of the constitution which enabled the executive and legislature to suppress the free workings of the media in the interests of national security, public order, public morality, the protection of rights and the freedom and reputations of other persons (Yeboah-Afari 1995: 1320). A 'presidential' constitution had not even been suggested for the Second Republic, and had not been a serious constraint on democracy in the Third, given the way in which the relatively unknown President Limann had only been drafted in as a late choice after his uncle had been disqualified from standing, but it was more important in the Fourth Republic when an office endowed with substantial executive powers was given to an already-powerful figure. The constitution made ministers only advisory to the President (Ghana Government 1992: 62–3), and Rawlings was able to appoint 54 of his 81 ministers, and 12 of his 16 cabinet ministers, from outside Parliament (Ghana Government Information Services n/d). As in much of Latin America, this looked like the formal United States model but without the checks and balances of an independent judiciary and congress, or a devolution of power to the states. Some of the more stridently 'antibourgeois' ministers of the earlier regime had gone, but ministers in the Fourth Republic appeared to have come into politics from similar backgrounds, and via similar routes, to ministers in the PNDC, even when they were not the same individuals. Some were technocrats, some claimed the advantage of a high status in traditional families (a position which became politically advantageous again after the initial revolutionary rhetoric had subsided), and several had climbed the ladder via organisations which had been in favour during the PNDC years such as student, youth and trade union groups, in addition to the armed forces, but virtually none had had any experience of party or parliamentary politics. Many of them were not so much hostile to pluralist democracy as perplexed by its very existence.

Parliament was dominated by members of the middle to lower-middle classes who had provided much of the sustenance for the PNDC, once the more proletarian revolutionary committees had become less dependable. Teachers were the largest single occupational group, with 63 of the 200 MPs, business and the public services provided 28 each and farmers 20. The teacher–farmer domination was not as great as in the district assemblies, and the bakers, hairdressers and canoe fishermen who had had a voice in the Consultative Assembly did not manage to climb to this rung of the political ladder. The nearest thing to working-class representation was the presence of eight people classified as 'self-employed and traders' and one diamond winner, but Parliament was still much less elitist than those of the Second and Third Republics. The lawyers and academics who been so dominant previously were reduced to 15 and 4 respectively (Ghana Parliament 1993). The virtual absence of any opposition meant the virtual absence of Ghana's previously dominant political class which, in turn, raised questions about the ability to heal political wounds. In terms of political influence, the mere existence of Parliament appears to have had some deterrent value, as ministers recognised the need to provide justifications for their decisions. Badly-drafted legislation had to be revised and unpopular budget proposals modified, and the Public Accounts Committee has had little difficulty in finding cases of mis-spent public money. Credit for the withdrawal of value-added tax might be claimed by the extra-parliamentary opposition rather than MPs, but again the existence of a Parliament provided a focal point for debate and for face-to-face negotiations with ministers.

This still leaves us with the question of whether a generally free press, freedom for public demonstrations and a lively Parliament are necessarily the best indicators of the consolidation of democracy. There are at least two reasons for unease. One is the way in which a presidential constitution enables much political recruitment and decision-making to take place outside any democratic framework. Not only has the President appointed most of his ministers from outside Parliament, but there appears to be a widely-held view that much political influence is wielded by presidential confidants who hold no political office. It is always difficult to separate hard facts from gossip in Ghana, but the name of Kojo Tsikata, the chairman of the state-owned Ghana National Petroleum Corporation, was frequently mentioned in interviews by opposition politicians and neutral observers, as indeed was Mrs Rawlings, whose frequently reported political pronouncements were in contrast to the self-effacing role of the wife of President Mwinyi in Tanzania. Secondly, much of the political protest, even within Parliament, may be a consequence of the government taking decisions with minimal public consultation in the first place, and perhaps without assessing the state of public opinion. Greater participation by groups in the earlier stages of policy-making might not make such good political theatre, but it might make for a smoother running, if less visible, democratic process. The ruling party appears to have a limited role in articulating interests, even compared with its predecessors in the Second and Third Republics. At least these parties had had histories (under different names) going back to the 1950s, and had roots in society. The NDC had emerged more as a Rawlings supporters' club just before the election, and many of its members were people who until recently had been opposed to the existence of political parties. While democrats might welcome the absence of a party with the intolerance, the corruption and the bullying that had characterised the CPP in the First Republic, the existence of a ruling party lacking the means, and possibly the will, to generate ideas and policies may also be damaging to democracy.

One of Rawlings's major concerns had been to try to ensure that what he saw as a populist, participatory form of politics could survive in a system of pluralist democracy, where the wealthy, the clever or the manipulators of new political structures might try to gain further power and wealth at the expense of the masses. Different Ghanaians will give very different answers on the extent to which he has succeeded, or indeed the extent to which there was much popular participation in major political decisions under the PNDC.

> The PNDC ... continues to remain unaccountable to the people. Decision-making is a restricted affair and few persons outside the higher echelons of the central administration are consulted.... Public debate on the ERP [Economic Recovery Programme] has hardly been permitted.
> (Tangri 1992: 108-9)

MPs will insist that their ears are close to the ground and that they can channel resources into the development projects most favoured by their constituents, and it is possible that the less elitist nature of Parliament, and the populist ideals that drew many MPs into the NDC, have helped them in this role. Similarly the social composition of the district assemblies, and the fact that MPs serve on them ex-officio, may have made them better vehicles for working alongside the people than were previous local councils dominated by either bureaucrats or self-seeking politicians. At the national level, ministers insisted in interviews that they did consult regularly with a variety of groups, but the suspicion lingers that much of this involved asking for responses to ready-formulated policies rather than maintaining 'policy communities' in which groups had an institutionalised role in policy formulation. This is an area for potential research, and it would be unfair to make any sweeping judgement. (One example of an attempt at outside consultation was the convening of a conference on environmental issues in Accra, which involved the private sector, local government, chiefs, fishermen and technical experts. See Accra Metropolitan Assembly 1995.)

All this micro–politics has to be set in the broader context of a macro-political environment in which, as Schmitter points out, attempts at democratic consolidation may be taking place alongside attempts to cope with an economy in which the terms of trade may be deteriorating, in which the shift to a freer market economy may be far from smooth, and in which the tax base may be inadequate, while more overtly political problems such as civil control over the military may still be unresolved (Schmitter in Tulchin and Romero 1995: 27). There are also likely to be the perennial Third World problems of a bureaucracy which lacks the will or ability to translate governmental decisions into policy outcomes, and inadequate resources for the level of social provision which voters may expect of their representatives. The economic recovery of the late 1980s may have put Ghana in a stronger position than many African states to deliver material benefits, but many of the problems highlighted by Schmitter are clear enough. The hasty withdrawal of the value-added-tax proposals was a reminder of the precariousness of the tax base, especially when considered alongside the inability of district authorities to raise the revenue due to them, which we noted in Chapter 4, and the impossibility of going back to the days when the government could effectively tax the farmer by buying his produce at an artificially low price and then selling it at a higher price on world markets. The room for manoeuvre for any elected government is also constrained by the terms on which foreign aid and loans are provided, which is conditional on continued public sector retrenchment. Again Ghana faces problems common to much of Africa in that democracy is difficult to practice if the capacity of the state, and therefore its ability to respond to the democratic will of the people, is weakened, and that many of the key decisions are not taken by authoritarians or democrats in Africa but by bankers or politicians in Washington or European capitals (see especially Jeffries 1993: 20–35; O'Donnell 1993: 1355–69).

We hypothesised in the previous chapter that a 'top down' transition to democracy, dominated by the government rather than the opposition, might make for relative stability, since there would be a thread of continuity, and no ousted rulers seeking to reclaim their political and economic gains, but that this stability would have to be set against the constraints on democracy imposed by the threat of military or elite vetoes. The stability has so far been maintained, and the disagreements between the main political contenders on policy questions are matters of degree rather than qualitative differences, in that there is a broad consensus on the need for a mixed economy, economic liberalisation, rural development and the maintenance of the chieftaincy, but the legitimacy of the government, given its authoritarian antecedents and its alleged ballot rigging, remains a matter of controversy. The different social and, to a lesser extent, ethnic backgrounds, of the rival leaders accentuates the conflict. Such a conflict, in turn, raises questions about the possibility of democratic choices being limited by an elite or military veto.

Opposition politicians would argue that an elite veto already exists because many of the anti-democratic devices created under authoritarian rule remain in place. The government may still use people's tribunals, rather than the regular judicial system, for trying defendants, allegedly in cases where it believes that such tribunals are more likely to secure a conviction, and the Serious Fraud Act allows 'economic offences' to be dealt with by an administrative body independent of the Attorney General. We have noted that reserve powers are in place which might limit the freedom of the press, and lawyers have complained of people being detained for long periods without charges being made against them. These may be regarded as matters that concern civil libertarian purists rather than the bulk of the population, but what may prove to be more serious is the preservation of groups established under the authoritarian regime such as the revolutionary committees, the June 4 Movement and the 31 December Women's Movement. They no longer have any executive powers, and the government sees them as useful bodies for carrying out public works and decorating ceremonial occasions, but there is the fear that they could be used again to harass the opposition. An elite veto on any serious opposition threat to the government might thus, according to the pessimists, be buttressed by extensive presidential power, the application of repressive legislation and the support of a hand-picked judiciary and public servants in key positions, with the revolutionary groups providing the weight of numbers at the mass level. One could also speculate about the possibility of a military veto, whether exercised independently of the government if the conflict between government and opposition created serious disorder, or in support of the government in an attempt to prevent the election of parties which might ask too many questions about the role of soldiers during the early Rawlings years.

Such speculation might be regarded as digressing from the question of the actual effectiveness of democratic consolidation so far, but the everyday interaction between government, opposition and civil society depends at least partly on calculations as to whether particular forms of political behaviour will provoke 'non-democratic' responses. It is easy to tolerate opposition parties if they mount little serious challenge, or boycott elections altogether. The major test of consolidation may come if and when a change of government through the ballot box appears to be a serious possibility. Would the government and its supporters allow a fair election and fair count, and would the losers accept the result? Outside election time, would government and opposition come closer to evolving conventions on their relations with each other, bearing in mind the fact that their roles might one day be reversed?

Before such questions can be faced, opposition parties have to arrive at a position where they do pose a serious challenge. How one judges the success of democratic consolidation so far depends largely on whether one emphasises the importance of basic freedoms of expression, association and assembly, where substantial progress has been made, or the importance of the checks imposed on the government by the realisation that an unsatisfactory performance may lead to people voting it out. At the time of writing there is still much room for doubt on the latter. The problem for opposition parties is not so much lack of policy, where the main challenger, the New Patriotic Party (NPP) continues in the Danquah/Busia tradition in offering more secure civil liberties, further progress towards a market economy and a slimmer state dispensing less patronage. These policies may be difficult to reconcile with those of the smaller Nkrumaist parties which are to the left of the government, but a common hatred of Rawlings could still bring them together, especially if they accept that the real scope for changing economic policy is anyway going to be severely limited.

The opposition parties also enjoy, in contrast to their Tanzanian counterparts, strong 'grassroots' bases. Indeed, long periods underground may have made cultivating the roots more important than the grass on the surface. As new democratic openings have appeared in the preludes to the 1969, 1979 and 1992 elections, old party networks have been revived with remarkable ease. But a major handicap may now be that long periods of fighting battles underground or in exile have made opposition parties too inward-looking, with a desire to punish Rawlings and his colleagues for their alleged misdemeanours and to demolish the structures they have created. This may divert their attention away from addressing the concerns of ordinary voters.

> [Opposition party leaders] believed the presidential election must have been rigged because they simply could not bring themselves, emotionally or logically, to accept that Rawlings could conceivably remain so popular amongst such large numbers of their compatriots. They had always

assumed party politics would spell the end of Rawlings and the dawning of a new political era ... this was in turn partly because of the distance – a distance they did not themselves fully acknowledge – in perceptions and experience between themselves and the intellectuals and professional elites on the one hand, and the mass of ordinary Ghanaians on the other. Talking, as they mostly did, to their fellow-educated citizens, they found scarcely anyone with a good word to say about Rawlings, and they tended simply to assume that they were opinion-leaders for the mass of their fellow-citizens

(Jeffries and Thomas 1993: 365)

Faced with a ruling party that looks like a somewhat rudimentary political party, and opposition parties which have yet to reach out effectively to a wider electorate, the Ghanaian political system has reached a curious pass. Many of the formal structures necessary for democratic consolidation are in place, and there is an underlying political culture which appears to be conducive to political competition, even if it is a rather unruly form of competition, yet political parties still hark back to past battles and past heroes, whether they be Nkrumah and the 'struggle for independence' in the 1950s, Busia and 'liberation' in the 1960s or Rawlings and the 'revolution' in the 1980s. Any further democratic consolidation may depend on the party system adapting more to the requirements of the 1990s.

9 Tanzania: Democratic Transition and Consolidation

A LONG AND LONELY MARCH

While Ghana's history has been marked by abrupt twists and turns, with radical changes of policy or unconstitutional changes of government often provoking violent responses, and with advances towards democracy followed by powerful repulses, Tanzanian history appears to exhibit greater continuity. Ghana has had seven heads of government since independence, of whom three were executed, two died in exile, one was deposed in disgrace and one other was deposed unconstitutionally. Tanzania has had just three heads of government (if we discount Nyerere's brief, nominal absence to concentrate on leading his party rather than his country). The first two presidents both retired as respected elder statesmen, to be replaced through an accepted constitutional process.

But constitutional change is not the same as democratic change. The first six presidential elections all returned unopposed candidates, and the seventh involved a contest which gave overwhelming advantages to the ruling party. According to Baregu

> The demands for multipartyism and democracy in Tanzania are the culmination of a long and cumulative (albeit uneven) struggle against authoritarian rule. At the time of independence in 1961, the Tanganyika African National Union (Tanu), led by Julius Nyerere, arrogated power to itself and forcefully imposed one-party rule. That move was resisted right from the start and continued to be resisted until 1992. Thus the political legitimacy of the one-party state has been contested throughout this period.
> (Baregu in Widner 1994: 159)

The march towards multi-party democracy was thus a long one, with not even temporary victories comparable with those in Ghana in 1969 and 1979, but it was also a lonely march for much of the three decades after 1961. There were occasional highlights, such as the resignation of Chief Abdullah Fundikira from the Ministry of Justice in 1963 in protest against the evolving one-party state, and the gaoling of Kasanga Tumbo, a former High Commissioner to Britain, for dissent against this development (McHenry 1994: 64), but there is a danger of equating any form of dissent with a demand for democracy or multi-party politics. There were workers' revolts against labour legislation, peasants' resistance to villagisation and attempted coups by dissatisfied soldiers, but the participants in these activities had more immediate concerns than competitive party politics. Enthusiasm for the latter appeared to be confined for a long time to a small group of intellectuals, in contrast to Ghana where every free, or even semi-free, election has been contested keenly, and where attempts by Acheampong and Rawlings to deny the people multi-party competition brought forth fierce resistance. But the long and lonely march in Tanzania did eventually attract new followers, and we must now seek to trace its ultimate success.

THE SEEDS OF CHALLENGE TO AUTHORITARIANISM

In a country where most political activity took place within the confines of the ruling party, it is perhaps unsurprising that many of the seeds of challenge to authoritarianism were sown by the party itself, or at least resulted from its actions. While Tanu, and later the CCM, was more successful than most African parties in maintaining a structure which facilitated such basic functions as political recruitment, policy making and the legitimation of the political system through intra-party elections, it was put under strain by both the inherent weaknesses in such a system and by economic decline. McHenry reports that by the mid-1980s the party was becoming increasingly remote from the people, with fewer attending meetings or paying subscriptions, and Nyerere criticising 'leaders' (that is, officers) for being increasingly office-bound and concerned with self-enrichment (McHenry 1994: 55–7; see also Mmuya and Chaligha 1992: 18). The myth of the party articulating the voice of the masses, while the state merely executed its wishes, became increasingly at variance with reality. As it became common for party posts to be held concurrently with state posts, the party lost much of its distinctiveness and autonomy. The government provided the party with 90 per cent of its funds, and controlled much of the necessary expertise and information, so that party control over the state became increasingly difficult (McHenry 1994: 57). There are few one-party regimes in the world that have not suffered stresses of this sort, as any initial enthusiasm for innovation gives way to more routine administration, but, in the case of Tanzania, the economic pressures of the 1980s made the legitimacy of the one-party monopoly increasingly difficult to sustain. Economic decline, with worsening terms of trade and the manifest failure of the command economy, led to both internal and external pressure for economic liberalisation. Wealth then depended increasingly on the private sector rather than on membership or control of the state bureaucracy, and politicians were quick to appreciate this. The abstinence of party officers from capitalist activity, which had been required by the Arusha Declaration, was abandoned, and there were growing reports of corrupt deals between politicians and foreign and indigenous Asian businesses, thus depriving the party further of claims to moral authority or legitimacy (Barkan 1994; 30). It could neither be claiming to lead a socialist crusade, nor to be following pragmatic policies which produced material benefits, and it was against this background that Nyerere called in 1990 for a debate on the merits of multi-party politics (McHenry 1994: 62). A major seed of challenge was thus planted by the major architect of single-party politics.

The economic problems of the 1980s, and the government's response to them, had other implications for one-party rule. The socialists in the party, who stood by the traditional faith, came to favour party competition in the hope (mistakenly as events proved) that the ideologically impure elements would find a home elsewhere, and that the CCM would thus restore its integrity (Barkan 1994: 31; McHenry 1994: 51). At a more practical level the party's claim to competence, let alone purity, was being exposed by the inability to finance essential projects, declining industrial capacity and a reduction in those areas of social provision, such as water, health and education, where Tanzania had previously boasted that its egalitarian socialism produced the best results. Mmuya and Chaligha suggest that these failures led to citizens developing greater confidence in alternative agencies, such as aid donors and non-government organisations (NGOs) (Mmuya and Chaligha 1992: 21, 33; see also Morna 1989: 25), which presumably raised further questions about the fallibility of the ruling party.

The contribution of economic liberalisation to political liberalisation, in the sense of pluralist, multi-party democracy, remains a matter of debate (see Pinkney 1994). It is clearly possible to have the former without the latter, as in Chile under General Pinochet and China more recently, yet economic liberalisation does frequently undermine authoritarian rule, whether by creating or strengthening groups independent of the state, by casting adrift groups which had previously remained compliant while the state had maintained their incomes or social security, or by the mere fact of opening debate on policy alternatives when previously the wisdom of the rulers had been under less challenge. We shall return to some of these points later in this chapter, but we may note Chege's description of an emerging opposition based on an independent, propertied, urban-based intelligentsia which was the product of a robust and expanding market economy that provided diverse independent opportunities outside the formal sector (Chege in Barkan 1994: 56), and Baregu's observation that economic liberalisation led to the breakdown of consensus in the party, with critics drawing attention in 1989 to 'the logical inconsistency in the government's espousal of economic liberalisation and its rejection of political liberalisation' (Baregu in Widner 1994: 168). Logical consistency may suggest that economic and political liberalisation should go together but, at an individual level, political and economic entrepreneurship may be competitive with one another rather than complementary. 'Some people have become preoccupied with material individual welfare. These people have become detached from politics' (Okumu 1995: 6).

Whether it is business people seeking new sources of profit or paupers seeking new sources of welfare in the absence of state provision, the new economic order will provide many individual diversions from politics. What happens in politics may depend less on the activities of those affected directly by economic liberalisation, and more on the ability of politicians to mobilise such people. To the extent that economic liberalisation increased doubt and uncertainty, and led to resources being allocated in ways which were less subject to any consensus, it contributed to a less monolithic political structure.

Beyond Tanzania's shores there were familiar developments which further undermined the authoritarian structure. The break-up of the Soviet Bloc had more serious implications for Tanzania than for Ghana, partly because Tanzania, and especially Zanzibar, had been more dependent on aid from the East, and partly because the breakdown of the one-party system in more 'advanced' countries led to renewed questions about whether such a system was desirable or workable in Tanzania. The Ghanaian government at least recognised that it was presiding over an authoritarian system that could only be transitory, while Tanzania was following a model (albeit in a more humane form) which was on the verge of extinction. Systems which had previously been admired for achieving rapid industrialisation, or putting men into space, were now exposed as politically and economically bankrupt. The West was quick to exploit this turn of events. In the absence of competition from the East, it could lay down more stringent conditions for aid, and these included political as well as economic adjustment. This reflected not merely the abandonment of dictators who had previously been useful bulwarks against communism, or who might be lured away from the communist camp, or even some passing democratic fad. The inefficiency and corruption of bloated party/state bureaucracies, and the lack of accountability or public scrutiny, were seen to be practical as well as moral problems, the ultimate solution to which was a more pluralist political order (see especially Barkan 1994: 2).

Yet another opportunity was thus created to challenge the old order though, as both Baregu and Barkan point out, demands for democratisation came initially from the indigenous population (and might perhaps have succeeded earlier if Western donors had been more discriminating in their choice of friends). Barkan suggests that not only Eastern Europe, but

South Africa, was important in giving Africans a new perspective. It was no longer possible to claim that African rulers in Tropical Africa were doing nothing worse than Europeans in South Africa (Barkan 1994: 3), and the sight of an opposition politician in South Africa going from a prison cell to the presidency must have raised the morale of opposition politicians elsewhere. The authoritarian mould had clearly been broken by blows from a variety of sources. We must now turn to the question of the scope for creating a new mould.

THE CONFIGURATION OF INTERESTS

The positions of different groups on the government–opposition and elite–mass axes are suggested in Figure 9.1. As in the previous chapter, the positions can be no more than suggestive, and other observers might well place the field differently, but we can again suggest the areas of government and opposition strength, and the floaters whose role might have been crucial in determining what sort of democracy emerged, and to whose advantage. In the 'north-western' corner of the table (the government/elite corner) are the cabinet and leaders of the ruling party, although even this corner was not immune to defections. One of the three opposition presidential candidates in 1995 had only resigned from the deputy prime ministership a few months before the election, and another candidate had recently been a presidential economic adviser. This suggests less rigidly drawn battle lines than in Ghana, although some left-wing defectors from Rawlings's government did join small, though largely peripheral, opposition parties. Below the government/party leadership was an apparently solid base of support in the form of bureaucrats, technocrats and army and police officers, all of whom had generally been treated generously by the regime, and had little reason to change sides. Nearer the bottom of the social scale were party activists, whose numbers were dwindling by the 1980s but who still had an enormous potential to convey the party message to the voters, especially in rural areas where other means of communication were sparse. The peasants formed the base of the pro-government forces. Their loyalty had been strained by villagisation but, as in Ghana, peasants

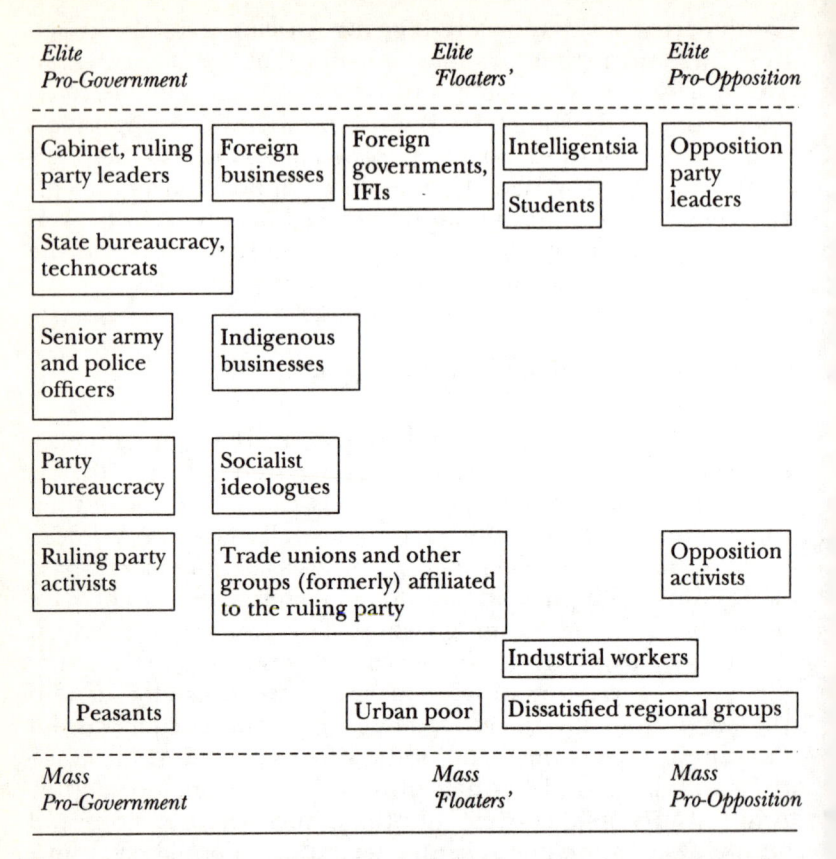

Elite Pro-Government	*Elite 'Floaters'*	*Elite Pro-Opposition*

Cabinet, ruling party leaders	Foreign businesses	Foreign governments, IFIs	Intelligentsia	Opposition party leaders
State bureaucracy, technocrats			Students	
Senior army and police officers	Indigenous businesses			
Party bureaucracy	Socialist ideologues			
Ruling party activists	Trade unions and other groups (formerly) affiliated to the ruling party			Opposition activists
			Industrial workers	
Peasants		Urban poor	Dissatisfied regional groups	

Mass Pro-Government	*Mass 'Floaters'*	*Mass Pro-Opposition*

Figure 9.1 Sources of initiative for democratisation in Tanzania: government and opposition; elites and masses

benefited from devaluation and the policy of allowing the price of agricultural exports to reach a realistic level. Any large-scale defection to the opposition was therefore unlikely.

On the opposition side, the leadership had generally come from the intellectuals and the urban middle class, with its strength mainly in Dar es Salaam (Mmuya and Chaligha 1992: 54–6; Chege in Barkan 1994: 56). Before the 1990s there were few links between ad hoc political protests and organised opposition, and it was not until 1990 that Chief Fundikira formed the Steering Committee for Multi-Party Democracy (Chege in Barkan 1994: 53). In March 1991 the Tanzanian

Legal Education Trust complained of the treatment of student dissidents, foreign economic domination and violations of civil liberties. It put forward an ambitious list of demands, including the release of the former chief minister of Zanzibar, a pardon for political detainees, the right to peaceful demonstration, the repeal of laws hampering free speech, the removal of the army from politics, the formation of a Commission to draft a new constitution and the establishment of a transitional government pending free elections (McHenry 1994: 64). Opposition parties were still not legal, but dissent continued to gain momentum. In June 1991 a 'multi-party workshop' was organised by dissident groups, which attracted an attendance of 800 to 1000, with the young, academics and students all well represented (Mmuya and Chaligha 1992: 134). These early manifestations of opposition set the tone for what was to follow. Elite groups predominated, and there was more talk about civil liberties and free elections than about the condition of the poor, although Zanzibar politics, as has so often been the case, remained an exception to the rule. Here politics took on a more earthy flavour, with the vanquished in the 1964 revolution wanting revenge over the victors.

The fact that early opposition demands focused largely on constitutional reform did not imply an indifference to the country's social problems or a lack of potential followers in the wider society, but constitutional reform was seen as the key which would unlock the door to other reforms. There was a potential opposition constituency beyond the narrow elite, but it was more difficult to reach than its Ghanaian counterpart. There were fewer dormant opposition groups waiting to be reactivated, no chiefs with any formal power or status to act as intermediaries, and no individual ethnic groups large enough to swing more than a handful of parliamentary seats. Opposition appeals appeared, paradoxically, to attract those who had benefited most and those who had suffered most from economic liberalisation. Chege refers to the independent, propertied urban groups which were the product of the 'robust and expanding market economy' that provided diverse, independent economic opportunities (Chege in Barkan 1994: 56) while, at the bottom of the social scale, opposition support came from badly-paid and unemployed urban workers whose real incomes had fallen as a result of retrenchment and the increased price of imports resulting from devaluation. This group included many recent migrants to the towns who eked out a living as petty traders and stall holders. Although poor, these groups were learning to struggle for survival through their own efforts, as state aid diminished. Mmuya and Chaligha suggest that their personal circumstances, together with increased literacy and exposure to foreign media, made them increasingly politically aware. Some formed themselves into 'grassroots associations' dealing with environmental or social problems or religious solidarity, and some forged links with opposition groups (Mmuya and Chaligha 1992: 18).

The 'winners' and 'losers' from economic liberalisation had in common the fact that they occupied less stable positions in society than the technocrats, state officials, soldiers, policemen and peasants who, for the most part, continued to be well protected by the government, even if it had not delivered extensive material benefits, and who were therefore less likely to change their allegiance. The 'winners' might have hoped that democracy would bring benefits with further economic liberalisation, or at least a more competently managed mixed economy. The expectations of the 'losers' are less clear, but they had little to lose in registering a protest vote against the party which had once offered a socialist utopia but which was now widening the gap between rich and poor. In the 'southeastern' corner of Figure 9.1 there were few urban mobs or protest movements comparable with those in Ghana, perhaps reflecting again a more passive culture, but there were, at least in the larger towns, impressive displays of support in poorer areas for opposition parties in the weeks before the 1995 elections. It might be stretching the concept to call these people opposition 'activists', but they helped to increase the visibility of an opposition presence.

The polarisation of opposition support between rich and poor was also manifested in geographical terms. The Kilimanjaro region voted heavily for the opposition in 1995, partly on account of the presidential candidacy of a fellow Chagga kinsman, Augustine Mrema, but also because this relatively prosperous region had suffered a decline in the price of coffee (see especially Kelsall 1996: 14), yet the greatest concentration of opposition support was on Pemba (the second largest of the Zanzibar islands) – the poorest region of the second poorest country in the world. Here the opposition made a clean sweep of all the parliamentary seats in 1995, as voters protested against government neglect and coercion, allegedly resulting from the island's opposition to the Zanzibar revolution.

Among the 'floaters' were some groups which were more likely to incline towards the opposition parties even if they had no formal affiliation to them, including the intelligentsia and students at elite level, and the urban poor and the disaffected regional groups we have just described at mass level. Industrial workers also appeared to be hostile to the government, even if their nominal leaders were, or had recently been, affiliated to the ruling party. These groups were not, for the most part, organised into any formal political structures, so their ultimate loyalty depended on thousands of individual decisions, and they were therefore open to persuasion from both sides, and were not all likely to float in the same direction. The mirror image of these groups were the indigenous and foreign businesses which found it prudent to be on good terms with the government, but whose support could not be guaranteed. This leaves a range of floaters which were more formally organised, including foreign governments, IFIs, the various former wings of the ruling party and (though organised in a somewhat different way) the socialist ideologues who had previously seen the CCM as their home but were now having doubts about some of their fellow occupants. For the opposition, the task was to win over enough floaters to ensure, both through weight of numbers and resources, that not only was there a transition to democracy, but that such a transition was on terms that would reduce or eliminate the opposition's handicap in fighting a party enjoying all the advantages of 24 years of incumbency. In numerical terms, the support of the intelligentsia, the newly-enriched, the marginalised urban poor and the disaffected peripheral regions would make little impression against the weight of an overwhelmingly pro-government rural population. But if foreign governments or financial institutions could be persuaded to make further aid conditional on constitutional reform, or if labour, co-operatives, military or women's groups recently affiliated to the ruling party could be detached from it, and therefore not used in promoting its re-election, the balance of forces might begin to look different. For the ruling party, the strategy was more a matter of defending the territory it already held but, in the new climate of economic liberalisation, growing dissent and the loss of the moral and material support of the Communist Bloc, a price would have to be paid to retain the existing bases of support. This price would have to be sufficient to satisfy waverers or potential waverers that enough progress was being made along the roads to political and economic liberalisation, but not so high as to jeopardise the party's prospects of winning a contested election.

Nyerere's call for a national debate on the question of multi-party politics in February 1991 was followed by the appointment of the Presidential Commission on the Constitution under Chief Justice Nyalali. The Commission held 1061 meetings all over the country and received 36 299 verbal and written submissions, which produced a response of 77.2 per cent in favour of the continuation of a one-party state and 21.5 per cent in favour of a multi-party system (United Republic of Tanzania 1992: 7–8). The large majority in favour of retaining a one-party state might be explained partly by the fact that the inquiry was perceived as a government/party exercise, with meetings held largely on government/party premises, and with people feeling that they should say what the party wanted them to say (see especially Mmuya and Chaligha 1992: 132). But on any calculation, this was not a country living unwillingly under an unwanted political order. The Commission nonetheless recommended that multi-party politics should be permitted on the grounds that this was what a substantial minority wanted and that 'undesirable features of the present system' could not be cured without multi-party politics (ibid.: 10). The patronage, corruption and incompetence condemned by many witnesses could not, it seemed, be tackled adequately by the old order. The CCM 'had become inactive and some party leaders were ineffective'. Democratic principles were being violated, there were shortcomings in the laws and the constitution, no genuine representation of the people in state organs, limited freedom of expression and association, and enormous presidential power (ibid.: 4–6).

It is a remarkable authoritarian government that allows a public body to make such sweeping criticisms, and a remarkable one that responds by apparently dismantling much of the apparatus it has created, without a shot being fired or threatened by its opponents. There did seem to be a genuine belief in the virtues of multi-party democracy, in contrast to the much more grudging attitude of Rawlings and his supporters, but such a democracy was going to be imposed on the terms that suited the ruling party, with the rejection of many of the Nyalali recommendations which had recognised that there was more to democracy than free elections. Among the recommendations that were rejected, or not even debated within the party, were those for an educational campaign to make citizens aware of their democratic rights, a constituent assembly to consider a new constitution, a federal political structure, elections by proportional representation using the additional member system and the repeal of repressive legislation (United Republic of Tanzania 1992: 12, 138–9, 148, 167–71). The implementation of such recommendations would have made for less of a top-down, government-imposed transition to democracy, and would have ensured that, even in the event of the CCM being re-elected, there could be no elective dictatorship.

THE RESOLUTION OF CONFLICTS

The Nyalali Report, together with the internal and external pressures already described, meant that there was little chance of resisting the coming of multi-party politics. It was now a matter of the CCM seizing and retaining the initiative. Nyerere was one of the first senior figures to support Nyalali (McHenry 1994: 65), and President Mwinyi followed somewhat reluctantly, still fearing the divisiveness and violence which multi-party politics might bring. As a Zanzibari, he had more cause for concern than mainland politicians. A CCM conference gave its support to multi-partyism in February 1992, having already held internal party debates over the previous two years (Ngasongwa 1992: 113–14), and it now set about converting itself into a potential competitor rather than a monolithic ruling party. Affiliated organisations such as trade unions, cooperatives, women's and youth groups were given greater autonomy as a preliminary to separation, party branches in the armed forces were abolished, party chairmen ceased to draw salaries, party secretariats at all levels were reduced in size, and ideological colleges were closed (Nyasongwa 1992: 116). In May 1992 the National Assembly voted to legalise a multi-party system with effect from 1 July, though all parties had to be 'national' in character with branches in every region, in order to avoid ethnic or religious appeals.

These appeared to be generous concessions on the part of the government/ruling party, but the rejection of the Nyalali recommendation of a constituent assembly to consider a new constitution made the transition even more 'top-down' than in Ghana, where at least the need to debate the new political order was recognised. In Ghana all parties started from scratch in the formal sense in 1992, even though the NDC had the advantage of government backing in practice, and they were working within a constitution approved by a national referendum. While other African countries were permitting multi-party politics as a means of overcoming national crises, the CCM liked to portray the Tanzanian position as one of 'business as usual', with the rulers changing the rules on the basis of their own judgement rather than in a state of panic. The absence of a constituent assembly or a new constitution gave the appearance of continuity rather than change, with the opposition invited to join in a game which had already been in progress for a long time under rules over which it had no control. This was probably humiliating psychologically, with opposition parties waiting as supplicants. After their June 1991 meeting, further opposition gatherings were prohibited until the law was changed in July 1992 (see especially Mmuya and Chaligha 1992: 138–9).

With the ruling party apparently holding most of the trump cards, how were the opposition parties to play their hand? We have seen that they lacked a geographical power base large enough to make any great electoral impression, and there were no dissident groups comparable with the churches in Kenya (where the government had antagonised religious groups much more) or the trade unions in Zambia (where workers on the Copperbelt constituted a significant group) which might have provided a nucleus around which opposition could build. There were no 'bogey men' in the government comparable with President Moi in Kenya or President Banda in Malawi who might arouse sufficient hatred to rally the opposition. Tanzanian rulers might be held responsible for driving the country into economic impoverishment, but they had not been responsible for the death or torture of large numbers of fellow citizens (Chege in Barkan 1994: 63). One advantage the opposition did enjoy was that, with Tanzania a latecomer in the democratisation process, international sympathy for groups challenging authoritarian rule was probably stronger and more open that it had been formerly. Leaders of embryonic opposition parties were able to hold meetings abroad, and Mmuya and Chaligha report that in April 1992 a meeting was held with representatives of most of the Western embassies to search for a common opposition front, with financial support provided by 'Western foreign agencies' (Mmuya and Chaligha 1992: 146). Around the same time, newspapers were beginning to appear which were owned by foreign companies, and which were frequently critical of the government or openly supportive of the opposition.

From legalisation in 1992, opposition parties had a little over three years in which to mount an electoral challenge. Contesting elections, like dining at the Ritz Hotel, was now open to everyone. The timescale compared favourably with the six months available to the Ghanaian opposition parties, but at least the latter had old contacts to reactivate, whereas Tanzanian opposition parties had few obvious starting points. We have already enumerated some of the obvious sources of opposition: business people, the urban poor, regions regarding themselves as victims of discrimination, and disillusioned former members of the ruling party. Various parties rose, fell, merged or split between 1992 and 1995, and by the opening of the election campaign in 1995 there were twelve opposition parties. Most of these contained idealistic men and women, many produced earnest policy proposals, and some had local pockets of support, often built around prominent members, which were sufficient to win one or two parliamentary seats, but it soon became clear that few had sufficient power bases or resources to mount a serious challenge. The main exceptions were the National Convention for Reconstruction and Reform (NCCR) and the Civic United Front (CUF).

The NCCR and its prototypes had been developed by long-standing dissident intellectuals such as Mwesiga Baregu, a professor of politics at the University of Dar es Salaam, and more recent converts from the CCM who retained their social democratic beliefs but were critical of the ruling party's actual performance and the growth of corruption. The defection of the Deputy Prime Minister, Augustine Mrema, early in 1995 gave the NCCR a big name, which most of the other opposition parties lacked and, with Mrema's selection as presidential candidate, support was built up both in his home region and amongst the urban poor. By polling day, a party which has its origins largely amongst the intelligentsia had its flag flying over thousands of shanty dwellings and market stalls. CUF's origins owed more to the complexities of Zanzibar politics, and the various groups which had either opposed the 1964 revolution or had since fallen out with the post-revolutionary government. The constitution prohibited purely regional parties, so it was necessary to establish a bridgehead on the mainland. This was achieved largely through the selection of Ibrahim Lipumba, an economics professor and former presidential adviser, as presidential candidate. Lipumba's horizons extended beyond Zanzibar and, as the only Muslim presidential candidate, he might have been expected to tap a large religious vote. Although religion has never played a major part in Tanzanian politics, it seemed possible that religious affiliation might tip the balance in a lot of voters' choices if policy differences were perceived to be narrow or unimportant. The only other opposition party to field a presidential candidate was the United Democratic Party (UDP), which offered the most rightwing policies. It attracted support from some prominent businessmen but had no obvious roots in society, and ultimately won only three parliamentary seats and 4 per cent of the presidential vote.

DEMOCRACY AS WHO CHOOSES WHAT, WHY AND HOW

The pressures to allow voters a democratic choice between competing parties had been irresistible, yet it was never entirely clear what the alternatives on offer were likely to be, or how people would arrive at a choice in the absence of any previous multi-party contests. I sought answers to these questions by interviewing officers of 11 of the 13 parties and distributing questionnaires to 105 party activists and voters (for details see

Pinkney in Hampsher-Monk and Stanyer 1996: 610–22). Such a small number of respondents cannot be presented as a representative sample, and opposition supporters, men and the capital city were all over-represented at the expense of CCM supporters, women and the provinces, but the results may shed some light on the political perceptions of Tanzanian citizens.

Table 9.1 lists the influences on people's decisions as to how to vote. Of the influences regarded as 'very important', party members ranked 'family and friends' first (83 per cent), and also gave prominence to 'persuasion by political parties' (57 per cent) and 'colleagues at work' (51 per cent), whereas ordinary voters put radio, newspapers and television at the top their list, with 'family and friends' accounting for only 43 per cent. This suggests that whereas party members saw political persuasion as a two-way process in which friends, relations, party members and colleagues could interact, ordinary voters emphasised the one-way communication of radio,

Table 9.1   Perceptions of 'very important' influences on Tanzanian voters

Party members	%	Voters	%
Family and friends	83	Radio	66
Radio	64	Newspapers	61
Newspapers	62	Television	48
Persuasion by political parties	57	Family and friends	43
Television	52		
Colleagues at work	51		

Table 9.2   'Very important' influences on Tanzanian voters: perceptions of two-way channels

	Party members %	Voters %
Family and friends	83	43
Colleagues at work	51	39
Fellow members of organisations	32	17
Persuasion by political parties	57	26

television and newspapers. This is highlighted again in Table 9.2, where party members consistently outnumber voters in their assessment of the importance of two-way channels of communication ('fellow members of organisations' here included trade union, social, religious and business groups), as opposed to the one-way channels through the media. The differences might reflect a tendency for party members to come from higher up the social scale, and therefore to be more confident of their ability to influence as well as be influenced, but they may also be indicative of a society in which national politics, for the ordinary voter, is something that comes down from on high rather than something that is the property of the ordinary citizen. As the diet offered by the media had, until very recently, been produced to the requirements of the ruling party, this did not augur well for the opposition.

Explanations of voting for different parties, for the most part, took refuge in generalities. Table 9.3 on voting for the CCM suggests a three-way split between the responses of CCM members, opposition party members and voters. Even CCM members ranked 'party identification and habit' (57 per cent) above 'satisfaction with government performance' (43 per cent), and opposition party members

Table 9.3 Reasons for voting for the CCM (the ruling party)

Opposition party members	%	CCM members	%	Voters	%
Fear, intimidation	35	Party identification habit	57	Ignorance	43
Bribery	38	Satisfaction with government performance	43	Bribery	35
Ignorance	28	Bribery	14	Satisfaction with government performance	22
Party identification, habit	8			Fear, intimidation	9
Satisfaction with government performance	8				

explained CCM support mainly in terms of 'fear and intimidation' (35 per cent), 'bribery' (32 per cent) and 'ignorance' (28 per cent). The latter was sometimes linked to the government's refusal to accept the Nyalali recommendation that a programme of political education should precede any election, and a belief that this refusal reflected a desire to keep voters in ignorance. (Only 8 per cent of opposition members mentioned 'satisfaction with government performance' as a reason for voting for the CCM.) The opposition perspective was thus a largely 'conspiratorial' one, whereas ordinary voters, although putting 'ignorance' at the top of the list at 43 per cent, gave much less weight to 'fear and intimidation' (9 per cent), much more to 'satisfaction with governmental performance' (22 per cent) and approximately the same amount to 'bribery' (35 per cent). Although such responses hardly indicated any great respect for the ruling party, there was a somewhat more 'instrumental' view of elections as a process of trading votes for favours, rather than winning votes by keeping people in fear and ignorance.

Explanations of support for opposition parties also emphasised the general rather than the particular. The largest single explanation was a desire for changes of leadership or policy (38 per cent of party members and 39 per cent of voters). The main divergence between the two groups was in the party members' greater emphasis on the inadequacy of the government's performance, especially the inadequacy of economic development (18 per cent of members and 13 per cent of voters), lack of social provision (9 per cent and 0 per cent), corruption in the government and ruling party (11 per cent and 4 per cent), or dissatisfaction with performance generally (26 per cent and 17 per cent). On specific differences of policy and principle, only 17 per cent of each group pinpointed the opposition parties' liberal, anti-authoritarian alternatives, and the perception of a free market, non-socialist alternative hardly emerged at all, despite the focus on this in the televised debate between the presidential candidates (Tasseni 1995: 6–7).

The lack of specificity in the answers may be the fault of the open-ended questions in the questionnaire, or the fact that the interviewees were not sufficiently articulate to spell out sources of satisfaction or dissatisfaction, even though they existed in their own minds. But it may also be that prolonged single-party rule, superimposed on a culture which placed little emphasis on political conflict, left voters with little notion of elections as a means of choosing between alternative policies. We should also remark on the issues which were not raised, perhaps because they were not seen as important, but possibly because they would have revealed aspects of Tanzanian politics which it was considered improper to raise in public. No respondents mentioned religious influences and none mentioned Mrema's Chagga background as a reason for voting for or against him, although his party received 78 per cent of the vote in his own region but less than 30 per cent over the whole country (*Tanzanian Affairs* 1996: 13). Indeed no one mentioned any of the presidential candidates, and only one respondent mentioned the influence of ex-President Nyerere, despite the publicity given to his nation-wide tour. The performance of the presidential candidates on television went unremarked, despite the general influence attributed to television and the fact that Benjamin Mkapa, the CCM candidate, appeared to have a much surer political grasp than his opponents, and that this perception was echoed widely even in the non-CCM press. Respondents may also have underestimated the appeal of the CCM as the party of internal peace and stability. The more articulate opposition supporters argued that the tolerance and non-violence embedded in the political culture was an explanation of prolonged CCM rule rather than an effect, and that few other populations would have tolerated such an abysmal economic performance so passively, but the CCM persuaded may voters that its stewardship had prevented violent conflicts such as those found in neighbouring Uganda, Burundi, Rwanda, or even Kenya (see especially Kelsall 1996: 12–15).

When we get to the level of national party officers, a much clearer perception of party policies emerges. Opposition officers emphasised their commitment to political pluralism and questioned the CCM's allegedly late and incomplete conversion, with repressive legislation still on the statute book, and many public appointments still in the gift of the government or ruling party, including appointments to the judiciary and the Electoral Commission. There was a broad division between parties such as the UDP, which openly advocated more rapid economic liberalisation, and those such as the NCCR which took a more social democratic line, and criticised the actual performance of the government rather than the existence of a mixed economy. Most opposition parties, even those taking the free-market line on the management on the economy, were critical of the government's inadequate social provision, especially in the areas of health and education. In contrast to Ghana, there were no fringe parties with a yearning for traditional socialism, which seemed to have been discredited more in Tanzania than in most African states on account of the extent, duration and ineffectiveness of the command economy, and even the CCM put a very broad interpretation on what socialism now meant. Mkapa saw it as 'building an economy with dignity, solidarity and equality' (Tasseni 1995: 6), though all the signs were that inequality was increasing while the public services continued to shrink. There was not a lot of mileage for opposition parties in advocating economic liberalisation when the CCM had already been travelling this road for ten years, and when opposition parties were anyway keen to restore higher standards of social provision. Even to advocate greater *political* liberalisation was to push at an open door. Tanzania was manifestly a much freer country in 1995 than it had been in 1985, with virtually no political prisoners, a critical press and few curbs on political activity.

For the connoisseur who was prepared to probe carefully, the policy differences between the parties were there and, as in much of the world, they provided inspiration for the efforts of a minority of activists to court voters who had little interest in these subtleties. The actual process of courting them was a tough one for all opposition parties. They had to convey their message to voters in constituencies which were, on average, twelve times the size of their British counterparts, travelling on dirt roads, supported by meagre resources, in a search for voters in largely scattered communities who had a minimal grasp of the concept of political competition. These voters had received little media exposure to opposition parties, and opinion leaders who might have been approached as intermediaries were often public employees, such as teachers, or people who had only recently been officers of bodies affiliated to the ruling party. Many of these people would therefore have had a sense of loyalty to, or dependence on, the CCM. A more dynamic campaign by the opposition parties would have helped, and there was a tendency to bemoan the unfairness of the system and the (allegedly deliberate) delay in releasing the state subsidies to which all parties were entitled, when an all-out attack on the government's social and economic record might have been a better strategy, but it is still difficult to conceive of issues or personalities being brought to the fore which would have produced a change of government.

The administration of the election did little to enhance the reputation of the government, the ruling party or the public service. The Commonwealth Observers monitoring the election reported on 'the chaos and confusion we witnessed on polling day, scenes we have not witnessed before when observing elections in other Commonwealth countries' (Haonga 1995: 1). The group reported that incidents of 'electoral materials shortage and cheating' were experienced all over the country: 'Government officials had openly supported the ruling party in some constituencies, and it concluded that the elections were not fair and free' (ibid.: 1).

Apart from blatant acts of cheating, such as transporting boxes of pre-marked ballot papers to polling stations, there were polling stations where insufficient ballot papers or ballot boxes were available. There were also reports of polling officials failing to report for duty as a result of disputes over wages, and of insufficient facilities for voting in secret (see especially Tanzanian Election Monitoring Committee [TEMCO], 1995: 8). As a result of these various irregularities, many polling stations opened late or not at all.

Some observers saw all this as plain incompetence; opposition parties saw it as an attempt to rig the results in the areas where they were strongest, and demanded that the elections should be re-scheduled throughout the country. The Electoral Commission denied any bias, and re-scheduled the elections only in the nine Dar es Salaam constituencies, where the chaos had been greatest. Whether a nationwide re-scheduling would have made much difference to the outcome is debatable. If fresh elections had been held a month or two later, is there any guarantee that officials would have been more competent, that there would have been less propensity to act dishonestly or that those caught in such acts would have been prosecuted any more rigorously? Any re-run election might well have dispensed the same rough justice as the original one. The ballot rigging thesis was anyway challenged by those who asked why the opposition parties were able to win 46 seats, and to defeat some prominent ministers in the government. The CCM's victory might as easily be attributed to the party's 'superior financial and grassroots organisation' (Karashani 1995: 4). The CCM might have dismantled the quasi-Leninist party–state structure but, in terms of available manpower to deliver the vote, whether through formal or informal contacts, it had no rival.

THE PROSPECTS FOR DEMOCRATIC CONSOLIDATION

The presidential election gave victory to Mkapa with 61.8 per cent of the vote, about 3 per cent more than that received by Rawlings in an equally controversial election. Mrema came second with 27.8 per cent. In the parliamentary election, the CCM won 186 of the 232 seats, CUF 24 and the NCCR 16 (*Tanzanian Affairs* 1996: 13–14). The most contentious elections were for the Zanzibar presidency and parliament, where CUF won 49.8 per cent of the vote to the CCM's 50.2 per cent. CUF questioned the accuracy of the count, as did many independent observers, and Zanzibar was left polarised with the opposition winning every single seat on Pemba and the CCM winning all but three seats on the main island of Unguja.

The aftermath of the election left a bitter taste, yet there had been much to admire. It had been a largely peaceful, good-humoured election, despite the occasional excesses of the police at opposition rallies, and rival party flags and posters had been displayed outside neighbouring homes and businesses without causing any obvious antagonism. The language of politicians and the press had been relatively temperate, especially by Ghanaian standards. Returning to the 'floating' groups enumerated in Figure 9.1, they had been influential enough to push the government into permitting multi-party elections, but not influential enough to ensure that the proverbial playing field was level or that the controversial results were annulled. Foreign donors were more concerned with the appearance of political competition than with the intricacies of lost ballot papers or absent poll clerks, and businesses were more concerned with the general direction of economic liberalisation than with the credentials of different parties to continue the process. Two peripheral regions felt sufficiently dissatisfied to give most of their votes to the opposition, but the remaining regions did not. Similarly, a minority of the urban poor, trade unionists and disillusioned CCM activists supported the opposition, but the majority did not, while the CCM's rural heartland, and its bureaucratic base, which allegedly enabled it to run elections to suit the party's convenience, held firm.

There is nothing inherently undemocratic about an incumbent party winning an election, and there are limits to what one can do to make an election 'fair' if a long incumbency has produced a bureaucracy in the party's image and a system of patronage that makes key groups and individuals reluctant to change sides. What is probably more important than recriminations over the election is the question of how far the democratic opening achieved in 1995, which would have been unthinkable ten years earlier, has created a potential for democratic consolidation.

Some of the handicaps under which the opposition laboured in 1995 might become less severe in the course of time. Although there had been a small nucleus of dissidents who had opposed authoritarian rule over many years, most of the opposition politicians were either defectors from the CCM or people new to politics. There was not therefore the same sense of shared identity and comradeship as is found in older-established parties, which have their own myths, heroes, martyrs and shared experiences. This may change as the parties mature, and the shared experiences of legal battles against the Electoral Commission may transform what were generally good fraternal relations between opposition parties into mergers to produce a more united front. The question of exactly which principles or policies might be proclaimed by such a front, given the CCM's extensive concessions to economic and political liberalisation, remains unclear, but the presence of 55 opposition MPs in Parliament (nine nominated women MPs were added to the 46 elected members) should make the scrutiny of government policy, and the formulation of alternatives, easier.

On the debit side, the problems of penetrating the rural hinterland, where the majority of constituencies lie, remain formidable. We return to the problem that civil society remains 'thin', with many of the opinion leaders, who might in other circumstances provide a point of entry, still tied to the ruling party through loyalty based on past patronage, or self-interest based on current transactions. There is also the question, posed in Chapter 6, as to whether the army or the civil bureaucracy would remain 'neutral' in the event of a serious opposition challenge. The alleged rigging of the count in Zanzibar in 1995, when the official figures put the opposition 0.4 per cent behind the ruling party, might suggest that the honesty of electoral administration varies inversely with the size of the opposition vote. Again I am not suggesting that democracy should be equated with governments losing elections but, if there is not even the possibility of a government losing, the scope for checks and balances, and for effective public participation, is likely to be minimal. With such heavy odds against them it would be easy for opposition parties, or at least some of their members, to give up the struggle. Whatever the democratic opportunities that social, economic or political changes create, much may still depend on the tenacity of those engaged in this unenviable pursuit.

On the more positive factors making for democratic consolidation, Tanzania's continued stability, and relative lack of ethnic or religious conflict, ought to give it advantages over neighbouring countries where violence has been much more widespread, though this stability can degenerate into fatalism or apathy. From a more dynamic point of view, much may hinge on the extent to which the forces that made the democratic opening possible will maintain their momentum. The development of a more heterogeneous society, and a free press reflecting a diversity of opinions, will not be reversed easily. The preference of foreign governments and IFIs for democracy rather than dictatorship, although not always matched by actions against authoritarian rulers, may continue to act as some deterrent against undemocratic tendencies. Possibly more important is the fact that authoritarianism in Tanzania operated on a rather different basis from authoritarianism in most other Third World countries, and that such a basis would now be difficult to restore. Some authoritarian governments, especially in East Asia, have owed their survival to economic success, with citizens' satisfaction with their material condition outweighing any concerns they might have about the denial of democratic rights. Other authoritarians, especially in Tropical Africa, have relied more on naked coercion.

Tanzania's lack of economic success is all too apparent, yet coercion, although not absent, probably played a much less significant role than in Uganda, Malawi and most of West Africa. Party/state penetration of society and the economy were more important, and resistance to authority could be punished less by guns than by threats to people's livelihood. With the dismantling of the command economy and the transformation of the ubiquitous 'ruling' party into a mere 'majority' party, wider opportunities were available for both economic and political freedom, and it seems inconceivable that either Tanzanian society or world political and economic forces would permit the old structures to be restored. The relationship between economic liberalisation and political liberalisation remains a complex one. Economic liberalisation may bring poverty and misery to large numbers of people, and may reduce politics to 'one dollar, one vote' rather than 'one citizen, one vote', and there may be regret that the pendulum which swung against 'socialism' did not stop at 'social democracy' instead of going all the way to 'free market economics', yet a measure of economic liberalisation may be necessary to stimulate political pluralism. Whether it is by new private businesses seeking to influence economic policy, increasingly impoverished workers learning new political skills as the state attends to them less generously, or intellectuals feeling freer to express their opinions without fear of losing their jobs, political participation may expand. And as it expands, still more groups may be persuaded of its efficacy. If this is to be the trend in Tanzania, and it is still too early to be certain, democracy may yet flourish despite the overwhelming government majjority in Parliament and the survival of a constitution which provides limited safeguards against elective dictatorship.

10 Conclusion

I suggested at the beginning that Ghana and Tanzania were interesting cases because they occupied an intermediate position between the countries which had apparently democratised successfully and those that had little immediate prospect of doing so. Ghana and Tanzania had a much more difficult task than Greece or Uruguay, where most of the ingredients for successful democratic transition were present, but not as difficult as Ethiopia or Iraq. At one time I had assumed that countries which democratised earliest would normally be those in which the conditions for democracy were most propitious, just as the most fleet of foot pass the winning post first, but now I am not so sure. Countries may be early democratisers because the incumbent regime is so oppressive that there is a widespread determination to remove it (Chile), because foolish decisions undermine the government's authority (the Argentinean invasion of the Falklands), because economic collapse renders the government ineffective (Benin) or because the country is swept along by the influence of democratisation in neighbouring or similar countries (some of French-speaking West Africa).

The late arrivals at the democratisation ball may be late not so much because they are ill-qualified to attend, but because they had difficult roadblocks to negotiate on the way. Having negotiated them, they may then consolidate democracy at least as successfully as the earlier arrivals. In Ghana and Tanzania one major roadblock was the perceived availability of a form of government which was neither military authoritarianism not multi-party democracy. Whereas Greece and most Latin American countries could do little other than revert to multi-party politics once military government proved too unpopular or ineffective to survive, Ghana (or at least its rulers) clung to the idea of a populist system without political parties and, at least in the short term, without national elections. Tanzania clung to intra-party competition, which appeared to satisfy the majority of the electorate but which confined electoral choice mainly to parochial issues. It was argued that Ghana did not need multi-party competition because it had worked badly in the past, and Tanzania did not want it because very few people had supported opposition parties in the past. It was only when a change in the balance of forces, whether from within the regimes or without, made it easier to challenge the legitimacy of the no-party or one-party state, that moves towards democratisation could make progress.

Yet if late arrival did not necessarily imply inadequate qualifications for sustaining democracy, as compared with Latin American and Asian countries which democratised in the 1970s and 1980s, Ghana and Tanzania did labour under greater handicaps in many respects. Not only did there appear to be plausible alternatives to democracy which could create a diversion, but these countries were more 'underdeveloped' on the basis of such indicators as per capita income, industrialisation and urbanisation. Tanzania had had no previous experience of pluralist democracy, and Ghana's experience of it had not been a very happy one. One country had no experience of handling national political conflict, and was fearful of the disunity it might cause; the other had a long history of conflict, but had never institutionalised it effectively. Both countries were young nation states compared with those in Asia, and very young compared with Latin America, so that a sense of national identity, within which the political process might operate, could not be taken for granted. There were also the idiosyncrasies of each individual country, such as the mutual lack of recognition between Rawlings and his opponents in Ghana, and the weakness or absence of structures in civil society on which to build political parties in Tanzania.

One of the questions raised in the Introduction was on the applicability of the explanations of democratisation in the earlier, and possibly 'easier' cases, to Ghana and Tanzania. On the whole, a similar framework of analysis seems to be helpful, and we looked at the seeds of challenge to authoritarianism, the configuration of interests and the resolution of conflicts, in general and specific terms, in Chapters 7 to 9. The actual seeds and interests, and the processes of resolution, will vary from country to country, but in most cases of democratisation one can discern significant actions, the rise or fall of particular groups, or various interactions between governments and their adversaries, which bring about processes of democratisation. In Ghana, Rawlings retained the support of the masses, but alienated the elite through his usurpation of an elected government and his creation of revolutionary committees and tribunals, and then alienated many revolutionaries and Marxists through his change of economic policy after 1983. He was not strong enough to resist the demand for party competition, yet he was able to win the support of, or at least secure the neutrality of, 'floating' groups whose position was crucial in determining the outcome, including foreign governments and businesses, IFIs, chiefs, technocrats and the churches, while using revolutionary committees, and possibly the state bureaucracy, to achieve the election result he wanted. Relative economic success enabled Rawlings to democratise without jeopardising his own survival, but in Tanzania it was economic failure which stimulated the challenge to authoritarianism, as the competence, legitimacy and honesty of the ruling party came increasingly into question. Economic liberalisation produced a modest recovery, but it also led to a more pluralist society which, in turn, led to increased demands for a more pluralist political system. The government's opponents were able to build bases amongst the intelligentsia, some of the urban poor and in two disaffected regions. The changed international climate probably weakened the Tanzanian government more than the Ghanaian, with the disintegration of the previously supportive Communist Bloc, and pressures for democratisation as a condition of Western aid, which was needed even more desperately than in Ghana. But the government retained most of its own power base, especially the peasants who comprised the bulk of the electorate, the dominant party and the civil and military bureaucracies, and achieved a form of democratisation which was sufficient to satisfy external donors while minimising the danger of electoral defeat. Democratisation in both countries might thus be seen as an anti-climax in that the previous authoritarian rulers retained power in competitive elections, yet in neither country could political structures be used to preserve the old authoritarian order. In Tanzania the ruling party had lost much of its effectiveness, and in Ghana the looser civil and military revolutionary groups became a potential threat to the government as well as to its opponents. In the end democracy, at least to the extent of permitting freedom of expression and association and competitive elections, became 'the only game in town'.

These were 'difficult' transitions compared with many of the earlier ones in Latin America, in the sense that there were fewer points of reference from earlier periods of democracy to guide the actors, and a less developed civil society to provide counterweights to the government and to negotiate transitions on terms which reflected a broader spread of opinions and interests. Indeed authoritarian rulers in Argentina, Brazil and Chile, unlike those in Ghana and Tanzania, all had to hand over power to leaders of political parties which would not have been their own first preferences. The Ghanaian and Tanzanian transitions were 'difficult' not so much from the perspective of the incumbent governments, which obtained much of what they wanted, but in the sense that, from a more detached perspective, it was difficult to establish an order that seemed genuinely democratic and was recognised as such by most groups in society. The accusation lingered that authoritarian governments had merely legitimised themselves through the ballot box, however unfair this accusation may have been. Yet compared with the 'most difficult cases', Ghana and Tanzania had clearly enjoyed advantages. There were no immediate threats of national disintegration, as in Rwanda, no major ethnic or religious conflicts, as in Uganda or the Sudan, and no intransigent rulers comparable with Mobutu in Zaire or even Banda in Malawi, insensitive to democratic demands. While opposition parties were generally excluded from consultation over the terms of transition, some attempts were made to consult the masses. In Ghana representation in the Consultative Assembly was heavily weighted in favour of the poorer sections of society, and in Tanzania the Nyalali Commission travelled the country to hear people's views on the future of the political system. The fact that these processes could be undertaken at all might suggest that some significant preconditions for democracy existed.

We examined the relationship between the nature of democratic transitions and the sort of democratic consolidation which is likely to follow. Where transitions were 'top-down', mainly government-controlled, executed gradually, and in pursuit of relatively moderate objectives, one might expect that the subsequent democracies would be relatively stable, but with the possibility of veto power being exercised by the civilian elite or the military. These groups would retain extensive power, and might intervene if the democratic process threatened to produce outcomes which threatened their beliefs or interests. Ghana and Tanzania seem to fit this hypothesis. The need for a veto had not arisen at the time of writing, and we do not yet know how stability in either country would be affected by the prospect of an opposition electoral victory. Related to this problem is the fact that, by freezing opposition groups out of any say in the form of democracy to be established, governments run the risk of establishing a democratic order which is not subject to a sufficiently broad consensus. This can be serious in countries like Peru where there is a wide ideological gulf between government and opposition. It may be less serious in Ghana and Tanzania, where it was often constitutional questions that were at issue rather than broader conceptions of the nature of democracy, but the damage done to government–opposition relations might still make the operation of the political process less smooth than it would have been if there had been a greater search for consensus.

This still leaves us with areas where the nature of democracy in Ghana and Tanzania depends more on local peculiarities, and where the sweep of any broad theory offers less help. Firstly, the structures of the authoritarian regimes which preceded democratisation, and which played the major role in shaping that democratisation, were built on foundations which it would now be difficult to reconstruct. The Ghanaian government of 1981–92 was not a military government in the normal sense, although military support was a necessary (though not a sufficient) condition for its survival. In its earlier years it relied heavily on Marxist ideologues and revolutionary committees, and later on technocrats who contributed much to economic recovery. The shattered state of the economy and society in the early years made resistance by civil society virtually impossible. In the later years the government's relative economic success endowed it with a certain legitimacy but, by their nature, neither of these conditions could endure for long, and it was difficult to see any long-term basis for government other than a democratic one. In

Tanzania it was the party-state penetration of society, through a command economy, that held the polity together, rather than authoritarian rule based on physical coercion. As the command economy became discredited on account of its inability to deliver material benefits, the old structures were gradually demolished and the party became increasingly ineffective. Again there seemed to be nowhere to go but in the direction of pluralist democracy. None of this is to argue that other forms of authoritarianism might not emerge in either country in the future, but what is important is the fact that, although the former authoritarian rulers of both countries retained power, through competitive but disputed elections, it is difficult to envisage them resorting to their former methods of governing. The bases of such rule have gone and are unlikely to return. The new democratic structures may work imperfectly, but it might be difficult to abandon them even if the rulers wanted to. The majority party in Tanzania is constrained not simply by the fact that it is faced by a small opposition in Parliament, but by the fact that it is only a 'majority' party and can no longer be a 'ruling' party. The majority party in Ghana only came into being when it was realised that a no-party state was not feasible, and it has neither the will nor the ability to model itself on the ubiquitous ruling party of the 1960s.

The second distinctive local feature is to be found in the ideologies of the previous authoritarian governments. These rulers were neither military rulers amassing personal power and wealth through force of arms, nor megalomaniac party leaders seeking self-glorification and attracting the support of sycophants seeking a share of the leaders' ill-gotten gains. The ideology of the rulers of Tanzania was spelt out in pronouncements such as the Arusha Declaration which espoused the objectives of common ownership, equality, popular participation and social justice. While it was never going to be easy to live up to such lofty ideals, and many were abandoned as economic liberalisation gained momentum, the mythology was never completely destroyed. Inequality and corruption did increase after 1985, but the notion that politicians are servants of the people and accountable to them is probably more deeply rooted in Tanzania than in most other parts of Africa, and may make pluralist democracy less of an exercise in exploiting the people than it is elsewhere. In Ghana the ideology was never so coherent, but it, too, emphasised a search for social equality and popular participation. The notion that a populist social order could be built on the base of the spontaneous activities of revolutionary committees did not survive for very long, but the local government reforms of 1988 emphasised the continued desire to empower the poor, and the Parliament elected in 1992, although far from a microcosm of the population, was much less elitist in composition than earlier Parliaments. Again it is possible that democracy will be consolidated in such a way as to incorporate elements of participation and equality as well as political competition.

A further influence is not so much local as temporal. The democratisations of the 1980s were not, for the most part, actively opposed by the major Western powers, but neither were they generally the result of overt pressure from them. By the 1990s the situation was different. Third World governments which failed to make progress towards democratisation were likely to be penalised by First World governments. The 1991 conference of Commonwealth heads of government produced the Harare Declaration which emphasised the promotion of democracy, human rights and equality for women, and the British Prime Minister stated that future British aid would be linked to 'good government' (Ravenhill in Harbeson and Rothchild 1995: 102). In the previous year the United States Agency for International Development (AID) adopted a 'democracy initiative' in which it set out to weigh the progress towards economic liberalisation and democratisation before deciding on the levels of assistance to be granted, and President Mitterand announced that France would link aid to institutional progress towards democracy (Diamond in Harbeson and Rothchild 1995: 257–8). The ending of the Cold War, a realisation that aid to authoritarian governments was frequently not cost-effective, and a realisation on the part of recipients of aid that they might lose resources to other aid-seekers if they failed to democratise, all had the effect of tipping the balance in favour of democratisation, even if the initiation of democratisation owed more to indigenous forces. What bearing does this have on democratic transition and consolidation in Ghana and Tanzania?

One conclusion would be that arguments about the one-party state, or no-party state, representing a more authentic African form of democracy than the 'alien' multi-party competition, were no longer likely to cut much ice. African governments seeking aid might, at the very least, have to permit opposition parties, even if they were eventually able to ensure that such parties had little chance of winning any election. (There was, of course, the alternative of calling the bluff of Western donors and announcing that the time was not yet ripe for multi-party competition, as in Nigeria, Zaire and even Uganda, but this could be a risky strategy unless the country's economic position was such that the West was willing to turn a blind eye to political events and to put commercial considerations first.)

A second conclusion might be that the late democratisers were pushed into political reforms which would not otherwise have occurred so soon (if at all), and that this created an 'artificial' democracy which it might be difficult to sustain. It is not so much a matter of arguing about whether countries are 'ready' for democracy, because there is no satisfactory means of measuring 'readiness', but it may mean that something has been established largely as a result of external pressure, which internal forces may have difficulty in sustaining. This in turn may lead to both external powers and indigenous populations being left with unfulfilled expectations. Aid may be made conditional on setting a date for multi-party elections, monitors may be sent in to ensure that the crudest forms of election rigging are avoided, and foreign resources may be used to finance televised debates between rival presidential candidates, or exhibitions on the virtues of 'good government'. Insisting on freedom of expression and association, and on the release of political prisoners, can do something to redress the concentration of power in the hands of incumbent rulers, but external pressure to expand civil society or create a more civic culture are much more difficult. Whereas the earlier democratisations in much of Latin America, South Korea, and perhaps even Pakistan, reflected a change in the balance of forces in society, with social movements often building up irresistible pressures, and former democratic leaders mobilising their erstwhile supporters, the pressures in Africa tended to be weaker. There were dedicated opposition politicians and civil rights activists, but their control over events was weaker and the public response to them more muted. Opposition politicians in both Ghana and Tanzania were genuinely surprised that they did not fare better in their countries' elections, or even that they did not win. The way in which the elections were administered certainly did not help them, but in the end the enthusiasm of opposition politicians and external donors for liberal democracy, and their revulsion at what had happened under authoritarian governments, was not matched by the majority of the electorate. In Tanzania, the relative internal peace and stability over which the CCM has presided, and in Ghana the relative probity and economic successes of the Rawlings regime, appeared to weigh more heavily in the minds of voters than concerns with the practice of democracy. This is important not just in explaining why the incumbents won, but in highlighting the hazards that lie ahead for democratic consolidation. The previous forms of authoritarianism may be kept at bay, but whither democratic accountability? Will governmental behaviour be based on standards of conduct and accountability so deeply ingrained that it will be difficult to depart from them? Will scrutiny by opposition politicians, and a belief that these politicians represent a serious challenge, ensure that governments accept a responsibility to all their citizens and not just to immediate clients? And will opposition politicians willingly assume the role of 'loyal' opposition? In the wider society one could go on to ask about the role of the state-owned media in detaching itself from the current government, and of the independent press in contributing to political debate rather than reporting or inventing scandals in high places, or of the ability of pressure groups to provide checks and balances.

Even to have asked such questions about Ghana and Tanzania in the early 1980s would have seemed eccentric. There appeared to be no reason why the party/state bureaucracy in Tanzania should not continue to confine democracy to the most parochial levels, while Ghana's prospects seemed to lie between a continuation of coercive military government, or alternations between military rule and unstable democracy constrained by military veto. Both countries have come a long way since then. Changes in the outside world have made a significant impact, but such changes can do no more than release (or sometimes constrain) forces within indigenous society. Politicians still have to decide what sort of bargains to strike and how to mobilise public support, and society has to decide how to exploit new opportunities. What has emerged may fit Schmitter's conception of 'unconsolidated democracy' but if, as I have argued, it is difficult to envisage a return to the previous bases of authority, this state of being could provide a workable, if less than perfect, form of government for some time to come. Schmitter speaks of regimes in this category being '*condemned* to democracy without enjoying the consequences and advantages that it offers' (Schmitter in Tulchin and Romero 1995: 16, emphasis added), but perhaps condemnation is in the eye of the beholder. If there is now less physical coercion, little or no arbitrary detention, possibly less corruption, less pressure for conformity, and at least the possibility of the ballot box being used as a constraint on political misbehaviour or even as a means of choosing alternative policies and personnel, unconsolidated democracy might be seen as an improvement on what went before. Whether it can be transformed into consolidated democracy is another matter.

We began this study by looking at the impressions of a fourteenth-century Italian artist on the nature of 'good' and 'bad' government. Then, as now, the bad version seemed easier to characterise than the good. Bad government went with tyranny, depravity and rulers living off the fat of the land – a state of affairs familiar to millions of present-day Africans. Good government went with order and prosperity, but the process by which such government emerged was not revealed by the artist. Many political scientists in the 1960s were equally ambivalent as they spoke of 'development' as the desirable goal. Some countries in Asia achieved this goal without much initial concern for democracy, but none in Africa did so. Authoritarianism invariably went with 'bad government' and with many of the vices depicted in *The Allegory of Bad Government*. Now, over six hundred years after the frescos were painted, the term 'good government' has come back into fashion, and it assumes that the virtues depicted by Lorenzetti can only be achieved through multi-party democracy. It is a bold assumption, yet 'bad government' seems as frightening to many present-day Africans as it did to the fourteenth-century

Italian. Human behaviour is not sufficiently rational for us to assume a happy ending, and to believe that democracy will triumph because most people recognise the horrors of the alternatives. But experience of bad government is still one factor which may, through a mixture of determination, luck and good judgement, enable democracy to survive. A twenty-first-century African artist's version of *The Allegory of Good Government* might yet include not only prosperous, well-dressed citizens occupying well-kept buildings and marketing their produce in an orderly manner from a well-cultivated countryside; it might also include a speakers' corner and a polling station.

Bibliography

ABUGRI, G.S. (1995) 'Public Account Report', *Daily Graphic*, Ghana, 18 August: 5.
ACCRA METROPOLITAN ASSEMBLY (1995) *Managing Sustainable Growth and Development of Accra*, mimeographed paper.
ADU, A.L. (1965) *The Civil Service in Commonwealth Africa*, London, Allen and Unwin.
AFRIFA, A.A. (1966) *The Ghana Coup*, London, Frank Cass.
AGGREY-FYNN, M. (1995) 'The management of District Assembly funds', *Daily Graphic*, Accra, 10 August: 5.
AGYEMAN-DUAH, B. (1987) 'Ghana, 1982–6: the politics of the PNDC', *Journal of Modern African Studies*, 25(4): 613–42.
AKE, C. (1984) 'Ideology and objective conditions' in J.D. Barkan (ed.) *Politics and Public Policy in Kenya and Tanzania*, Eastbourne, Praeger: 127–39.
ALLEN, C. (1992) 'Restructuring an authoritarian state: democratic renewal in Benin', *Review of African Political Economy*, 54: 42–58.
ALLISON, L. (1994) 'On the gap between theories of democracy and theories of democratization', *Democratization*, 1(1), Spring: 8–26.
ANSAH-KOI, K. (1993) 'The socio-cultural matrix and multi-party politics in Ghana: observations and prospects', in K.A. Ninsin and F.K. Drah (eds) *Political Parties and Democracy in Ghana's Fourth Republic*, Accra, Woeli Publishing Services.
APTER, D. (1961) *The Political Kingdom in Uganda*, Princeton, New Jersey, Princeton University Press.
ARMAH, K. (1965) *Africa's Golden Road*, London, Heinemann.
AUSTIN, D. (1964) *Politics in Ghana 1946–60*, London, Oxford University Press.
AUSTIN, D. (1976) *Ghana Observed*, Manchester, Manchester University Press.
AUSTIN, D. (1985) *Ghana: Less than a Revolution*, Institute for the Study of Conflict.
AUSTIN, D. (1993) 'Reflections on African politics: Prospero, Ariel and Caliban', *International Affairs*, 69(2): 203–21.
AUSTIN, D. and LUCKHAM, R. (eds) (1975) *Politicians and Soldiers in Ghana*, London, Frank Cass.
AYEE, J.R.A. (1994) *An Anatomy of Public Policy Implementation: The Case of Decentralisation Policies in Ghana*, Aldershot, Avebury.
AYEE, J.R.A. (1995) 'Good governance and decentralization in Ghana: retrospect and prospects', unpublished paper, Institute of Economic Affairs, Accra, 8 August.
AZARYA, V. and CHAZAN, N. (1987) 'Disengagement from the state in Africa: reflections on the experience of Ghana and Guinea', *Comparative Studies in Society and History*, 29(1), January: 106–31.

BAREGU, M. (1994) 'The rise and fall of the one-party state in Tanzania', in J.A. Widner (ed.) *Economic Change and Political Liberalization in Sub-Saharan Africa*, London, Johns Hopkins University Press: 158–81.

BARKAN, J.D. (ed.) (1984) *Politics and Public Policy in Kenya and Tanzania*, Eastbourne, Praeger.

BARKAN, J.D. (ed.) (1994) *Beyond Capitalism Versus Socialism in Kenya and Tanzania*, London, Lynne Rienner.

BARKER, P. (1969) *Operation Cold Chop*, Accra, Ghana Publishing Corporation.

BATES, R.H. (1994) 'The impulse to reform in Africa', in J.A. Widner (ed.) *Economic Change and Political Liberalization in Sub-Saharan Africa*, London, Johns Hopkins University Press: 13–28.

BERG-SCHLOSSER, D. and SIEGLER, R. (1990) *Political Stability and Development: A Comparative Analysis of Kenya, Tanzania and Uganda*, London, Lynne Rienner.

BOAFO-ARTHUR, K. (1993) 'Political parties and the prospects for national stability', in K.A. Ninsin and F.K. Drah (eds) *Political Parties and Democracy in Ghana's Fourth Republic*, Accra, Woeli Publishing Services: 224–45.

BROKENSHA, D. (1966) *Social Change at Larteh, Ghana*, Oxford, Clarendon Press.

CALLAGHY, T.M. and RAVENHILL, J. (eds) (1993) *Hemmed In: Responses to Africa's Economic Decline*, New York, Columbia University Press.

CHAZAN, N. (1988) 'Ghana: problems of governance and the emergence of civil society' in L. Diamond et al. (eds) *Democracy in Developing Countries, Vol. II: Africa*, London, Adamantine Press: 93–139.

CHAZAN, N. (1991) 'Political transformation in Ghana under the PNDC' in D. Rothchild (ed.) *Ghana: The Political Economy of Recovery*, London, Lynne Rienner: 21–47.

CHEGE, M. (1994) 'The return of multi-party politics', in J.D. Barkan (ed.) *Beyond Capitalism Versus Socialism in Kenya and Tanzania*, London, Lynne Rienner: 47–74.

CLEARY, S. (1989) *Tanzania: Surviving Against the Odds*, Catholic Fund for Overseas Development.

COMMONWEALTH OBSERVER GROUP (1992) *The Presidential Election in Ghana, 30 November 1992*, London, Commonwealth Secretariat.

CROOK, R. (1983) 'Bureaucratic politics in Ghana: a comparative perspective' in P. Lyon and J. Manor (eds) *Transfer and Transformation: Political Institutions in the New Commonwealth*, Leicester, Leicester University Press: 185–213.

CROOK, R. (1990) 'State, society and political institutions in Cote d'Ivoire and Ghana', Sussex, *IDS Bulletin*, 21(4), October: 24–35.

CRUISE O'BRIEN, D.B., DUNN, J. and RATHBONE, R. (eds) (1989) *Contemporary West African States*, Cambridge, Cambridge University Press.

DAHL, R.A. (1971) *Polyarchy*, New Haven, Yale University Press.

DANOPOULOS, C.D. (ed.) (1992) *Civil Rule in the Developing World*, Boulder, Westview Press.

DIAMOND, L. (1995) 'Promoting democracy in Africa: United States and international policies in transition' in J.W. Harbeson and D. Rothchild (eds) *Africa in World Politics*, Boulder, Westview Press: 250–77.

DIAMOND, L., LINZ, J.J. and LIPSET, S.M. (eds) (1988) *Democracy in Developing Countries, Vol. II: Africa*, London, Adamantine Press.

DODD, C.H. (1979) *Democracy and Development in Turkey*, Beverley, Eothen Press.

DRAH, F.K. (1993) 'Civil society and the transition to pluralist democracy' in K.A. Ninsin and F.K. Drah (eds) *Political Parties and Democracy in Ghana's Fourth Republic*, Accra, Woeli Publishing Services: 72–115.

DUNN, J. (ed.) (1978) *West African States: Failure and Promise*, Cambridge, Cambridge University Press.

DUNN, J. and ROBERTSON A.F. (1973) *Dependence and Opportunity: Political Change in Ahafo*, Cambridge, Cambridge University Press.

DUODU, C. (1992) 'Rawlings & Co, specialists in fancy rigging', *Observer*, London, 29 November: 20.

ECONOMIST, THE (1994) 'Why voting is good for you', 27 August: 17–19.

FOLSON, K.G. (1993) 'Ideology, revolution and development – the years of J.J. Rawlings' in E. Gyimah-Boadi (ed.) *Ghana under PNDC Rule*, Senegal, Codesria: 74–99.

FREE PRESS (1995) 'The shame is out', Accra, 21–7 July: 1.

FRIMPONG-ANSAH, J.H. (1991) *The Vampire State in Africa: The Political Economy of Decline in Ghana*, London, James Currey.

GHANA GOVERNMENT (1977) *Report of the Ad Hoc Committee on Union Government*, Accra, Ghana Publishing Corporation.

GHANA GOVERNMENT (1992) *Constitution of the Republic of Ghana*, Accra, Government Publishing Corporation.

GHANA INFORMATION SERVICES DEPARTMENT (n/d: circa 1993–95) *Fact Sheets: Government of Ghana*, mimeographed paper.

GHANA PARLIAMENT (1993) *Parliamentary Election – Ghana 29.12.92*, mimeographed paper.

GREEN, D. (1995) 'Ghana's 'adjusted' democracy', *Review of African Political Economy*, 22(66), December: 577–85.

GYIMAH-BOADI, E. (ed.) (1993) *Ghana Under PNDC Rule*, Senegal, Codesria.

GYIMAH-BOADI, E. (1994) 'Associational life, civil society, and democratization in Ghana' in J.W. Harbeson et al. (eds) *Civil Society and the State in Africa*, London, Lynne Rienner: 125–48.

HAMPSHER-MONK, I. and STANYER, J. (eds) (1996) *Contemporary Political Studies*, Belfast, Political Studies Association.

HANSEN, E. (1991) *Ghana Under Rawlings: The Early Years*, Oxford, Malthouse Press.

HAONGA, M. (1995) 'Observers: what they witnessed', *Guardian*, Dar es Salaam, 3 November: 1.

HARBESON, J.W., ROTHCHILD, D. and CHAZAN, N. (eds) (1994) *Civil Society and the State in Africa*, London, Lynne Rienner.

HARBESON, J.W. and ROTHCHILD, D. (eds) (1995) *Africa in World Politics*, Boulder, Westview Press.

HAYNES, J. (1992) 'One-party state, no-party state, multi-party state? 35 years of democracy, authoritarianism and development in Ghana', *Journal of Communist Studies*, 8(2), June: 41–62.

HAYNES, J. (1993) 'Sustainable democracy in Ghana: problems and prospects', *Third World Quarterly*, 14(3): 451–67.

HERBST, J. (1993) *The Politics of Reform in Ghana 1982–91*, University of California Press.
HERBST, J. (1994) 'The dilemmas of explaining political upheaval: Ghana in comparative perspective' in J.A. Widner (ed.) *Economic Change and Political Liberalisation in Sub-Saharan Africa*, London, Johns Hopkins University Press: 182–98.
HUNTINGTON, S.P. (1984) 'Will more countries become democratic?', *Political Science Quarterly*, 99(2): 193–218.
HUNTINGTON, S.P. (1991–2) 'How countries democratise', *Political Science Quarterly*, 106(4): 579–616.
HYDEN, G. (1994) 'Party, state and civil society: control versus openness' in J.D. Barkan (ed.) *Beyond Capitalism Versus Socialism in Kenya and Tanzania*, London, Lynne Rienner.
HYDEN, G. and LEYS, C. (1972) 'Elections and politics in single-party systems: the case of Kenya and Tanzania', *British Journal of Political Science*, 2: 389–420.
IMAM, A. (1992) 'Democratization processes in Africa: problems and prospects', *Review of African Political Economy*, 54, July: 102–5.
INSIGHT (1995) 'A 'natural' disaster', Accra, 26 July–1 August: 3.
JEFFRIES, R. (1980) 'The Ghanaian elections of 1979', *African Affairs*, 79.
JEFFRIES, R. (1989) 'Ghana: the political economy of personal rule' in D. Cruise O'Brien et al. (eds) *Contemporary West African States*, Cambridge, Cambridge University Press.
JEFFRIES, R. (1991) 'Leadership commitment and opposition to structural adjustment' in Rothchild, D. (ed.) *Ghana: The Political Economy of Recovery*, London, Lynne Rienner: 157–71.
JEFFRIES, R. (1993) 'The state, structural adjustment and good government in Africa', *Journal of Commonwealth and Comparative Politics*, 31(1), March: 20–35.
JEFFRIES, R. and THOMAS, C. (1993) 'The Ghanaian Elections of 1992', *African Affairs*, 92: 331–66.
KARASHANI, B. (1995) 'Many Newcomers take parliamentary seats', *The East African*, Nairobi, 13–19 November: 4.
KELSALL, T. (1996) 'Party identities and electoral competition in Tanzania: the 1995 elections', unpublished paper, *Political Studies Association Conference*, Glasgow.
KRAUS, J. (1987) 'Ghana's shift from radical populism', *Current History*, 86(520): 205–29.
KRAUS, J. (1991) 'The political economy of stabilisation and structural adjustment' in D. Rothchild (ed.) *Ghana: The Political Economy of Recovery*, London, Lynne Rienner.
LEE, J.M. (1963) 'Parliament in Republican Ghana', *Parliamentary Affairs*, XVI (4): 376–95.
LEGUM, C. (1995) 'The goal of an egalitarian society' in C. Legum and G. Mmari (eds) *Mwalimu: The Influence of Nyerere*, London, James Currey: 186–95.
LEGUM, C. and MMARI, G. (eds) (1995) *Mwalimu: The Influence of Nyerere*, London, James Currey.
LEWIS, P.G. and POTTER, D.C. (eds) (1973) *The Practice of Comparative Politics*, Harlow, Longman.

LIJPHART, A. (1977) *Democracy in Plural Societies*, New Haven, Yale University Press.
LIPSET, S.M. (1959) 'Some social requisites for democracy: economic development and political legitimacy', *American Political Science Review*, 53(1): 69–105.
LOFCHIE, M.F. (1993) 'Trading places: economic policy in Kenya and Tanzania', in T.M. Callaghy and J. Ravenhill (eds) *Hemmed In: Responses to Africa's Economic Decline*, New York, Columbia University Press: 398–462.
LUCKHAM, A.R. (1971) 'A comparative typology of civil-military relations', *Government and Opposition*, Winter: 8–34.
LUDWIG, F. (1996) 'Is religious revival a threat to Tanzania's stability?' in D. Westerlund (ed.) *Questioning the Secular State*, London, Hurst: 216–36.
LYON, P. and MANOR, J. (eds) (1983) *Transfer and Transformation: Political Institutions in the New Commonwealth*, Leicester, Leicester University Press.
MALIYAMKONO, T.L. (1995) *Who Votes in Tanzania and Why*, Dar es Salaam, Tema Publications.
MARMO, P.S. (1989) 'A one-party state: the role of Parliament in Tanzania', *The Parliamentarian*, 10(2), April: 65–71.
MARTIN, M. (1993) 'Neither Phoenix nor Icarus: negotiating economic reform in Ghana and Zambia 1983–92' in J.M. Callaghy and J. Ravenhill (eds) *Hemmed in: Responses to Africa's Economic Decline*, New York, Columbia University Press: 130–79.
MASANJA, P. (1990) 'Industrial workers and the politics of incorporation' in N. O'Neill and K. Mustafa (eds) *Capitalism, Socialism and the Development Crisis in Tanzania*, Aldershot, Avebury: 207–32.
McHENRY, D.E. (1994) *Limited Choices: The Political Struggle for Socialism in Tanzania*, London, Lynne Rienner.
MMUYA, M. and CHALIGHA, A. (1992) *Towards Multi-Party Democracy in Tanzania*, Dar es Salaam, Dar es Salaam University Press.
MORNA, C.L. (1989) 'A grassroots democracy', *Africa Report*, 34(4): 17–20.
MOXON, J. (1984) *Volta: Man's Greatest Lake*, London, Andre Deutsch.
MUKANDALA, R.S. (1983) 'Bureaucracy and socialism in Tanzania: the case of the Civil Service', *The African Review*, 10(2): 1–21.
MUNUSHI, G. and MTENGETI-MIGIRO A.R. (1990) 'Rombo: the dynamics of election organisation in a one-party democracy' in H. Othman et al. (eds) *Tanzania: Democracy in Transition*, Dar es Salaam, Dar es Salaam University Press: 182–201.
MVUNGI, S. C.A. and MHINA, A.K.L. (1990) 'Dodoma Urban: searching for a people's MP' in H. Othman et al. (eds) *Tanzania: Democracy in Transition*, Dar es Salaam, Dar es Salaam University Press: 103–20.
MWAKYEMBE, H.G. (1990) 'Mbezi: the end of a honeymoon' in H. Othman et al. (eds) *Tanzania: Democracy in Transition*, Dar es Salaam, Dar es Salaam University Press: 134–49.
NGASONGWA, J. (1992) 'Tanzania introduces a multi-party system', *Review of African Political Economy*, 54, July: 112–6.
NINSIN, K.A. (1993) 'Strategies of mobilisation under the PNDC government' in E. Gyimah-Boadi (ed.) *Ghana Under PNDC Rule*, Senegal, Codesria: 100–13.

Bibliography

NINSIN, K. and DRAH, F.K. (eds) (1993) *Political Parties and Democracy in Ghana's Fourth Republic*, Accra, Woeli Publishing Services.

NOVICKI, M.A. (1984) 'Flt. Lt. Jerry Rawlings, Chairman of the Provisional National Defense (sic.) Council, Ghana', *Africa Report*, March–April: 4–8.

NOVICKI, M.A. (1991) 'Flt. Lt. Jerry Rawlings: constructing a new constitutional order', *Africa Report*, May–June: 34–8.

NYONG'O, P.A. (1992) 'Democratization processes in Africa', *Review of African Political Economy*, 54: 97–102.

NZOUANKEU, J.-M. (1991) 'The African attitude to democracy', *International Social Science Journal*, 43(129): 372–85.

OBSERVER (1995) 'More and more become less and less educated', Dar es Salaam, 15 October: 7.

OCRAN, A.K. (1968) *A Myth is Broken*, Harlow, Longman.

O'DONNELL, G. (1993) 'On the state, democratization and some conceptual problems: a Latin American view with glances at some postcommunist countries', *World Development*, 21(8): 1355–69.

OKEMA, M. (1990) 'Some salient changes in the Tanzanian parliamentary system' in H. Othman et al. (eds) *Tanzania: Democracy in Transition*, Dar es Salaam, Dar es Salaam University Press: 37–57.

OKUMU, A. (1995) 'Voter registration fiasco: minority to pick leaders', *Guardian*, Dar es Salaam, 18 September: 6.

OKUMU, J.J. and HOLMQUIST, F. (1984) 'Party and party–state relations' in J.D. Barkan (ed.) *Politics and Public Policy in Kenya and Tanzania*, Eastbourne, Praeger: 45–69.

O'NEILL, N. (1990) 'Politics and development strategies in Tanzania' in N. O'Neill and K. Mustafa (eds) *Capitalism, Socialism and the Development Crisis in Tanzania*, Aldershot, Avebury: 1–21.

O'NEILL, N. and MUSTAFA, K. (eds) (1990) *Capitalism, Socialism and the Development Crisis in Tanzania*, Aldershot, Avebury.

OQUAYE, M. (1980) *Politics in Ghana 1972–79*, Accra, Tornado Publishers.

OQUAYE, M. (1992) *The Military and Democracy in Ghana*, unpublished Ph.D. thesis, Legon, University of Ghana.

OTHMAN, H., BAVU, I.K. and OKEMA, M. (eds) (1990) *Tanzania: Democracy in Transition*, Dar es Salaam, Dar es Salaam University Press.

OWUSU, M. (1970) *The Uses and Abuses of Political Power*, Chicago, University of Chicago Press.

OWUSU, M. (1992) 'Democracy and Africa – a view from the village', *Journal of Modern African Studies*, 30 (3): 369–96.

PINKNEY, R. (1972) *Ghana Under Military Rule 1966–69*, London, Methuen.

PINKNEY, R. (1990) *Right Wing Military Government*, London, Pinter.

PINKNEY, R. (1993) *Democracy in the Third World*, Buckingham, Open University Press.

PINKNEY, R. (1994) 'Economic liberalisation and political liberalisation', unpublished paper, *International Political Science Association Congress*, Berlin.

PINKNEY, R. (1996) 'The Tanzanian elections of 1995' in A. Hamsher-Monk and J. Stanyer (eds) *Contemporary Political Studies*, Belfast, Political Studies Association: 610–22.

RATHBONE, R. (1978) 'Ghana' in J. Dunn (ed.) *West African States: Failure and Promise*, Cambridge, Cambridge University Press.
RAVENHILL, J. (1995) 'Dependent by default: Africa's relations with the European Union' in J.W. Harbeson and D. Rothchild (eds) *Africa in World Politics*, Boulder, Westview Press: 95–123.
READ, J. (1995) 'Human rights in Tanzania' in C. Legum and G. Mmari (eds) *Mwalimu: The Influence of Nyerere*, London, James Currey: 125–45.
RILEY, S.P. (1992) 'Political adjustment or domestic pressure: democratic politics and political choice in Africa', *Third World Quarterly*, 13(2): 539–51.
RILEY, S. (1993) 'Africa's 'new wind of change'', *World Today*, 48(7), July: 116–19.
ROTHCHILD, D. (ed.) (1991) *Ghana: The Political Economy of Recovery*, London, Lynne Rienner.
ROTHCHILD, D. (1994) 'Structuring state–society relations in Africa: toward an enabling political environment' in J.A. Widner (ed.) *Economic and Political Liberalization in Sub-Saharan Africa*, London, Johns Hopkins University Press: 201–29.
ROTHCHILD, D. and GYIMAH-BOADI, E. (1989) 'Populism in Ghana and Burkina Faso', *Current History*, May: 221–44.
ROTHCHILD, D. and LAWSON, L. (1994) 'The interactions between state and civil society in Africa: from deadlock to new routines' in J.W. Harbeson et al. (eds) *Civil Society and the State in Africa*, London, Lynne Rienner: 255–81.
RUSTOW, D.A. (1973) 'How does democracy come into existence?' in P.G. Lewis and D.C. Potter (eds) *The Practice of Comparative Politics*, Harlow, Longman: 117–32.
SAM, K. (1995) 'Assemblies misapply district funds – team', *Daily Graphic*, Accra, 19 August: 3.
SAMOFF, J. (1982–3) 'Pluralism and conflict in Africa: ethnicity, institutions and class in Tanzania', *Civilisations*, 32–3 (92–1): 97–130.
SCHMITTER, P.C. (1995) 'Transitology: the science and the art of democratization' in J.S. Tulchin and B. Romero (eds) *The Consolidation of Democracy in Latin America*, London, Lynne Rienner.
SHILLINGTON, K. (1992) *Ghana and the Rawlings Factor*, Basingstoke, Macmillan.
SHIVJI, I.G. (1976) *Class Struggles in Tanzania*, London, Heinemann.
SHIVJI, I.G. (1990) 'Workers' struggles' in N. O'Neill and K. Mustafa *Capitalism, Socialism and the Development Crisis in Tanzania*, Aldershot, Avebury.
SIDDIQUI, R.A. (1990) 'Socialism and the ujamaa ideology' in N. O'Neill and K. Mustafa (eds) *Socialism and the Development Crisis in Tanzania*, Aldershot, Avebury: 22–57.
SKLAR, R.L. (1983) 'Democracy in Africa', *African Studies Review*, 26(3/4): 11–24.
STEIN, H. (1985) 'Theories of the state in Tanzania: a critical assessment', *Journal of Modern African Studies*, 23(1): 105–23.
SUNDET, G. (1994) 'Beyond Developmentalism in Tanzania', *Review of African Political Economy*, 59(21): 39–49.

TANGRI, R. (1992) 'The politics of government–business relations in Ghana', *Journal of Modern African Studies*, 20(1): 97–111.
TANZANIAN AFFAIRS (1996) 'Were the elections free and fair?', January–April, 53: 12–18.
TANZANIAN ELECTION MONITORING COMMITTEE (TEMCO) (1995) 'TEMCO preliminary statement on the October 29, 1995 general elections', *Guardian*, Dar es Salaam, 11 November: 8.
TASSENI, M. (1995) 'The debate that was ...', *Guardian*, Dar es Salaam, 7 October: 6–7.
TORDOFF, W. (1977) 'Residual legislatures: the cases of Tanzania and Zambia', *Journal of Commonwealth and Comparative Politics*, November: 235–49.
TORDOFF, W. (1994) 'Decentralisation: comparative experience in Commonwealth Africa', *Journal of Modern African Studies*, 32(4): 555–80.
TRIPP, A. M. (1994) 'Rethinking civil society: gender implications in contemporary Tanzania' in J.W. Harbeson et al. (eds) *Civil Society and the State in Africa*, London, Lynne Rienner: 49–68.
TULCHIN, J.S. and ROMERO, B. (eds) (1995) *The Consolidation of Democracy in Latin America*, London, Lynne Rienner.
TWUMASI, Y. (1975) 'The 1969 election' in D. Austin and R. Luckham (eds) *Politicians and Soldiers in Ghana*, London, Frank Cass.
UNITED REPUBLIC OF TANZANIA (1992) *The Presidential Commission on Single Party or Multiparty Systems in Tanzania*, Dar es Salaam, Dar es Salaam University Press.
VAN DONGE, J.K. and LIVIGA, A.J. (1986) 'Tanzanian political culture and the cabinet', *Journal of Modern African Studies*, 24(4): 619–39.
VAN DONGE, J.K. and LIVIGA, A.J. (1989) 'The 1985 Tanzanian parliamentary elections: a conservative election', *African Affairs*, January: 47–62.
WESTERLUND, D. (ed.) (1996) *Questioning the Secular State*, London, Hurst.
WHITEHEAD. L. (1993) 'Introduction: Some Insights from Western Social Theory', *World Development* 21(8) August: 1245–61.
WIDNER, J.A. (ed.) (1994) *Economic and Political Liberalization in Sub-Saharan Africa*, London, Johns Hopkins University Press.
WISEMAN, J.A. (1993) 'Democracy and the new political pluralism in Africa: causes, consequences and significance', *Third World Quarterly*, 14(3): 439–49.
YEAGER, R. (1989) *Tanzania: An African Experiment*, Aldershot, Dartmouth.
YEBOAH-AFARI, V. (1995) 'The media and the Fourth Republic', *West Africa*, 21–27 August: 1320.
YEEBO, Z. (1991) *Ghana: The Struggle for Popular Power*, London, New Beacon Books.
ZIRKER, D. (1992) 'The preservation of civilian rule in Tanzania' in C.P. Danopoulos (ed.) *Civil Rule in the Developing World*, Boulder, Westview Press: 107–23.

Index

Acheampong, I.K.   40–4, 54, 70, 71, 140, 161
Adu, A.L.   69
Afrifa, A.A.   37–8, 44, 71
Agyeman-Duah, B.   20–1, 22
Ansah-Koi, K.   52
Armah, K.   37
Army, Ghana   70–4, 160–3, 166, 168, 181
Army, Tanzania   118–23, 207
Arusha Declaration   89, 105, 117, 186, 214
Austin, D.   20, 22, 35–6, 48–8, 52, 53
Ayee, J.   80–81, 84
Azarya, V.   51

Baregu, M.   23, 103, 116, 132, 184, 187–8, 197–8
Barkan, J.D.   98, 106, 114, 117, 188–9
Bates, R.H.   149
Berg-Schlosser, D.   87, 98–9, 100, 127
Britain   154–6
Brokensha, D.   66
Busia, K.   38, 53, 54, 58, 69, 74, 159, 161

Chaligha, A.   97, 109, 110, 187, 192, 197
Chama Cha Mapinduze (CCM)   96, 103, 108, 114, 128, 185–7, 193–7, 200–6, 214, 217
Chazan, N.   51, 52, 64
Chege, M.   187, 191–2
Civic United Front (CUF)   197–8, 205
Civil Service, Ghana   68–70, 161, 166
Civil Service, Tanzania   118–23, 207, 210
civil society, general   156, 216
civil society, Ghana   62–8, 212, 213

civil society, Tanzania   112–18, 207, 212
clientelism   101
Cold War   121, 139–40, 215
Committees for the Defence of the Revolution (CDRs) (*see also* People's Defence Committees, Workers' Defence Committees)   9, 47, 51, 60, 72, 79, 80, 162, 163, 166–9, 174, 181, 213, 215
consociational democracy   14–5
Convention Peopie's Party (CPP)   35–7, 38, 66, 74, 79, 165
corruption   42–4, 71–2, 82, 141, 149, 186, 188, 198
Crook, R.   23, 64, 67, 68

Dahl, R.A.   128–9
December (31) Women's Movement   60, 166–7, 172, 181
Drah, F.K.   66
Dunn, J.   19

economic liberalisation   108, 115–19, 150, 163, 165, 186–8, 191–2, 203, 208, 211

Folson, K.G.   55
Frimpong-Ansah, J.   49

Gbedemah, K.   78
Ghana Bar Association   74
'good government'   1, 2, 164, 171, 215, 218–19
Gyimah-Boadi, E.   65–6

Hansen, E.   9, 11, 57, 116, 168
Harare Declaration   215
Harbeson, J.W.   24, 63
Haynes, J.   164, 173
Herbst, J.   26, 51, 65
Holmquist, F.   101, 103

Index

Huntington, S.P. 4, 134
Hyden, G. 91, 97, 103, 107, 114

Imam, A. 16–17
International Monetary Fund (IMF) 46, 50, 73

Japan 155
Jeffries, R. 18, 26, 64, 172–3
judiciary, Ghana 74–7
judiciary, Tanzania 123–6
June 4 Movement 57, 60, 166–7, 181

Kraus, J. 58

Law Reform Committee 76, 126
Lawson, L. 25
Lee, J.M. 124
Legum, C. 104, 106
Leys, C. 91, 97
liberal democracy 9–12, 15–16, 35, 83
Lijphart, A. 15
Limann, H. 44, 54, 69, 75, 78, 176
Lipset, S.M. 26
Lipumba, I. 198
Liviga, A.J. 23, 115–6
local government, Ghana 77–85, 169, 179
local government, Tanzania 126–9

Maliyamkono, T.L. 113
Masanja, P. 129–31
McHenry, D. 12–13, 101, 109, 185–6
Mhina, A.K.L. 98
Mkapa, B. 202, 203, 205
Mmuya, M. 97, 109, 110, 187, 192, 197
Movement for Freedom and Justice (MFJ) 165, 172
Mrema, A. 192, 198, 202, 205
Mtengeti-Migiro, A.R. 98
Mukandala, R.S. 119
Munushi, G. 98
Mvungi, S.C.A. 98
Mwinyi, A.H. 108, 195

National Convention for Reconstruction and Reform (NCCR) 197–8, 203, 205
National Democratic Congress (NDC) 59–61, 85–6, 174, 178, 214
National Liberation Council (NLC) 38
National Redemption Council (NRC) 40–4, 71
New Patriotic Party (NPP) 182
Ninsin, K. 79, 84, 169
Nkrumah, K. 12, 13, 22, 35, 53, 58, 66, 74
Nyalali Commission 18–19, 110, 140, 194–6, 212
Nyerere, J. 12, 13, 22, 88–95, 108, 139–40, 185–6, 194, 195, 202
Nyong'o, P.A. 149
Nzouankeu, J.-M. 17–18

Okema, M. 123, 124
Okumu, A. 101, 103
O'Neill, N. 106
Oquaye, M. 79, 80
Owusu, M. 77, 80

Parliament, Ghana 74–7, 176–7, 179
Parliament, Tanzania 123–6
Pemba 192–3, 205
People's Defence Committees (*see also* Committees for the Defence of the Revolution) 45–7, 56–7, 168, 176–7
People's National Defence Council (PNDC) 45–7, 58, 72, 84, 162, 178
populism 40–7, 54–5, 59, 72, 81, 83, 152–3, 171, 215
Progress Party (PP) 38–40, 165

Rathbone, R. 77
Rawlings, J.J. 43–7, 54–6, 58–60, 69, 72, 73, 79, 83–6, 160–2, 165, 170, 172–3, 176–7, 182, 210–11, 217
Rawlings, Mrs N. 178
Read, J. 125

Robertson, A.F. 19
Rothchild, D. 25, 174

Samoff, J. 118–19, 127
Sandbrook, R. 15–6
Schmitter, P.C. 154, 156, 179, 218
Shivji, I. 114–15, 119, 130–2
Siegler, R. 87, 98–9, 100, 127
Sklar, R.L. 16
socialism 12–14, 35–7, 88–96, 109–11, 115, 152–3, 187, 203
South Africa 188–9
Spain 155
Stein, H. 94
Sundet, G. 95, 101
Supreme Military Council (SMC) *see* National Redemption Council

Tanganyika African National Union (Tanu) 88–96, 131, 185
taxation (*see also* value-added tax) 82, 127, 179–80
theocracy 2
Thomas, C. 18, 172–3

Tordoff, W. 123, 128
trade unions 129–32, 170
Tripp, A.M. 117
Tsikata, K. 177–8

Ujamaa villages 92, 105–6, 121
United Democratic Party (UDP) 198, 203

value-added tax (VAT) 75, 175–7, 179
Van Donge, J.K. 23, 115–6

Whitehead, L. 157
Workers' Defence Committees (WDCs) (*see also* Committees for the Defence of the Revolution) 45–7, 56–7, 168
World Bank 50

Yeager, R. 95, 100–1, 119
Yeebo, Z. 56, 116, 168

Zanzibar 90–1, 96, 97, 104, 191, 192–3, 198, 205, 207